HOMECOMING

HOMECOMING

Voices of the Windrush Generation

Colin Grant

JONATHAN CAPE
LONDON

1 3 5 7 9 10 8 6 4 2

Jonathan Cape, an imprint of Vintage,
20 Vauxhall Bridge Road,
London SW1V 2SA

Jonathan Cape is part of the Penguin Random House group of companies
whose addresses can be found at global.penguinrandomhouse.com.

Penguin
Random House
UK

First published by Jonathan Cape in 2019

penguin.co.uk/vintage

A CIP catalogue record for this book is available from the British Library

ISBN 9781787331051

Typeset in 13/16 pt Dante MT Std
by Integra Software Services Pvt. Ltd, Pondicherry

Printed and bound in Great Britain by Clays Ltd, Elcograf S.p.A.

Penguin Random House is committed to a sustainable future for our
business, our readers and our planet. This book is made from
Forest Stewardship Council® certified paper.

MIX
Paper from
responsible sources
FSC® C018179

Contents

HOMECOMING

Introduction

Homecomings without Home

My parents, Ethlyn and Bageye, came to England in the late 1950s. I was born here. As a teenager, I worked out a neat little summary for the times when people asked me where I was from. I'd say I was British by birth but Jamaican by will and inclination. If ever Bageye overheard me he'd berate me. 'Stop talk tripe. You born right here. You are English; I am British. Now let's get that straight. Don't let the man take you for fool.'

Though Bageye never really expressed much enthusiasm for Britain, he had an uncomplicated attachment to his moral right to be here. His British passport bore the stamp: 'Right of Abode'. And so what more was there to discuss? 'Argument done,' as Jamaicans say.

But the argument is not over. Growing up in the 1960s, it was always a mystery to me why we were here, living in an unhappy house in Luton, thousands of miles from Jamaica. It would not have been wise, though, to ask Bageye such a foolish question. Bageye was a 'simple sense' man. The answer would most likely have been: 'We're here because we're here. You have some place else to go?' My mother, Ethlyn, was far more reflective and philosophical, but she seemed to be forever singing sad plaintive hymns to keep such questions and answers at bay, as much from herself as from her children.

In almost every West Indian family I knew, there was this division between adults, between the dreamers who were given to nostalgia about the West Indies and the sacrifice they'd made, and those who focused on the hard-nosed reality of life in Britain. As a child, parked in draughty hallways when my parents visited friends and relations, I eavesdropped on the strained and hushed disputes between couples as they argued over 'the plan', such as there was one, that they'd agreed on when setting out for Britain. But there didn't actually seem to be any plan other than a vague commitment to an impossible-to-imagine future. With hindsight, they seem to me now arguments over what had been lost by leaving the islands, what emotional wealth had been traded for small gains of financial security – the absence of sunlight and warmth, the impossibility of living outdoors or sheltering under palm trees from sudden thrilling downpours of rain, and the unlikelihood of finding breadfruit or ackee in the market.

That tension was there from the beginning. You can see it in the newsreel footage, in the faces filled with hope and apprehension of the smartly dressed men in suits and fedoras disembarking from the HMT *Empire Windrush* at Tilbury in 1948.

The month before the new British Nationality Act was given royal assent on 31 July 1948 (conferring British citizen status on colonial subjects), the *Windrush* started picking up passengers from the Caribbean. Some commentators and Members of the Houses of Parliament disapproved of the new legislation, fearing the ship steaming towards Britain would change the mind set of people from the Caribbean; they'd now feel encouraged, it was argued, to try their luck in Britain. The fact that government officials planned to meet the newcomers at Tilbury on 22 June 1948 piqued media interest in the *Windrush*'s arrival. Though the *Evening Standard* alone believed it warranted front-page coverage, Pathé newsreel's brief report captured a moment which (especially since the fiftieth anniversary celebrations in 1998) has become emblematic.

Looking back now, the attention paid to the arrival of that ship seems extraordinary. The popular image of *Windrush* has also reduced the story – not least because it excludes more than 200 women who were also passengers. It also threatens to eclipse the bigger picture of the impact of mass migration, as some 300,000 adventurers made their way to Britain from Trinidad, St Kitts &

Nevis, Antigua & Barbuda and other West Indian islands over the next fifteen years.

But the *Windrush* is only a small part of a magnificent story of the changes wrought to this country by the arrival of that generation. Of course, Caribbean travellers to the UK had preceded the *Windrush* in the decades and centuries before. When Flying Officer Ulric Cross, a tall black man with a plummy voice, was introduced on the 1943 Ministry of Information film, *West Indies Calling*, the bomber navigator from Trinidad revealed the degree to which West Indians saw Britain as the motherland; they felt awed, privileged and protected by it, and were keen to 'do their bit' in the fight against Hitler. 'It's a job to know where to begin,' says Cross. 'There are so many of us doing so many different things, pilots, navigators, wireless operators, gunners and ground staff.'

British viewers also were able to see, many for the first time, people from the imagined far-off colonies who, strangely, but for a slight sing-song Caribbean lilt, sounded just like them. For a brief moment, the boundary between Britain and Empire collapsed.

The early West Indian émigrés were often exoticised in similar ways to visiting African-American performers. In the 1940s, Ken 'Snake-hips' Johnson and his West Indian Orchestra had a lucrative residency at the elegant subterranean nightclub Café de Paris in Soho – at least until it was bombed during an air raid, killing at least one band member and badly injuring the others. Such men little knew that they were outliers for those who would follow their lead and head to Britain.

The idea for this book was partly spurred by the urgent need to capture the voices of those pioneering West Indians, now elderly and towards the ends of their lives, before their stories disappeared. But just a few months after I started to compile their accounts, the British government gave a new twist to the story, ensuring that the word 'Windrush' will now also forever be associated with scandal. The reprehensible treatment of that

West Indian generation caught up in the government's creation of a hostile environment resulted in some being deported 'back home' decades after they'd arrived.

In *Homecoming* we will hear from some of them: nurses in Manchester; bus drivers in Bristol; Vauxhall Motors workers in Luton; ball-bearing engineers in Cleckheaton; virologists in Crawley; seamstresses in Birmingham; merchant seamen in Ipswich; teachers and child psychologists in Croydon; welders in Leeds; dockers in Tiger Bay; poets in Watford; inter-racial romancers in High Wycombe; Black Power activists in Smethwick; slum landlords in Notting Hill; Carnival Queens in Chapeltown; and Calypsonians in Salford.

These are stories that have rarely been recorded; they're tales of ordinary people but together they reveal a rich tapestry of Black British lives which too often have been cast as problematic; a pattern that seems to have been established in the decade after the *Windrush*'s arrival, with Pathé news headlines such as 'Our Jamaica Problem' (1955) and 'Racial Troubles in Notting Hill' (1959).

In this book I focus on the years of West Indian migration to Britain – from its beginnings in the late 1940s to the Commonwealth Immigrants Act of 1962, which severely restricted the movement of Commonwealth peoples to Britain – to construct an oral history of the Windrush Generation. I was determined to throw out a wide net to represent the region. Jamaicans made up three-quarters of the West Indians who came to Britain, but authors, filmmakers and broadcasters have been guilty of focusing too heavily on them. To redress the balance, I spent much more time with the Guyanese than with Jamaicans, and in Leeds I became an honorary Kittitian. I interviewed more women than men, partly because they had outlived partners and partly because they were more generous with their anecdotes, more humble and prepared to interrogate their interior lives. In their company I was more likely to be fed as well. I also wanted to reflect the diversity of the West Indian region. So my interviewees include people of African, Indian, Chinese, Madeiran and Lebanese descent.

Although West Indians seemed to lead separate, parallel lives to white British nationals, there were inevitably interactions between the two cultures at work and play (on the factory floor or dance floor, as it were). By including a number of white people in *Homecoming*, exploring their perceptions and assumptions about West Indians in the 1950s and 1960s, I began to glean the range, limits and evolution of interracial love and hate.

When interviewing people of my parents' generation, whom West Indians refer to as the elders, a veil of respectability usually descended just as I turned on the recording device, but that soon lifted. And, as these octogenarians became ever more frank, I found myself asking, 'Are you OK to talk like this?', especially when unbidden tears began to flow. This happened several times when people remembered that, after setting out from the West Indies, they'd never seen their parents again. Years later, by the time they'd saved up enough to return for a visit, their parents had died.

If they had stopped to think about the scale of the challenge of uprooting themselves from islands to settle over 4,000 miles away, maybe they would never have embarked on the huge adventure in the first place. But the stories of this pioneering generation have been obscured by a West Indian reticence and reserve, as well as the immigrants' anxiety about not wanting to attract attention. 'Me don't like chat people business' is a phrase you'll commonly hear in West Indian households up and down the UK. I've been aware of it all of my life. Growing up in their company in 1960s Luton, there seemed to be a suspicion and brittleness around sharing personal information. If you had dared to ask an adult, 'How are you?', they'd have thundered back, 'Not as good as you!' It was more than thoughtless obfuscation. I was sure of it even as a boy, but never knew why.

That attitude was burned into Bageye's being. Like many of his friends, or his spars, Bageye might have appeared ungenerous or even curmudgeonly, but his guarded manner was born, I suspect, of superstition and self-protection. If people had information about you, you never knew what they might do with it – especially 'the white man' (a term used to describe figures of authority). That nervousness in part explains why his identity was obscured through the moniker Bageye (he had baggy eyes). All his friends had similar nicknames like Tidy Boots, Shine, Pumpkin Head, Summer Wear and Pioneer. None of these men addressed my father as Clinton George; he was always just 'Bageye'.

The same code, a West Indian omertà, was present in many households. It extended beyond names, to reflections on life in the Caribbean, a reluctance or inability to say very much about the past. It meant that children of my generation grew up in ignorance, scratching around in the dark, picking up, and being grateful for, crumbs of information about the lives of parents back in the cinnamon-scented past.

The setting for my interviews, mostly in front rooms, was always intimate, at times bordering on the confessional. Often the grand-children and protective adult children of the elders sat in, listening attentively, occasionally correcting and attempting to tidy up anecdotes, sometimes shaking their heads in awe and disbelief. Time and again they'd tell me at the end of a revelatory interview, 'I have never heard half of those stories before.'

In the final years of Bageye's life, perhaps because he was much closer to the end of his adventure than to its beginning, there was also a loosening, and he was prepared to talk, to dig up the ground where the totems of his past lay lightly buried. I learned more about him than I'd gleaned in the first dozen or so years of my childhood, when he'd been at least present physically, if not emotionally. With those last surprising conversations, he was no longer so determined to forget – or at least to resist answering my questions. I discovered that Bageye had four sisters; that his mother had been a pastor and that, aged sixteen, he'd disappointed his family by signing on with the Merchant Navy as a galley boy.

How do we account for the past silence? Was it just that newspaper editors and publishers were not interested, as one agent told me when I approached him thirty years ago, in 'ethnic writing'? It seemed to me as a child that people who wrote books were as little interested in West Indians as they were generally in the working class. Even so, bizarrely, the idea of the working class seemed separate from us, so that we were even more marginalised than our white counterparts and not part of the wider discourse on class division and disparities in this country.

Perhaps when West Indians were considered, we were too passive in ceding our stories to others. I remember the gratitude we felt when some white writers attempted to shine a more positive light on our lives. Mostly, though, there was silence.

West Indians may have seemed complicit in the omission but, fundamentally, that silence had its roots in slavery. The Middle Passage was an area of darkness best left unilluminated; best to hurry towards the future light. People in the British colonies were discouraged from looking back. The British, aided by their colonial administrators, executed a kind of genius of propaganda in the decades and century after emancipation; Britain was admired for its part in Abolition rather than for the plunder of Africans or for setting up and running an Atlantic Slave Trade in the first place. 'We never knew!' Joyce Estelle Trotman told me, her voice rising with disbelief. It seems incredulous to the ninety-year-old that, as a girl in British Guiana, she'd blithely walked on land that had been worked under the driver's whip by ancestors just a century before. Somehow it remained hidden.

There was something thrilling about growing up in West Indian social circles in the 1960s. These young parents seemed enormously impressive. Walking through the West Indian neighbourhoods of Luton was like walking through the musical *Guys and Dolls*: we had our own pious Sister Sarah Brown, smart-suited Big Jule, Benny Southstreet and Nathan Detroit. Bageye, of course, approximated Sky Masterson. In gambling, if asked to give an inventory of his life, he'd always say he was 'ahead'.

There seemed only the odd 'character' among the British, but the West Indian population was awash with them. Some did become cartoonish figures, like the fellow West Indians V. S. Naipaul cruelly lampoons in his 1994 novel *A Way in the World*: 'shipwrecked men ... in pin-stripe suits and bowler hats, with absurd accents'.[1] But I could forgive them the pose. Aren't we all absurd, even Naipaul?

Fatherhood was a different matter. At some level, men like Bageye, unschooled in the ways of Britain and unable, therefore, to school their children, absolved themselves of the responsibility of fatherhood. The women were left to take up the reins. Like many of my peers, the sober truth was, to borrow the Barbadian writer George Lamming's phrase: 'my father who had only fathered the idea of me had left me the sole liability of my mother who really fathered me'.[2]

I conceived of *Homecoming* as an excavation of the past in which I would elicit truths from simple questions about the intentions of the elders. What was the plan? What were the West Indians who migrated here in the 1950s and 1960s thinking? Can they really have set off 4,000 miles without a road – or psychological – map for where life would take them?

I began to see patterns among the answers. Most of the elders had lived in Britain much longer than they'd ever envisaged on arrival. I remembered words and ideas from past conversations with my mother. It was as if she had worked it out and provided the answers all along. Her husband, Bageye, she'd often lament in the sixties, was a man who 'like tek chance.' He was addicted to uncertainty; his friends were too. When my mother would occasionally chastise me for my own indirection in life as I turned into a man, she'd say, 'You're bluffing. C'mon now what do you really want? Right now you're only bluffing.' The West Indians I'd admired had settled for bluff. As a child I couldn't, at first, make out the shape and contours of their lives. Somewhere along the way, they had accepted that this is what life was: a blur, a fudge, bluff.

How, then, to delineate these lives? I imagined not a quick snapshot or a succession of Kodak moments. No, I would spend hours with them, in the comfort of their homes, and listen. I would sit with them as if I'd brought with me a huge sheet of tracing paper and we would trace and map their great adventure.

There were many surprises. Some of the distressing landmarks which are associated with the time – the Nottingham and Notting Hill riots in 1958; the anti-immigrant Commonwealth Immigrants Act of 1962; Smethwick's 'If You Want a Nigger for a Neighbour, Vote Labour' campaign in the general election two years later; and Enoch Powell's notorious 1968 'Rivers of Blood' speech – were not necessarily felt as viscerally by these West Indians as we might imagine today. People were too busy getting on with their lives to be distracted by hate and foolishness. West Indians might have been aggrieved and resentful about prejudice, but they were also phlegmatic. 'The Englishman can't help himself,' Bageye used to say. 'It's just his way.'

Growing up in suburban Britain back then, it felt as if West Indians and their children had been abandoned or, at best, overlooked by the mainstream, as if we were the graft that didn't 'take' to the host. In our initial headlong focus on the wisdom of assimilation, it took a while, and some nerve, to step back, to process what was going on, even, as Stuart Hall was to discover, to 'turn to your blackness'.[3] But thank God he did. Others lacked the emotional intelligence or ability or luck to be much help in navigating Britain and locating our place in it. Writers such as Andrea Levy – with works like *Every Light in the House Burnin'* – dropped a stone in the great pond of English literature and created a ripple to show we existed, if only for a while. It may have been my own ignorance and narrow-mindedness, but

I did not want to read what white but sympathetic British writers like Colin McInnes had to say. I didn't hold out much hope for a nuanced depiction of the zoot-suited black spivs in 1950s Notting Hill whom he depicted in *City of Spades*. A more attractive and resonant work came with Sam Selvon's sad but funny reflections on early West Indian migrants in *Lonely Londoners*. And I often wondered what would have become of his characters, Moses, Tanty and Sir Galahad, if their stories were updated today. That question animated the research for this book. I hope readers will find the glow of their afterlives here, in these pages.[4]

If I felt any resistance from potential interviewees during the compilation of this book, I'd always enlist the support of Chinua Achebe. In fact, he often came up in interviews anyway. Chinua Achebe once commented on the importance of story-telling for black people who have been marginalised in mainstream cultures: 'Until the lions have their own historians then the story of the hunt will always glorify the hunter.'[5] In this book there are many lions and lionesses, and they are all telling their extraordinary stories and unashamedly 'chatting their business'.

In addition to these new interviews, to create a tableau of West Indian life in Britain, I draw on my personal archive of interviews amassed over the last twenty years. They are woven into the text alongside other richly rewarding sound archives from institutions like the British Library and the BBC, as well as other discrete oral history projects begun in places such as Leeds and Manchester, and individual collections, like those accrued by the filmmaker and DJ Don Letts, and the writer and artist Michael McMillan for his 'The West Indian Front Room' installation. I also follow the paths of other writers like Andrea Levy, Stuart Hall, V. S. Naipaul and, of course, Derek Walcott.

I'd forgotten about Derek Walcott's great poem, 'Homecoming: Anse la Raye', when I was searching for a title for this new book. Retrospectively, I was struck by Walcott's lines: 'but never guessed you'd come/to know there are homecomings without home'.[6] I'd assumed the St Lucian poet was considering the nature of return to the Caribbean literally after such a long time abroad. But, actually, his canvas is much bigger. Home is not home; home is elsewhere. Walcott is talking metaphorically and universally. 'I don't think we ever have complete homecoming,' Walcott later explained. 'There is always a little extra left that we need to occupy, or something to contradict the elation of being home.'[7]

That same sentiment – the complicated elation of being home – was expressed by many of the people I interviewed for this book. On setting out from their British colonies in the Caribbean to come 'home' to Britain in the 1950s and 1960s, they never felt that they'd fully arrived.

England Was No Muma to Me

My siblings and I would sometimes nag my mother Ethlyn as she put us to bed in Luton to describe her life in Jamaica – a place we'd never been. She would conjure up a 1940s world that was magical and mysterious. Ethlyn had lived on Kingston's Outlook Avenue, a residential area – she rolled the r and drew out the word 'residential' so we understood its societal importance. At the bottom of Outlook Avenue there was the Bournemouth Beach Club where she and her friends met to listen to jazz. In her halter-neck dress she swooned on the dance floor and sipped cocktails at candle-lit tables around a swimming pool with steps down to the sea. 'Can you see it?' said Ethlyn. 'No? If you want to see glamour, close your eyes and imagine it.'

Ethlyn talked fondly (proudly even) of her middle-class home with uniformed servants; of joining the Girl Guides and taking part in the ceremonial folding of the Union flag; of practising cursive handwriting from a *Vere Foster's New Civil Service Copybook*; of standing to attention in the Rialto Cinema at the end of a screening of the latest film, to sing with lusty enthusiasm 'God Save The King'; and of learning by rote and reciting Alexander Pope's 'The Rape of the Lock' and the sentimental ending of Rudyard Kipling's 'Gunga Din'.

As much as she was steeped in English poetry, Ethlyn's language was also laced with Jamaican proverbs and sayings. On the question of motherly love, for example, she would say: 'Cook pickney give muma, muma can't eat it. Cook muma give pickney, pickney nyam.' The meaning of the parable – the mother who couldn't eat her child yet the child ate the mother voraciously – was that mothers would always love their children more than children love mothers.

Ethlyn, like many of her friends in Jamaica, had a romantic attachment to the notion of England as a motherland. The values of England were her values; her belief in England was an article of faith. In a sense, I owe my education to those reveries. Ethlyn immersed herself, 4,000 miles away, in a fictionalised idea of Britain found in *Tom Brown's School Days* in particular. That quintessentially British novel, film and culture held a grip on her imagination and that of her peers. Decades later, this fuelled her determination to give me the kind of 'polish' offered by a British public school, even though she could ill afford to send me to such a place.

Another favourite poem of Ethlyn's was Kipling's 'English Flag', which included the memorable line: 'And what should they know of England who only England know?' Directed at the British who'd never travelled to the colonies to grasp the ambition of Empire, Kipling's question might also be asked of West Indians who'd never left their islands and whose knowledge of England, grounded in arcane ceremonies and history, was drawn almost exclusively from text books imported from Britain. West Indians only knew England in the abstract: in the eccentricity of Ealing comedies, in paintings of Salisbury Cathedral and in playground songs of dancing around the exotic 'mulberry bush'.

Today, the south London home of Joyce Estelle Trotman brims full of memorabilia and the legacy of Empire. There are even copies of her old school text books, Nelson's West Indian Readers series – a standard educational tool that included extracts of Dickens and reflections on Constable's paintings. There were never examples available of any locally made art or literature. As she remembers the English country dance they learned at school, the sprightly ninety-year-old Joyce gets up to demonstrate the dance she'd performed as a seven-year-old in British Guiana, knowing nothing of its origins.

The bodies of West Indians may have been in the Caribbean, but their heads were in British clouds. George Lamming has this in mind when he asserts in *The Pleasures of Exile* that 'most West Indians of my generation were born in England.'[1] Though they'd never left the West Indian islands, they'd bought into the idea that the colonies were an extension of England. To pack your bags and book passage on a steamship to England was to journey to the centre, like Dick Whittington striking out from Lancashire to London.

West Indians were part of something bigger than just England; subjects of an imperial experiment. These nineteen Caribbean islands (and Guiana on the mainland of South America) had been colonised by the British over the course of three centuries. They would continue to be governed by the British until they became independent from the 1960s onwards. On Empire Day (24 May) each year, millions of children from all corners of the globe were encouraged to stretch out hands, forming a ring around earth to celebrate their membership of an extraordinary extended family – including those British territories in the West Indies.

But where were these so-called Caribbean people from? They were not Caribs. In the 1960s the Rastafarians would spell out the anomaly in song: 'Jamaica is an island but not I land'. The British subjects in the West Indies were a forced admixture of African and European; not Afro-Caribbeans then but, more accurately, Afro-Saxons.

Whenever I asked Ethlyn about our heritage and family line, she would recite almost as a litany the names of our ancestors. Ethlyn's mum was Pauline. Before her was Granny Reid who was preceded by Marmie. Finally there was Gong who was a slave. That was it. Ethlyn could go back no further. And all she knew of Gong was her name.

Considering Britain's role in the toxic Atlantic Slave Trade, I was surprised by how little antipathy there was towards Britain from my West Indian interviewees. But for many, like Ethlyn and Joyce Trotman growing up in the region, slavery and its legacy – its psychological impact, reparations or indentureship of mainly Indian labourers hired to work on plantations after the newly freed slaves refused – had never been a topic of conversation, other than when celebrating William Wilberforce's role in abolition. While British history was taught and absorbed in the colonies, there was little recognition of African ancestry. Africa was an embarrassment and a pitiful 'dark continent', only thought about when the collection plate came round in church services. Africa was not the motherland; England owned that title.

★

Joyce Estelle Trotman

I was born in Stanleytown village, West Bank, Demerara, British Guiana. It's a little village on the Demerara River. The Dutch had two polders [sections of drained land] and two canals dug by slave labour, and Stanleytown would be the first village. My grandparents were farmers, planting cassava and eddoes and so on.

My grandfather was a chief pan boiler. Sugar! Slavery is sugar! The pan boilers were the workers in the sugar factory. When you got all the juice out from the cane it was boiled and boiled until it became like molasses. Then it was boiled again in a big copper pan until it crystallised; they said that the Guyanese pan boilers were the best in the West Indies.

By the time, in 1936, I wasn't even nine yet; by that time, I could do the times tables from two to seventeen. It's true! Teacher was like a circus master with a cane, and I'm in the middle there, and I'm doing seventeen times table by rote. I didn't even know what it was for! The cane was like a whip, and it had some joints in it, and they were imported from England!

And then, we had to do English country dancing; [sings and dances] 'If all the world were paper, and all the seas were ink, if all the trees were bread and cheese, what would you have to drink?' Up

a double, back a double, set and turn. English country dancing, to
the tune of 'If All the World Were Paper'. One year I was looking
at *Poldark* on TV and they were doing the country dancing and I
thought, 'Oh! That's Black Nag [an English country dance, aka the
Galloping Nag] they're doing there!'

For the scholarship, books were imported and they were all
English, and they would have dictation passages, because you have
to learn the hard words. In one year, one of the passages was all
the flowers of England, and among them was 'delphinium' and
'antirrhinum' and you had to learn to spell them, and I spelled
'antirrhinum' with one r and I got licks; so every time I look at the
one in my garden I say, 'You caused me a headache!'

Now in those days secondary education was not free. If you
were a girl, and you were illegitimate like me, you couldn't
go to the Bishops High School; you had to go to the convent,
because Bishops High School was very English. You had to
be rescued by St Joseph's Convent – Ursula Convent wouldn't
take you because you were black. Who went there were white
and Portuguese.

So this friend of my mother's, he opened this school called
Enterprise High School in somebody's big two-storey house, and
twelve of us turned up that first morning, Friday 1 September
1939, when Hitler invaded Poland. I heard the [sings out] 'WAR
BULLETIN!' That was the first time I heard war bulletin.

Later the government decided they had extra money, so they
offered four free places ... and I went to the Bishops High
School. The Deputy was Mr Ogle. One day one of the girls,
in the presence of Betty, the Deputy's daughter, called Olive
Dennison a nigger and Betty Ogle said to her, 'You apologise to
Olive now.' But do you know what it was? Betty Ogle's mother
was white Jamaican, so she was different – so Betty had a different
upbringing from the girl, and stood there and made her apologise
to Olive Dennison.

Everything was English! Look at the books! [points to her bookshelf] *Ivanhoe, Henry V*, Keats and Shelley and Wordsworth, Matthew Arnold. Talking about Keats, in the primary school, when you read, on the page, there was a poem called 'The Naughty Boy':

> There was a naughty boy,
> And a naughty boy was he.
> He ran away to Scotland,
> The people there to see ...

But, if you see the page, it had 'John Keats' at the bottom; well, we were rapping without knowing that we were rapping:

> So he stood in his shoes
> And he wondered,
> He wondered,
> He stood in his shoes,
> And he wondered
> John Keats

Nobody told us that this 'Keats' at the bottom wasn't part of the poem!

Trevor Rhone

In Jamaica, we grew up on the iambic pentameter and Chaucer and Shakespeare. And all our lives going to the cinema; there'd be Ealing comedies or Noel Coward dramas, films of Shakespeare, Laurence Olivier; big stars on the screen. So little of our own. And I remember going to my school library in the 1950s and out of the blue jumped this book at me, *The Hills Were Joyful Together* by Roger Mais. It was the first time I'd come across any locally written literature. Poems were about snow and daffodils, which we really couldn't relate to at all. There was nothing that reflected our own life experiences.

Colin Carter

In Barbados we have got Hastings, we have got Worthing, we have got Yorkshire, we've got Lancaster, we have got Tetley. You name it. We have a Nelson statue in Barbados that is older than the one in London, and it also stands in Trafalgar Square.

We had a warped knowledge of English people. Barbados was swamped with the middle-class Englishman who conveyed a certain image, a certain air about England; he done it so well it was natural for Barbadians to visualise England through the eyes of those kind of people. And I'm talking about our Civil Service – the Commissioner of Police, the adjutant, the regimental sergeant major instructor, the Governor – all these were people who were dispatched from England to run the administration.

George Mangar

I was born in British Guiana, now called Guyana, in 1937. 42 Broad Street, Charleston, Georgetown, British Guiana. It was a multi-racial area, and in those days people of all walks of life lived next to each other, and we all lived harmoniously together, all races of people. We were so cosmopolitan. I'm of Indian extract and my neighbours were Negro extract, Chinese and Portuguese. If you came to my house and expect to have curry and rice you'd be wrong. My grandparents came from India, three of them, two from Bihar and one from Kashmir. They came as indentured labour at the end of slavery. And my mother's father was from Ireland. My father was a medical practitioner, my mother was a housewife.

I always knew I was British. Everything rotated around being British, we spoke English. When you got to school you have to speak English correctly – you can have accents after, but we learned from a book. Because all the churches run everything in English, we had to aim to learn one thing, English history. I knew more about England than I knew about Guiana.

My father studied in England and he adapted English customs as well, like egg and bacon for breakfast, and cornflakes and milk, and roast lunches. My father followed all the British customs. Then the Church, of course, brings along that line as well. All the priests were from England. The governor of our country was from England, the Home Secretary was from England. We had a parliament which was local people, but you always had the English influence.

Bookers came from England, Bookers Brothers, and most of the big stores, and so on. [The London-based Booker Company was the colony's largest landlord, manufacturer, retailer and employer.] We had Sandbach Parker, we had Fogarty's [which was Irish]. Everything came from England: our clothing, K shoes. Booker Brothers' managers were from England, Scotland and various places – all white people. They all employed people of fair colour in these stores. In my time I only saw about two or three non-white people working there; they had to be Catholic as well. The banks as well; we had Barclays Bank, the Royal Bank of Canada. Barclays Bank, I hardly ever saw a black person working there until years and years after. Royal Bank of Canada as well, there were one or two non-whites in there. In later years they took people from other nationalities. I thought nothing of that.

My aspiration was to come to England and study like my father. My father died from a brain haemorrhage when I was only eight years old. He died very suddenly, while we were having dinner one evening. I was sat next to him, his face went into his bowl of soup and I took his glasses off and moved the plate. I didn't realise what was happening, and the next thing I knew all these doctors came to the house and said my father was dead.

We had so many different things under the English rule that you never had under the local rule after. I think it was positive in the sense; because we were educated in English, we had a culture. We played cricket, football, rugby. We had a lot of things which the English brought to us – dancing the waltz, the classical music, which I love.

In Guiana everybody had a club that they go to for their entertainment, like the white people had their own club, the GCC, the George Cricket Club. The Indians had the British Guiana East India Club; they had dances, they played cricket and at the weekends they played bridge – all the English things they did, and tennis. The Negro people had the DCC, Demerara Cricket Club, then the Chinese Association had theirs, the Portuguese had theirs; everybody had a club to go to, but everything was English.

We could go to all the clubs, except the white clubs; you had to be invited. We had a place called the Carib which all the elite went to – the Saturday night dances – the crème de la crème, lawyers and doctors. I was never invited to the white club, you had to be invited to these things; my father [a doctor] was invited to things like that – he treated people who were white.

We had a radio and the end of the programmes at night, they played the national anthem of England. At the cinemas at the beginning of every film there was the national anthem of England; everybody stood up. When I came to England in 1959 in Ipswich, my sister-in-law took me to the movies and they played the national anthem, and I was the only person who stood up! She grabbed me, said, 'Sit down, what are you doing?' I didn't know anything different.

Learie Constantine
BBC Third Programme, 1943

My grandparents were slaves. It's queer now to think back to my childhood, to see my grandfather sitting in the hot sunshine on the top step of his little bungalow leaning his back against the door and to realise when he was a youth he was a slave, and my grandmother too.

I remember my first cricket bat when I was four or five. It wasn't a cricket bat in the sense that English boys know them; it was made from a branch taken from a coconut tree and the ball we played with was a young orange or grapefruit dried in the sun until the rind came off and rolled around until it became flexible and we could get forty or fifty runs off it before we demanded a new ball. All the boys in our family played cricket. My father first came to England with the West Indies team in 1900 and when he was first over he made friends with two Irish men called Learie and Vivian. They gave him such a good time in Ireland that he said he would call his son after one of them.

Vivian Durham

The ambition of every black Jamaican in those days was to be a white man. In those days, our conception was based upon the story of the rich man in his castle; the poor man at his gate. God made them high and lowly and ordered their estate. There was a perversion of the fundamental principle of theology. You'd be shocked to know that up until we got universal adult suffrage in 1944, a black man could not be Inspector of Police – he couldn't go further than Sergeant Major. It would have been incredible to think of a black man being a prelate of the local parish. It would have been incredible to have a black man like me being a justice of the peace, and so those were the kind of rapacious conditions [we lived under].

Wilford Lawson

Montego Bay [Jamaica], where we were from, was a tourist place, so I used to mingle with people from foreign. I met some well-known film stars like Gary Cooper. I remember getting a dollar from him. We used to go and entertain them at the Casablanca hotel, spitting fire out of we mouth with kerosene, things like that. It was at the Casablanca that Gary Cooper chucked a dollar to me.

I had plenty little job as a youth. I was also a cabin boy on Lyndon Johnson's little 37ft yacht – when he and his wife Ladybird came out I would serve them. It was more or less like a work/ friend thing, it wasn't really a master and servant situation; I used to sit and talk with Lyndon Johnson and Ladybird.

I used to sing at the Boys Club. The club was run by Mas' Charlie and was funded by the founder of the *Daily Express*, Lord Beaverbrook. I was kissed by Lady Jeanne Beaverbrook. When I say kissed, I mean she come and kissed me on my lips at the Boys Club. We were singing for her and her husband.[2]

I also got building work in and around Montego Bay. I had a friend who knew this millionaire Captain Saunders, his house was like a fortress, he had a pilot house that send the sea water straight up to the swimming pool. A chap called Basil controlled the millionaire and Basil was a friend of mine. I used to do all the work he was commissioned for. Basil was a showman, right; when you see him, you see light; when you see him the whole place light up! He used to have a white horse and used to dress in a white suit when he'd be riding the horse on the main road. Whatever Basil said to the captain, he do. Somebody said he was a bit gay or something. Anyway Basil was able to control him.

You can get on with white people in Jamaica but you have to know to deal with them. I was quite privilege, I was always mingling with white people, English people.

Linette May Simms

I was born in St Catherine, Jamaica, 5 January 1930. I love St Catherine. My father's land was his father's land, Orange Hill, all ten of us born there. We farm coconut, breadfruit, thing like cassava, callaloo, sugarcane. My father used to have a donkey and it had two hampers, and my mother would sit in the middle on the back of the donkey and the two hampers at the sides have the coffee or the chocolate or the breadfruit, whatever she'd going to sell; that's how she get to Linstead Market.

I went to elementary school; no secondary. Empire Day was a day you dress up. You don't wear shoes to school but on Empire Day we wear shoes. We were celebrating the King. I had friends from the village. My favourite friend was white because her father wasn't Jamaican; he was Mas' Percy. She was called Myrtle. She don't friend no other girl, just me. People would look at me and wonder what was so special about me to have a white friend. She was at school with me but she could go to High School but I couldn't afford to go there.

I was twelve when I leave school. Because we had a school inspection and you change classes, I skipped from B to second; I was brighter than my friend [Kathleen] at the same school. Because I skipped a class I leave her behind. When playtime come we go for dinner and I used to tease her, 'Catch you and pass you'; she was crying and I didn't know she was going to tell her mum about my singing. The mum said something to the daughter, and when I got to school there was a bump or a boil that came up on one of my feet. And the teacher start to sniff and say, 'What smells?' I tell my mum, 'Mum, the teacher say there's a funny smell, and a lump come up on my foot and it getting bigger.' My mum looked, she see the boil and she say, 'It must be this Miss Birdie smell. You know what, stay home from school today, don't go back today.' And she look after it. When they call for me to go back to school, she say, 'You have to leave her here and I'll have to look after her foot.' And from that day I never went back to that school [crying].

It was some kind of obeah,[3] yes. And my father brought a man called Mr McKenzie to our house. He's far away from my district and when he came he rode on a horse, a big lovely white horse, and he rode the horse through the gate and around the house three times, and as he did he was talking to himself, saying, 'I am here now, and since I am here you have to go, now!' Then he said, 'Bye bye, I see you again.' And my foot improved. He was spiritual man and we called him 'healer'. I never bother with Kathleen again.

From there, I work on helping plant my father's land. I remember when the Queen father died I was in the bush picking gungo peas and heard the church bells far and wide tolling, and the people were bawling and wailing because the King died. In my mind I had pictures of the Queen. Even the dogs were barking because the King died.

Bert Williams

I was born in Jamaica in 1944 in the mountains, in a place called Coleyville in Manchester. It's cool and high up. A lot of white English settlers settled in those areas, because they were high up in the mountains, so it's more like English climate really. Coleyville is a village and that's where the post office is, but where I was actually born was a little village called Ticky Ticky. It's a beautiful name but when we were away from home we wouldn't tell anyone that we were from there, because Ticky Ticky meant bush.

It's no neighbours, just my uncle who was our neighbour, and he was around a quarter mile away from where our house was. It's very bushy and very stony and the road wasn't made up for cars. My dad was a farmer. He farmed sugar, everything, kept chickens, ducks, pigs, cows, goats, donkeys.

We lived in the mountains and there was no running water, no electricity, no gas and the cooking was done by wood. I wake up in the morning and my brother and I would take a bucket to the spring. In the dry season, we had a tank to collect water, but even when I was there, there was improvement; they put a pump in, a hand pump, otherwise we have to go up on the tank with a rope, put a bucket down and pull the water up. When there's no rain, for the animals we had to go and carry the water in a bucket. It was heavy work; you carry what you can on your head and that was it. Even now I could balance a glass on my head.

I'd say I had a royal education. You'd see the Royal Family in school books, on the wall in the school. Don't forget we were educated the same as people in England. Our exam paper, our 'O' Levels, were sent from and had to come back to England to be marked in the first place. So all our history were about Churchill and the war; the geography was all about England; the economy was all about Bristol iron works and Sheffield steel, and we knew all about them. We knew about Ford's and different factories and machinery that you'd seen. You hear 'Sheffield steel' and you didn't realise that Sheffield was a place; it was always a brand name.

All the books we had came from England and was written by English writers. Even the cartoons in the newspapers ... there used to be a cartoonist and they would show a cartoon of two English tied up in a pot with a couple of African Pygmy-type people dancing around with bones through the nose, and that's the impression you had of Africa – lion going to eat you kind of thing, that sort of attitude. That's what was going on at that time.

We always thought we weren't Africans; we were better than the Africans and they were actually really slaves. Well, that's how you was taught. It does stick to your memory. They used to say, 'The Master's always right,' and 'You got to pray to the Master.' Well, who is the Master? One minute they say god is the master, and the next minute they say the white man up the road is the master, you know?

My sisters left for England and I knew my time would come, so I start to misbehave, knowing it wouldn't be long before I gone. And if I got into mischief or something like that, there was no way my dad could catch me. I was faster than him, but he used to get another guy to go and catch me and then he'd tie me up ready for beating me. He'd give a penny or a sweet or drink or something and say, 'Catch the boy.' Tie you up till him ready to beat you. You try to wriggle out. Sometime the guy might not tie you tight enough; tie you to a tree or to the house post. Belt or a bit of stick; same stick that he'd beat the dog with. You weren't treated no better than the dogs, I tell you. You don't know any difference because you feel everybody's got the same situation, because you go to school and the children say, 'Oh, I got a good beating from my father.' Or something. Everybody is in the same boat. The teacher beat you as well and you can't complain, because you go home, and the teacher is never wrong according to your parents, so they beat you as well. So you're in a catch-twenty-two situation.

Ken
Journey to an Illusion, 1966[3]

My father kept a cupboard in the schoolroom full of flags. On the slightest provocation – a holiday, a Royal death, a British victory – he tore them out. Rule Britannia! Half-naked children, some without food, some sick, but all loyal, would come out to school. Their voices were loud and clear, innocence drowning the subversive rumblings in their empty tummies. In the dining room of our schoolhouse, there was a Manufacturer's Life map of the world which my father would unfurl after reading the papers and on which he would, with the help of tacks, trace the British frontline [in World War Two]. I was a white supremacist with a dark skin, a champion of white people against the injustices of the blacks. How unspeakably offensive that you should address a white man with hands in your pockets! My father, though a headmaster, saw nothing wrong with books we had to read – books which saw Trinidadians through the eyes of lesser-known English writers. Trinidad was a string of mud huts relieved by the colourful landscape, exotic, green – a romantic paradise for English adventurers.

I never knew anyone as a child who had actually been to Britain. Yet this far-off country where the King lived, completely swamped my mind with things like the Colonial Office, the appointing of Governors, the final word in authority! It was also the home of gentlemen. I was impressed by their manner, the bowler hats and their tightly rolled umbrellas.

Louise Smith
I was born in St Thomas, Jamaica, Fonthill district. It was beautiful growing up, but my dad died and leave my mum with six of us.

And I tell you, it wasn't easy for her, it was very very hard. She have to work hard. She have to walk many miles to Morant Bay to buy fish and then string them up and she walk with a basket 'pon her head to sell it to look after us, and it wasn't easy. When she comes home her foot them swollen from walking. It wasn't a bed of roses for my mum but, thank God, we all grew up, the six of us. My mum has a piece of land from the government and we plant gungo peas, everything, and we have to don't go to school. When she dig the hole, we drop in the peas or the corn. And sometimes the sun hot, and we fed up, we children. Sometimes, we're not supposed to drop more than four, we drop eight or ten, because we want it for finish. When it done, sometimes she said, 'How come the corn done so quick?' We don't answer, me and my brother, we don't answer a word. But it was good still, everything was there, food – we have fruits, we raise chicken, some people have their goat, they get milk from the goat. In the district everybody's the same. We club together, and if you have plenty food and I don't have none, you give me bunch of banana, yam, anything – we share with each other.

When I was growing up I didn't think I was British. Me Jamaican and me Fonthill where I grow up so. Me not talk about no British. One time I remember my brother says the Queen coming to Jamaica and you can have this flag, and everybody was so excited. My mother say, 'I'm not going to see no Queen. Why?' Listen, Jamaica have some white people. Them say they are white people but bwoy, I'm not sure. They live on the level part; they capture it, they have the better part in Jamaica. We is up in the hills where goat run; they, the white man, on the level. They have nanny and cook. My cousin was the cook for one of them and she get me to help out with the woman children, and that time I was still a child, you know. I never forget this English woman, oh she was mean; when you put the food on the table, any food left, she tell you, 'Put it up, you can't eat it.' She say, 'Put it up for tomorrow.'

When she buy a piece of meat, like a leg of lamb or pork, she score it so it's marked so she know if any missing. That's how they stay, English man and woman. And I thought, when people said they going to the mother country, them fool if them think they go up here and treated good, you know. They say England mother country, but she was no muma to me.

Arthur France

I'm from a village was called Mount Lily in Nevis, born in 1936. We had maybe 200 people in the village. A white man was held in high esteem, you don't question him. The family who owned the estate that my father worked on was a man name of Sir Arthur Lees. He was there, the wife only had one daughter and they had lots of toys you couldn't play with, they had a little pedal car and a tricycle, and we used to sneak up and ride around; but you couldn't get caught on them, your dad would beat you.

Apart from managing coconut plantation on the estate, he had to drive them. Sometime daddy wouldn't get home till two, three o'clock in the morning, because they're going to another part of the island to visit a friend and he have to drive them, wait for them and bring them back – he was kind of a manservant.

He worked very hard because they had three cane fields as well, and another three that were cotton, and they grow a lot of livestock. He was a very hard-working man but he had fun as well because he had a friend. We had three horses, two donkeys and we had a mule whose mother was a horse. There's two kind of mules. The mule whose mother is a horse becomes big like a horse; where the mule whose mother is a donkey becomes small like a donkey. Anyway, he had a friend with a carriage. And I remember my dad, sometimes on Sundays, would put the mule in front of this carriage. They go through town, visiting people.

We used to go down, me and my mates, we used to gather the coconuts, so we'd get them in a big pile, and a vehicle would come and take them to the yard. We used to make copra, which is something that you make soap from. I think they had a factory in Nevis. We used to collect them when we were little boys and we used to get four pence to collect a hundred coconuts. We'd have ten or twelve in a big sugar bag.

I join the Boys' Brigade. Everybody wanted their children to be part of a group. Methodists had a brigade but the Church of England had Boy Scouts. One Sunday in every month you'd go charge parade – and your parents there, smartly dressed – and you're in your uniform, going to church, marching down. At school you had to know the make-up of the Union Jack back to front.

What I couldn't understand was my father used to order his suits from Halifax in England; he always used to be well-dressed, and I couldn't understand why he had his suits from Halifax. In those days you didn't have a wardrobe, you had a trunk, and the trunk had a tray at the top of it, and all your cufflinks and your ties were in the tray, and your shoes were in the bottom. On a Sunday morning my mother had to take the suit that my father was going to wear out the trunk, hang it up and brush it.

It's like magic to see 'Made in England' and people cherished things from England. Like a car, Austin of England, which was one of the cars Daddy used to drive. When they see something 'Made in England', that was it, you don't ask any more questions.

In fact, we had a flagpole on the house and every morning we had to raise the flag.

Clinton Cameron

I was born in St Catherine, Jamaica in 1939, same year as the war, in a district called Mendez. Jamaica is a very mountainous place and we were on top of the hill. The school was about three miles away, called Point Hill – at that time there was the Baptist school. My parents didn't go to church; as I grew up my parents had some links with Jehovah Witnesses so that's what I grew up.

I remember as a boy, aged nine, they introduced the scouts at school, and after school it was all boys dressed up in their khaki uniforms marching and saluting, and I was really taken by it. I wanted to join, so I went home and asked my mother if I could join. She didn't say yes and she didn't say no. Eventually, she said, 'Right, you want to learn to kill people, do you?' And that was the end of that. I never asked again.

My dad was a farmer, farming every little thing – planted yams, potatoes, grew coffee, oranges and all sorts of fruits. My mother would go to the market every week. There were two markets, one in Linstead, about ten miles away. Everybody going from Kingston to the north coast would go through Linstead. You know the song by Louise Bennett,[4] 'Carry me ackee go Linstead market not a quatty would sell'? A quatty was two pence ha'penny in old money at a time when the pound was made up for 240 pence. So it would have been a bad day at the market.

We all grew up with Louise Bennett, who was like a travelling poet through the island, and I remember at school more than once she would come and teach us the songs, particularly trying to get us to write the language as is spoken, and also to get us to write in verse. She came one day and it was raining and usually we do all our learning outside, so now we were inside and she was trying so hard to get us to open up our heads, but nothing much came of it.

I grew up in a time of Empire and every Empire Day you go to school and after assembly you go outside for the little displays; there was something of a show, but my parents were always against anything to do with a kind of Empire loyalty and were against anything that might be interested as worshipping the flag. I think part of it might have been political. They did not support worshipping the Queen or giving her special status or worshipping the symbol of the flag. We were told, 'Yes you go to school on Empire Day, but as soon as they go outside and start the celebrations you just come home'; so we did.

Waveney Bushell

I was born in the then British Guiana, in Buxton, a village on the east coast, Demerara in 1928. My mother's name was Gertrude Ogle and my father, they called him Woody. I didn't know him at all, Woody Ogle, he was a lawyer. He was Woodbury. Waveney is an English name; there's a river called Waveney, it's near Diss. I grew up as an orphan in a way, with my aunt. My mother died and I remember her clearly; she died when I was six. Her husband wasn't around and my godmother used to say, 'Your mother died of a broken heart.'

Being a colony, everything was British. There were clubs, which we were not allowed to enter on the grounds of our colour. We weren't slaves then but, because we were the product of slaves, we were always downgraded. The treatment that we got was second class, made us feel as if we were second-class citizens. For example, black people's involvement with English people, even with the mulattoes, was an involvement of servitude. We were their gardeners or their servants, we were not allowed to walk up their front steps. A cousin of mine was a seamstress and she sent me with a dress, a parcel, to deliver to a home and you knew instinctively that you walked up the back step. The black servant would tell you, 'You have to use the back step.' I lived for the day when I would be able to earn a living and feel, myself, that I'm the same social status as anyone else.

We were indoctrinated into feeling that Britain was *the* place in the world. When you think of literature, up to the days when I was doing teacher training age nineteen, twenty, I would say that until then I felt everything English was the best, for example was better than American. A good example of that is when we studied literature, we somehow got the impression that these English books were better – that the English people spoke was somehow superior to the English that the Americans spoke. It wasn't until – we had a very good teacher called Johnny Rodway, who was from one of the islands. He was a very well-read man and he started telling us about short story writers, he told us about O. Henry, Guy de Maupassant, he gave us a spread of people from all over the world. I realised there was no distinction to say one was better than the other. One of the reasons was that our library only had English books. There was no Caribbean literature in those days.

Franklin Jackson

I was born in a likkle place called Prospect, Prospect District, Clarendon, Jamaica, up in the hills on 18 March 1950. I went to school in Prospect. School was not important to me. When they send me to school sometimes I would end up at the river instead, and sometimes I would go shooting birds in the woods. I was very good at it; we made a slingshot. We had to make everything, we didn't have toys. I never had a toy. We used to make things like banjo from bamboo. We made our cricket ball from the root of bamboo tree. Everything we used to have to make ourself. I often wonder why they call it Prospect, because I don't think the people who live up there have any prospect at all. I think it might be a bit ironic.

My parents were not skilled and not highly educated. Most black people were not highly educated. They used to grow their own food and sell a likkle bit where they can. Or my daddy would saw wood for other people to make money, or they would join together, a group of men, and they all go and do it in the morning, call it their morning work, so by eleven or twelve o'clock they finish.

In Jamaica when we was young and growing up, a lot of us grew up quite a little bit backwards, because the elders – whether they were older kids or were our parents' age – we couldn't be in those conversations or sit around them when they're having conversations, we had to move away; so therefore, if children are always just talking to themselves or with themselves, then they don't really learn much. What can one child teach the other? So fundamental things like making facial expressions, we not learn what one thing or another meant because it was ill-mannered to look up into their faces. When we talked to them we supposed to look down, just like the slave master would teach us, and it transferred down through a lot of them – because in my parents' age, it wasn't that long through slavery, don't forget.

Discipline was strong, yes. If I'm late from school, ten minutes. I get home, 'Where've you been, why you're late? Go and cut me a piece of whip.' And what we used to do, we used to use one knife and cut little circles in these whips so when it was brought down it would break. And if we bring a whip that is not big enough, we better not do that, because they'll go and pick one for themself. So the discipline was installed. We all used to fear our parents. They brought us up with a whip just like their grandparents did from slavery days or whatever, because it takes a long time to re-educate or de-educate or change a nation of people. It's a whole attitude of people you've got to change and it takes a long time.

I never seen a film, never read a newspaper, never been to a dance or anything like that, or seen any people going to a dance or anything, never even turned on a radio. I turned on my neighbour's radio once. I was in the house with one of my friends and I said, 'Can I turn the radio on?' I turned it on and music was playing, wow!

And growing up where I came from, I never saw a white person until I went to the airport [to come to Britain]. It was very different, I couldn't stop looking at him, I thought there was something wrong with him.

Barbara Gloudon

We started to come into our own voice through pantomime in Jamaica. Pantomine had been founded by British ex-patriates. So they did the old pantomimes which were found in the West End in London, *Puss in Boots*, *Cinderella* and things like the Widow Twanky and all that; very few black people were in it, for a start. And then Louise Bennett came into it, and she began to write using the stories of Anancy the Spider God, which were ready-made stories, and she then developed them.[5] And I remember as a very young reporter, I went to do an interview with a lady who sat on the board of the Little Theatre, and when she talked, she said she stopped being associated with the theatre when they started putting market women on the stage. All these things with market women and sun-kissed people rushing around the stage singing 'Where you a-go Miss Janey where you a-go', she found it unbearable.

Reginald Davis

I was born in Falmouth, capital of Trelawny, 7 May 1933. I am the last child for my mother. She was in Falmouth at the time. My father was a police in Falmouth. After my birth my mother went back to Clarkstown and she set her home up, and she send both of us to my grandfather – he was living in Jacksontown. I was an infant when my mother died. My father transferred from Falmouth about the same time as I was born.

So I grew up in Jacksontown and I go to school there. I knew they call me Reginald Davis. But I was grown up by my grandfather, he was capable of maintaining my sister and I. When I was about seventeen, after I finished school, there was two estate in Trelawny, Longpond and Vere Royal, about four miles apart. It wasn't a good environment. To me it was degrading, because where we originated from, our ancestors were taken from Africa and the British brought them here, to the Caribbean, to work on the sugar plantation.

And growing up, I knew that when you work on the sugar plantation you are actually repeating your ancestor's experience. I went to work in the laboratory at Vere Royal Sugar Cane, the sampling, testing and so on, it was quite attractive to me, but the pay wasn't very good, about six or seven pounds a week.

After I'd worked there, although it was a prestigious job, the beginning of chemist work, I asked the engineer there – his name was Nash, he's from somewhere in England – and I asked him if I could get a better job in the factory, and he said, 'Oh yes Reggie, ask Mr Antony, that is the head chemist.' I wash his bicycle and fix it up, and the boys say, 'Oh, you are fixing up Mr Antony's bicycle.' Because when you are doing chemist work you feel you are a better class, but I knew I'd need that relationship with someone in a position where they could help me, and when I want the job in the factory, he say, 'Oh yes Reggie you can go and I will find somebody to replace you.' So I get the job down there.

That was in the 1950s and I manage to buy a bicycle. At that time you have a bicycle and you feel like you have a car. So the estate get it for me and I pay a pound a week out my wages, and then I feel quite chuffed. At that time there is a road from Jacksontown to Clarkstown. They call it the Queens Highway from the first time the Queen come, and that's four miles, so it was smooth and pretty. So, Sunday evenings the girls and the boys, we have a bicycle and the girls who want a ride, we act like we have motorcars. You give them a ride and they have to look nice, you give them a little ride and so on.

We always send to England and buy the suit length to make my trousers, and there was some shoes from foreign; I bought those, so I look quite smart. We put together with a few boys and we get our suit length, we get flannel; the cloth from England is proper wool, very strong and it lasts very long. Jamaicans, when you are poor, you gravitate towards what you call style. Though you don't have money, it make you feel as though you're achieving something, that's what happen.

James Berry

When I was a small boy growing up in my Jamaican rural village, the idea of being British made us special; we were not African, not American, we were British. Our teachers stirred in us great pride in being part of the Empire; through songs: 'God Save The King', 'Rule Britannia', 'The Ash Grove'. On 24 May every year, I march in fresh khaki shorts. We wave the flag, I march and sing, 'Britons never never shall be slaves'.

We had somehow fallen for the idea that they [the British] were a fair-minded Christian nation. Despite the history of slavery, we had come along feeling that we were much better off being part of the British way of life than being part of the African. This meant that we had inherited nothing and poverty was always at our door. I tried to express this ambiguity towards the British in a description of Empire Day in my poem 'New World Colonial Child':

I arrive to doubtful connections,
to questionable paths,
to faces with obscure
disclosures, with reticent
voices, not clear why
my area is inaccessible,
my officials are not promoters.

Odd farthings drive the circles
bare, around the houses, like
goats tethered and forgotten.

I can't endure like my father.
I wait bowed. I wait
in rain-saturation,
in sunlight-dazzle.

Dark valleys and snow domes
are elsewhere. I am a piece
of disused gold mine, sometimes
a feather of shot game, other
times a seedbed of obsessions.[6]

Viv Adams

I was born in Kingston, Jamaica in 1948. I never questioned the importance of England as a major country that had shaped us, but I didn't feel that shape was aggressively against my interests, it was just a cosy framework that one naturally fell into. The only time – there were moments when I had a sharp recognition that this was a false world I was living in. One such moment occurred when I was about twelve. In Kingston they had these taxis that were chequered cab, yellow cab, all kind of private taxi companies. Anyway, my mum and I and Percy [his brother] I think, we're in one such cab, and there was an altercation at a road junction between the taxi driver and another cab that was carrying three or four uniformed English soldiers. They had the khaki; they had the short trousers, reprising that Kenyan kind of thing, and I don't know what was the cause of it, but all I remember was these soldiers clambering from the car and coming over to our cab and remonstrating with the driver in a very rough way. I'm not sure if they man-handled him, and I'm not sure if I'm reconstructing it to say they did, but they were sufficiently vocally aggressive – superior in language; tone – that left a deep impression on me to say, 'Well, you know what, these men know that they've got power behind them, that our taxi driver does not have, because they are representatives of the mother country beyond the seas, England, and that's where the real authority lies, that's where the power base lies.' Although they were just common soldiers, nevertheless they seemed to me to have something of power and authority that the taxi driver couldn't resist.

The eccentricity of the English intrigued us, but it didn't have a power hold on us, we saw the English man as quite a weird character – feeble and fragile and effete in his distance but, nevertheless, as a repository of something beyond the boundary.

When you grow up as we did, seeing only a handful of white people – we had white neighbours when I was four or five, there was a German–English couple across the road from us – the Whitlers. The man had a big bush of white hair and his wife was similarly like that, and we saw them as the English family. They were nice; they were nice to me. But the man had a congenital heart condition that meant the ambulance had to constantly be called for him, so I lived in fear of his dying. I wasn't ignorant of white people, but at the same time, I knew they were not like us, they belonged to something more important – even if they did not give anything to suggest that they were behaving that way, we just knew that they were cut from a different cloth.

The American thing was different. America had clout, financial clout, and it could change your life. England didn't seem to have a willingness to give financial support to the local thing. When I was growing up in the 1950s, if you were making a head start in life and you had some kind of financial sustenance, you bought an American car. Nobody bought English cars. English cars were seen as kind of dinky toys that only English men would drive, because they were so clunky and misshapen and lacking in glamour. When a man made it he would drive an American car.

I grew up with an understanding that we were living in the place that did not define us because we did not originate from there. Our true origins were somewhere else. Our father, after the war, decided that he would take the whole family, lock, stock, and move and emigrate to Canada, and he officially applied to the Canadian authorities for the whole family to be immigrants to Canada and we had to take these family photographs, everybody, for the Canadian authorities. But something happened beyond my focus, and he changed his mind and didn't bother with it in the end. But that had set a tone in the household, that this thing you're faced with in Jamaica is not real, it is only temporary, because the real thing will happen soon. A ship or a plane will come to take you away. Something will miraculously happen that will move you away from this place.

Last One Out Turn Off All the Lights

A few months before his death, my father, Bageye, sat me down and told this story. In 1943, aged sixteen in Jamaica, he had secured a job as an assistant in a hardware store. It was a good job and his family was delighted. He was required to wear a white shirt and tie. 'And,' he emphasised, 'that shirt was clean!'

But Bageye was restless; all of his friends had gone to sea, some had subsequently migrated ('gone to foreign' as Jamaicans say). Bageye resolved to join the Merchant Navy one day and do the same. The manager of the hardware store was amazed that he'd prefer to work as a 'dirty seaman'. There would be no job waiting for Bageye, the manager warned, when he woke up to his terrible mistake.

Bageye signed on with a cargo ship called the *Lombardy* as a galley boy and within a short while began to hate it. But he had no choice now but to stick with it. In the course of ten years he rose, promoted through the ranks, from galley boy to chief steward. He had men under his command and some of them were white (he emphasised the word 'white', shaking his head in disbelief) – white Englishmen, who had to take orders from him! From him, a little black man! Bageye was inordinately proud. He now wore a white uniform and, with this change in fortunes, his ambition to leave the island was renewed.

Jamaica was a pigmentocracy: society was arranged for the benefit of white and light-skinned, middle-class brown people. A job in a hardware store marked the limits of possibility for a black boy, but surely England would see the potential of a man who rose from galley boy to chief steward in a decade. In England he wouldn't be known or judged, he could be anything he wanted to be. And so he would not squander the opportunity for betterment. He left.

This is true of so many. They left the Caribbean with few prospects and went to Britain to better themselves. They could readily do so because they held British passports and because of the British Nationality Act of 1948. The Act clarified their status and, inadvertently, held open the door to nationals in the Dominions and Colonies, as it established that they were legally entitled to live in Britain as British citizens. Mass migration may not have been expected but the Act had been introduced partly as a way of encouraging colonial residents to come to Britain to help with the reconstruction after World War Two. They were needed because of the shortages in the workforce, fuelled by the huge numbers of Britons who had emigrated to Australia and Canada in the later 1940s and 1950s. In 1947, Winston Churchill had implored the more than half a million 'lively and active citizens in the prime of life' who had applied to immigrate to mostly white Commonwealth countries not to desert Britain. 'We cannot spare you!' he warned. But such pleas fell on deaf ears. Over the next two decades West Indians, Irish, Indians and displaced Europeans would take their place.

Although not universally welcomed in Britain, West Indians were encouraged by employers such as London Transport, who stepped up their drive to recruit personnel in 1956 by setting up a recruitment office in Bridgetown, Barbados.

Caribbean people have always been mobile. Thousands headed to Panama to build the canal at the beginning of the twentieth century. They travelled to Costa Rica, Cuba or Florida for seasonal work. Edith Stanley from St Kitts recalls, 'Had I not come to England I would have gone elsewhere. All of my family have travelled ... [to] the Virgin Islands, America, Bermuda.'

And of course some, such as Marcus Garvey (in 1912 and 1935), had even managed the 4,000-mile journey to England. Caribbean people had been coming to Britain (in much smaller numbers) in the decades and centuries previously. But in the two decades after the 1948 Act, it is estimated that more than 300,000 took up the opportunity to book their passage on a ship or seat on a plane to try their luck in Britain.

It was a trickle at first (a few hundred each year) but the numbers exploded after the US government changed its own immigration rules in 1952 with the McCarran-Walter Act, which drastically reduced the numbers of seasonal farm workers allowed entry to the USA and effectively closed their doors to immigration.

For many, this was a galvanising moment. Whereas Harlem in New York, the great 'Negro Metropolis', had been the place to get to, now the default destination was Brixton (for Jamaicans), Leeds (for Kittitians), High Wycombe (for Vincentians), Reading (for Bajans). Major cities like Birmingham and Manchester attracted people from around the West Indies. Jamaicans constituted the biggest group by far – more than 75 per cent – of migrants. From 1955 to 1961, over 150,000 Jamaicans migrated to Britain.

Initially, the majority who came to Britain were single men and a smaller number of women; partners and children would follow later. If they had a plan, then it was to 'work some money' (save and prosper) and then to return to buy that plot of land they'd always dreamed of back home, to build a house and a life on the back of funds accrued in Britain.

The arrival of the *Empire Windrush* has been widely championed by the mainstream media as a foundation story but, in fact, it wasn't the first ship bearing hundreds of West Indians to Britain. Earlier ships included the SS *Almanzora* and the SS *Ormonde* in 1947. Hannah Lowe memorialised her father, Chick's, unheralded arrival from Jamaica in her poetry collection *Ormonde*:

and all the passengers step from the ship
and through a coverlet of mist, then slip
like whispers into tenements and backstreets
as *Ormonde*'s deep horn bellows her retreat –

and from this little piece of history
she slowly creaks her way back out to sea.[1]

Like Chick Lowe and his fellow West Indians who came on board
the *Ormonde*, the first passengers on the *Windrush* were offered a
special one-off fare of £28. By the late 1950s £60 or £70 could buy
you passage on a ship to Britain. Journeys by sea, which took two
to three weeks, were £10 cheaper than the airplane Ethlyn climbed
aboard in 1959.

These were young and dynamic adventurers (the average age of
passengers on the *Empire Windrush* was twenty-four) and, like Bageye,
they succumbed to the urge to leave. They called it 'England Fever'.
There was tremendous excitement at the possibility of starting over.
Equally, there was the real terror of missing out and being left behind.
So many were 'gone to foreign' that a joke quickly emerged and
was heard throughout the region: 'Will the last person out please
turn off all the lights?'

★

Pastor Sydney Alexander Dunn
The Colony, BBC TV, 1964

Well, I had nearly twenty acres of good land, and the crops that
I grow on it are bananas, ginger, coffee – if there was market for
it. I couldn't make a decent living. You see, Jamaica is a farming
country – oranges, bananas, sugar, rum, coconuts – and one of our
biggest markets is England. During the years gone by they have
taken the stuff off us at a cheap rate which leaves us very little for
helping ourself financially, so there wasn't any money to make in
farming and, though you slave twelve months of the year; but when
the crop comes in there isn't much, not even to pay back your debts.
Most of the time the little funds that you could get were sometimes
just enough to buy you a meal, it was hardly a matter of existing.

Archippus Joseph

I was touting around for a job at the age of twenty. At that time, educated people used to be given priority for certain jobs; what we call decent jobs, they were few and far between. A lot of the job owners were white people, so most of those jobs were already ear-marked for their people. And not only that, but especially if you're from the country, to get a job in the town, they're very hard because all of those people who are already in town, they get first choice. So what they did eventually, the government, [even if] you only went to elementary school you could still become a teacher – they held those jobs for people like myself, until you find something more in line with what you want or you're qualified for. I went to St Kitts looking for work but could not find anything, any decent job. I met the same stumbling block, so after a month I came back. So I went back home.

I used to play cricket a lot, just knocking around practising, and one day I was on the cricket field and my father sent for me, and I was wondering what's going on, and he said to me, 'Do you think that it's right for a man like you to walk up and down playing cricket all day? Tomorrow I'm going to give you some money; you go and take out your papers. You're going to England.' Simple as that. In the Caribbean, if you living at home and your father says, 'Jump,' you ask, 'How high?'

People had just started getting the bug to come to England [in 1954], a few came over to England and started working and we got the news that they were earning good money and the news spread like wild fire.

My father gave me the money to get my papers ready. At the same time other chaps around me were doing the same thing, schoolteachers were doing the same thing. If it was up to me I wouldn't have come, but it was him, my dad, who financed the trip ...

It was about a month later ... local friends got the bug as well. Things worked out; as you know, we only had light clothes. I had to buy a suitcase, not a trunk, as I didn't have enough to fill it, no coat or umbrella, but I had a felt hat – a fedora.

We had a party but there were more tears than anything else; you cry when things are bad, sorry to see the person go, you're going to miss your friend. My sister and friends came with me to the small ship to Dominica. My father didn't come – it was just one of those things, it didn't really matter. Well, who needed him?

My father said, 'Here's some money, on your way.' He had to give me money as he didn't know what was going to happen on the other side.

Ethlyn Adams

In Jamaica at the time there was high unemployment and no work. You see the boys leaving colleges and going down to the store Monday morning with their certificates in their hands but there was no work. There was no future in Jamaica at that time. It's not a nice feeling. So I was glad to get away and try somewhere else. We had that opportunity in coming to England and trying to get jobs and better yourself. 'Cause you'd only be sitting in Jamaica, idle.

C. W. W. Greenidge

Letter to *The Times*, 24 June 1948
When I was in Jamaica in December [1947], recruiting offices were opened in the capital for 100 and 300 men respectively. About 9,000 men went to each, and on one occasion the disgruntled majority, in a fury of disappointment, began to pull down part of the recruiting office and had to be dispersed with tear gas. The streets of Kingston teem with beggars, some so desperate that they even state how much alms they want given them.

Wallace Collins

Jamaican Migrant, 1965
I lost my job in Jamaica late in 1952 and stayed unemployed for over a year; during which time I seemed to mellow from idleness

and to bear with ease the hardships of unemployment. I thought and thought, and I could not invent anything else but to migrate.[2]

Devon

Journey to an Illusion, 1966

By this time almost every family had a representative in the 'mother country'. People were now wearing ill-fitting English clothes and were grumbling that, 'No matter what English people do, them can't touch the Yankee people.' It was no good dreaming about serving in the United States. The waiting list for prospective migrants was ten years long, and growing. With Britain it was different. The old ones said that it was just like the days when a man could simply pay his passage in a ship and sail away to Cuba or Costa Rica.

Britain which had been revered had suddenly, in the 1950s, become something that could be touched. Besides the larger British cities about which we learned at school, there were other names such as Brixton, Handsworth and Moss Side. The image began to build up that if you went to Britain you belonged to Brixton the way if you went to the United States of America you belonged to Harlem. It does not take much to let people think this way. From the papers everyone was certain that if he went to Brixton he would find friendlier people and was sure to meet a long-lost cousin or school pal. The names of Colonel Lipton and Fenner Brockway were things you learned and tucked away in a reserve corner of the mind. Some day you might break in and make use of something there.

Rena Khublall

I always wanted to leave Guiana to go to America or England to do nursing, but my father stepped in and said, 'No, my daughters are not leaving home!' Girls are supposed to stay home. Do whatever there is to do at home: cook, do the house and wait to get married.

And if you get too old they will find someone and you have to get married whether you like them or not. I didn't argue with my father; if he says no that is that. I would make myself useful, doing sewing at home. I felt a little bit hurt, I thought it was a good thing to do because there was nothing for young women, no college, no university, so you couldn't do anything. The only thing I was able to do, I went to commercial school where I did shorthand and typing, hoping that one day I'd be working, but I never did. I was stuck.

David Khublall (with Rena)

I was working for the Department of Agriculture. Where it was, there was a police station, post office etc and I used to work in the office, and anyone that turned up at the office where I was working, if they need any advice I would pass it on to them; or in those days the people who had animals, like horses and donkeys and cows, they used to come for a permit to get molasses to feed their animals. But do you know what they used to do with that black stuff? They used to make rum and they used to call the rum 'bush rum'.

During that time with my boss, he said, 'Dave, you always say you'd like to go away to England, I tell you something, don't wait.' He said, 'Politics in this country, I don't like the way it's going, because it's dividing the people of Guiana, there's one for the blacks and one for the Indians and I don't like that at all. If you have got the money go and book your fare and go.'⁴ I took his advice and within a few days, as soon as I got my booking – I didn't need a visa or anything, I'd got my original British passport – I resigned my position. Within a week I was travelling to England. I went on my own; my wife [Rena] was at home with three children.

Linette May Simms

All I wanted was to leave Jamaica because I thought England was a better place than Jamaica, because the English people in Jamaica live so well and I thought I would live like that. You had to tip your head to them English people if you see them in the street. We grow that way so we had to. We glad to bow to them when we walk past them. If their name Alec we say, 'Morning Mas' Halec.'

Jamaica on the whole was hard and I didn't want to go lower than I was; I knew I was poor, but I didn't want to go lower. In Kingston, the woman where I stayed paid for me to learn sewing but only when she could afford it, and I do a few jobs. I look after the children of some Chinese people and I save the money. And there was a Tropical Theatre – the owner there, Mr Graham, English man – and I get a job there. It shows films.

I saved some money and I say to my parents, 'I'm going to England.' And they said, 'Do what you like.' So I went across the river to see my grandparents to tell them that I am going to England. My grandmother said, 'How can you?' This was my mother's mother. I buy the ticket from the theatre for my passage. It was for the ship, and you bought the ticket from the theatre. Them sell every ticket. I save, I borrow, I get help to get £16. When I tell my grandmother to help me, she wouldn't help me, she said, 'You can't go England.' 'Why not?' 'Don't argue with me, me born in slavery days, don't argue with me! You can't go!' I couldn't say another word to her. It went in one ear and out the other. I had to keep it from her. A friend in town make a coat for me. It was between February and March; went on the ship SS *Colombie*. My parents knew I was going. When I get to the wharf and I look out, who did I see sitting there? My grandmother. She had heard; she came, and she was crying.

It take me sixteen days on the sea to come to this country. Other people were on the ship, but me have no one to come to; I don't know where I am going, but I am going to England. We made friends on the ship but I didn't know anybody.

Bert Williams

In 1955 Princess Margaret came to Mandeville [Jamaica]. Me and my brother, Roy, were in the Boys Brigade. I was eleven, and my brother and I went on parade in our uniforms but, because we come from so far, the two sisters accompany us to look after you. I can't remember seeing Princess Margaret because there was a massive crowd and you was small. My sisters remember picking up two magazines about recruiting nurses to come to England; and when we got back home, they applied to five hospitals from this magazine to come to England, and they chose Brighton General because they were the first one to respond.

One came first, in 1956, and the other sister and my brother came over in 1957. He went and signed up join the RAF for life, which was twenty-two years.

So I knew I was coming to England. I knew my parents couldn't control me, because to get rid of me I was playing badder than I was bad. Because I wanted them to get rid of me, and I knew that you do, as children know – if I play bad they'll get rid of you – and I think they wanted everybody to have a better education. That was the idea. So I knew I was coming to England, so I was quite excited about it for a long time.

Armet Francis

Before I could come here I had to go to Kingston to get a passport picture and that's the first time I became aware of photographs. I'd never seen a photograph before – I was about seven or eight. That was my first magical introduction to photography. To get to Kingston, which was ninety miles away, you had to get a market truck and it would cost so much to get the picture done, it was an absolute fortune in relation to what you earned on your small farm.

I came by boat with my guardian, Novell, who was about twenty-five and was emigrating and coming to work. Her father's sister was married to my uncle, but I knew her very well. When we got on the boat I thought I'd be with her in the cabin, but what they did was separate the men and women. So all of a sudden I was thrown in with all these men. I was a child and had never really known the world of men at all, so it was a bit of a shock for all of us. We were separated and then I became a man, I guess. If there were other kids on a three-week journey on the ship, you'd soon make friends with them. It was an adventure.

The thing that I can remember is my granny on the wharf and me on the front of the ship saying goodbye to her. She started to cry and that finished me off. At first I thought it was like going to Kingston for the day. I think I'd only ever seen the sea once and that was down by the beach. I had no idea of distance so I thought, 'What's she crying for? I'll be back in a couple of hours.' Or whatever.

I used to pretend that I wasn't frightened and I had this sense of survival, like – if your foot can't reach the bottom, it's too deep. So my child logic was that if this thing that I'm on starts to sink, then I've got to be on the top of the deck. But I got pneumonia after being on the deck (for a boat drill) for one or two hours. I'd just ran up in my pyjamas and I got pneumonia. I actually didn't know I was so cold, as I was so scared. I was in hospital (on the boat) for about a week. I was sweating and thought I was going to die.

Shirley Williams

I did my high school, which my parents paid for, and it can't have been easy for my parents to make that sacrifice, pay for a house, pay for school, books, everything. Because, dad being a pharmacist for a start – and, because we had several on my maternal side that were doctors in Guiana – my father could help us [Guiana only had one nursing training school] to get the British qualification. As a young girl a lot of the decisions that are going to be made, it's not you making them, it's your father – as the head of the house, he's making them. 'I think you would do well if you went to England.' Not me saying. I didn't have a clue about England. He did all the research about the schools. But we also had two relatives already training to be nurses in England and they were training at the General Hospital in Brighton. My dad said, 'Let's try applications to three schools in England.' And I got into Brighton General at eighteen.

I was terrified. I'd been in a light aircraft to go touring the interiors with my dad, because he was a pharmacist he had to fly to spray the crops, because of the mosquitoes, and give worm medicine to the aboriginal children. BOAC [British Overseas Airways Corporation, the UK's state-owned airline created in 1939] was the flight. My mum, dad, sister, brother all came, aunties, uncles. We were a very close-knit family, meaning that, the Indian community – in-laws, children, they would all come, it was massive. I had woollies but I don't know where they came from, a little jacket, not even a coat. Mother had things like socks or thick tights in there. Because friends had family that were nurses over here, so it would go around the grapevine, 'So and so's daughter is going to England to study.' It's a big thing.

V. S. Naipaul
The Enigma of Arrival
I asked the stewardess to sharpen my pencil. I did so partly to taste the luxuriousness of air travel. The plane was small, but it offered many little services, or so the airline advertisement said. This request to the stewardess was in the nature of a challenge; and to my amazement the stewardess, white and American and to me radiant and beautiful and adult, took my request seriously, brought the pencil back beautifully sharpened, and called me, two weeks away from being eighteen, sir.[5]

Louise Smith
My brother came to England first and he asked me to come, but I said, 'I'm not coming.' And then my mother said to give it a try, so, 'OK.' They say, 'It's cold and it snows.' And I don't know, and this lady been to America and she tell me about it, she say, 'It come

from heaven.' Me say, 'Mm hm.' She say, 'It come from the cloud.' I couldn't believe that. Anyway I decided to come.

The woman from America, she had a coat and she said, 'Love, you'll need this.' And I was glad for that coat, one of them mohair, and it warm. My brother sent a plane for me. That's the way it seemed, for me.

When I grow up I live in the country. I was with my uncle in Kingston and then my uncle died and when my brother said he'll help me come up, I say, 'OK.' And then, when I was ready to come, there was more people coming so we all kept company on the plane. It was horrible: bad weather, that dip. My grandmother call it 'devil buggy' [the plane]. She would never go in airplane, she ride horse to church – she would never go into a car even. Some of the hostess were very courteous. But I didn't kiss the ground when we land because I was so cold – snow coming in my mouth and nostril. The same brother, Albert, met me off the plane. It was a good while, about five years since I'd seen him, it was joy to see him!

Arthur France

Funnily I had an overcoat, someone from America bought an overcoat for me. It was amazing because, when people were coming over, no matter how poor the family was, you had to make sure you had a tailor-made suit, because you're going to England and you have to look well-dressed. I still can't come to terms. My father came to Charlestown for the boat, my father took me by the pier and I think he was a very sad man that day, and I remember I looked around and I see him turn away [crying]. He's a man I can never get out of my head, and that's the last time I saw him.

Edwin Hilton Hall

The reason I came to England was because I wanted to better myself. Although my father had a very substantial business, I used to be the book keeper. So, liking to be independent, I decided to come up on the *Empire Windrush* to England, which was known as the mother country, as we were brought up under the British flag. I am from British Guiana. There was lots of entertainment aboard ship. There was singing, there was dancing; there was boxing which I participate in ... that was my line. There was live music and the music was quite nice – my line of music and I loved dancing – but I had more time gambling. I used to be down there playing cards and dice most of the time.

Sam King

During the Second World War, we were aware that Nazi Germany was a bad thing and, being a part of the British Empire, we ... many thousands of my people ... volunteered to serve King and country. The British people accepted us as a part of their family. We did our job and by the grace of God, Nazi Germany was defeated and later Japan. Then, after the war, we had it to return to the colony of Jamaica. But, in 1944, there was a hurricane and most of the plantations were destroyed. So, we went back to a set period or an area of great tribulation.

I went back to Jamaica [from England] in 1947 on the SS *Almanzora*[6] and about a half mile outside of Kingston Harbour, I saw men diving for pennies and shillings, risking their lives. It was sad. I had seen Britain, including some of America; I read a bit and was not going to live in a British colony. My mind was set to return to England. There was an ad in the *Jamaican Gleaner* that the SS *Empire Windrush* will be leaving Jamaica for England in May and if anybody wants to go, they have to pay £28 10s on a certain day. We had to sell three cows to get the £28 10s, and the average man did not have that amount at that time. I arrived there in the morning and I was shocked. There was about 200 people in the line with passport documentation. I remember my mother washing the very black thing I use to clean my shoes. She said, 'You're going back to England. Everything must be clean.' And the morning of the 24 May 1948, I boarded the SS *Empire Windrush* bound for London.

Wilford Lawson

There were a few lads who were stowaways to England and they used to send back pictures to Jamaica showing some off themselves in scissor-tail suit and bow tie blah blah blah, with trilbies.

None of them pay for the passage. The banana ships would come in to Montego Bay and the lads would have ample time to hide themselves away from the workers. What inspire me to leave was seeing them photograph. And I said, 'Damn it I'm going to England.' I decide I'm going as well.

There was a famous ship used to come on there named *Eros* and there was this chap who used to stowaway on it so often we called him Captain Eros. His name was Sydney Palmer. People would come down to Montego Bay and he'd show them how to get on and hide on the ship. He knew all the tricks of the trade. So in 1954, I was nineteen, I decide to stowaway with him on a ship call the *Jamaica Producer*.

I never tell no one. I never told my parents as I knew it would put them too much in a trance like, they would be very very anxious. Only one friend, Sam, knew and he would publicise it afterwards.

We hid behind bananas and had quite a few to eat; we were never hungry. Well, after a few days at sea we come up from the hiding place 'cause we knew by then they wouldn't turn the ship around. And the Chief Steward, a white Jamaican called Chambers, ordered me to scrub the deck. I told him, 'I'm not scrubbing no damn deck.' Well, he took my passport, Eros's passport and another chap called Okra (George Williams) and he threw them, all three passports, overboard.

Now when the ship docked [we went in front of a judge and] they sent the three of us to Brixton Prison in a Black Maria; we had to stay there till the ship unload and ready to go back. It was good in the prison because we got on with the warden 'cause he know we never commit a crime as such. We spent twelve days in prison and then they send us back to Jamaica.

When we were coming back a lot of the chaps who work in the galley take sick and, because we were now seasoned like almost seamen, we helped out. We went into a storm, Hurricane Hattie, the ship went in the tail-end of that storm. The fellas and me we just played cards waiting for the ship to sink. Luckily we rode out the storm.

Back in Jamaica we were sent to Central Jail in Kingston. Eros got thirty days in Spanish Town Prison. But because I help out on the ship, they was lenient; I only spend another twelve days in jail. I tell you, though, it was worse than Brixton; in Brixton the meals were quite good, we put weight on. But back in Jamaica flies used to get your dinner before you. Within two years I save and buy a passage this time. I learn my lesson. No more prison for me.

Carlton 'Stanley' Gaskin

As a little boy I always aspired to come to England because it mean there'll be more food and better clothes in England, economically – and funny thing is, I always read anything I could about England.

I went to bed on the floor and lied on old clothes, no blanket, no, no. Old clothes. And sometimes you get up and there's a button mark on your face.

At the beginning of the war no black person could get in the Air Force. And, as I found out later, it was not because you were from Guiana. It was wherever you were from. We knew why we did join the Air Force and I mean, let's face up, we didn't come to kill any Germans. What did we know about Germans? It was an economic situation.

One thing really struck me [when I returned on the *Windrush*] was this Jamaican woman who stowed away. I accept the fact that men did that sort of thing, but it was the very first time I heard of a woman stowing away. She must have been given specific instructions because she waited until the boat had reached so far to England that they wouldn't turn back. She gave herself up.

Now this is where West Indian solidarity came up, because we decided to raise the money to pay for her passage. On the *Windrush* there were Calypsonians, Lord Kitchener, Lord Beginner. There was a famous pianist from Jamaica. There was this young lady from Trinidad, Mona Baptiste, who used to sing on the local radio.[7]

So all these talented people were able to perform. So we had quite an interesting little concert. And the money that was collected paid the fare of this rather courageous woman who decided to stow away.

Agnes DeAbreu

I was born in a place called South Rivers in St Vincent. We were from Madeira originally and they took us to Guiana after the slave trade; that's how there is the Portuguese in the Caribbean. It was about 1854 and they wanted workers after the slave trade. The Indians went there as well, they took the Indians and the Portuguese. They weren't slaves, they were paid and they worked on the sugar plantations. I don't know why it was the Portuguese. From Madeira some went to New York, some went to Brazil. So it was my great-grandparents who came to St Vincent from Madeira.

My parents were farmers growing sugar cane, arrowroot, sweet potatoes, vegetables and fruit trees, and at one time they had peanuts as well. I never liked to work on the farm. I used to go with them, my dad always used to take us. When it was the arrowroot time. I suppose we were middle class.

My parents liked him [my boyfriend Jim] to a certain extent. But they think he doesn't have anything so it's going to be hard for me and they didn't like that. I was eighteen in 1958. My parents wanted me to go away [to Britain] to get away from him [Jim]. People said it was because he wasn't my colour but it wasn't that at all. The older Portuguese are a bit like that, maybe I'd have to use the word racist, but you know the world is like that; Indians want their people to marry Indians, so it's not just the Portuguese who will say that, not being offensive; but some black people are like that too, you know, them who don't want their children to marry into another race; but it's all mixed now and you can hardly see a Portuguese in St Vincent; they all inter-marry. My eldest brother, he married an Indian. My dad was always a mouthy mouthy but he see his hard life and he want the best for them [his children]. When you're young you just want to go; it's to explore, you read about places and you'd like to go. I wanted to go and when you have strict parents it's like freedom.

Nobody wanted to stay and work on the farm. I booked on the *Iripinia*, Italian ship, met people there who I knew from St Vincent. My dad bought my ticket. I wore a pair of jeans. I packed summer clothes, no cardigan or nothing, in a medium suitcase; I've still got it. Especially bought by my mum, lots of nice clothes were made for me and my mum tied a pillow on my case and a little enamel basin inside to have a wash. I'd never been off the island before.

It was kind of sad and joyous but you think, 'Oh, it's England, and I want to see what it's like.' Some people had a plan to stay for five years but I had no plan to go back. Just going and leave it open. My dad was talking to be careful, 'Honesty is the best policy and be careful where you go and who you're with and there'll be better fish than what you caught already.' He was kind of worried. He was a serious man. He used to say, 'See that tree … you bend it when it's young … you wait till it's grown and you can't bend it no more.' He said, 'Be careful with your company.'

George Mangar

After my father died and I was growing up with my mother, my brother came to England to study. She wouldn't allow me to come with him. I could have been here before he was because I passed my exams. He came in 1956. He came to England, I stayed at home and I became the chauffeur of my mother and sisters, taking them to dressmakers, to weddings at the weekend and I resented that,

I resented being the chauffeur. I applied to join the police force. The Commissioner of Police was English. The Deputy Commissioner was English, the Commandant of the school was English, the whole thing was run by English people. We wore blue uniforms, we rode motorbikes that were made in England; everything was British. I was just seventeen and a half. When you finish your training and you're sent out to the street you have this power, a young man's power; you have the golden whip to stop somebody and arrest them, you have this attitude, and I'd just finished training!

Soon after, I tried to arrest a man and I didn't know I'd been stabbed in the heat of things happening. I got to the station and my colleague said to me, 'You're bleeding.' I had this cut in my arm. So I was taken to the hospital and the surgeon sewed me up. My mother came that night, very irate, and she took my uniform and threw it through the window. She told my senior officer, 'My son's just resigned.'

I was embarrassed about my mother's behaviour, but then what happened after that, after my sick leave was over, I went back to work and my mother was going on at me, then she had an asthma attack one night and said it was because of me working on the beat. It meant that I could come to England now.

My mother did my shopping for my shirts and clothes and things. She packed over a hundred shirts, because I was coming away. When I got to England I would wear three shirts, plus my vest. I had three huge suitcases. There was clothing, some rum for my brother, the travelling money was [hidden] in the suitcase.

I got on the TS *Venezuela*. Huge ship, over 1,000 people on that ship. It's an Italian ship, it was a freighter, Grimaldi line, and it went up to Venezuela and picked some people up, and in Venezuela plenty of ladies in black came aboard the ship because they'd lost their husbands. It then went to Trinidad and Guiana then we went to Barbados and picked up in Barbados and then we went to sea.

When I wrote home to my sister I said, 'All I've seen is sea and sea and more sea.' That was all we saw. I saw two ships in a week pass by, one at night and one in the daytime.

The food was not the kind of food that we're used to; it was Italian food – and wine at every meal. I was a first-class passenger and all my friends who I'd met in Trinidad, they were not in first class, so I used to come down and join the boys, played dominoes and table tennis, make friends.

Our first stop was Tenerife. There was a Chinese girl I knew from Guiana and an Indian girl and another girl called Zena Ramos, she was a Negro girl, beautiful girl from Trinidad, she was a table tennis champion in Trinidad. I played table tennis with her and I tried to beat her. She was excellent; she was a champion, taller than me, a very good-looking girl. Every night, we'd go dancing on the ship.

When we got to Victoria station, there were all these desks, with people recruiting the people coming off these ships to go and work in various places, and Zena's going to Birmingham where her family lived; she was going to the university to do teacher training, and that's what she did. I called her the day before Christmas Eve and I came on the train to see her in Birmingham. We had a long talk. She was beautiful, we became very good friends, and we kept in touch for years.

Sheila Howarth

I was born in Leeds in 1957 at St James Hospital; my parents came from St Kitts, my mum came over first, she came over in 1955, and then my dad came over two years later. They got married in Leeds. Her [my mother's] parents sent her to get rid of my father who was chasing her. He was from the village and she was from the town. She was very, very posh, they owned the shops, and my dad was from the village. But he wouldn't leave her alone. She ended up getting pregnant with my older brother, and after he was born, they sent her to England to get rid of him [my father], to stay with my aunt.

I can see her parents' point of view. If you've got children and you think their partner's not good enough for your child, you'd try to break them up. If they're still living in your house, under your roof then yes, you'll interfere, because they're bringing their problems into your life. But if they've got their own life you're just there as a stand-by to support them.

My mum was born in 1935 and my dad was born in 1930. In those days you left your children with their grandparents, but she didn't realise that she was pregnant again. She was sick for twenty-one days on the boat and didn't know if it was seasickness or the pregnancy and only knew she was pregnant when the doctor on the boat told her. She went straight to her aunt in Leeds. Later my father followed her; he came over.

Sam King

We had to call into Bermuda, because they stated that the [*Windrush*'s] engine was wrong and needed repairing. We felt that they did not want us to come to England and that is why we went to Bermuda. Having spent three days in Bermuda officially repairing the ship, we are out at sea again. We notice HMS *Sheffield* that we have left in Bermuda, a pocket battleship was always on the horizon. In the morning, you can just see smoke coming out of her funnel. And about five days out of Tilbury, I saw a man crying. This was about 6:15 p.m. 'They're going to send us back.' I said, 'What are you talking about?' He said, 'I heard on the six o'clock news that in Parliament they said that black people should not come to England and if there is any disturbance on the ship, they will turn us back to Jamaica.' I said, 'They will not send us back.' I got two ex-RAF wireless operators to play dominoes underneath the windows where wireless operators were stationed [so that they could hear the official communications]. We learned that the *Daily Dispatch* stated that no black people should land in England and the Rt Honourable Arthur Creech Jones, Minister for the Colonies said, 'Do not worry. These people are just adventurers. They will not last longer than one British winter.'[8]

Edwin Hilton Hall

Going to be docked at Tilbury dock, we passed through the white cliffs of Dover and I tell you it was something fascinating. It was all rocks and white as ever. It was something beyond imagination. I always remember that. Even sometimes when I do see it on the television ... sometimes I will always remember that day. Arriving at Tilbury docks, it was so exciting seeing the cameraman and the dock. Lots of people actually, probably to welcome the *Windrush* arriving. I just came out having something to eat in the mess hall and I saw this crowd with the cameramen and I was waving my cup ... teacup that I had ... waving to be noticed.

Clinton Cameron

I grew up with people leaving the island, a lot of people I knew, went to school with, were always going off to England, people from the district, just about everywhere. But it had never occurred to me, because my image of England was a cold place; not much fun. It came from books and from films. America seemed to me to be a place worth going to but not England. But one day in the back end of 1959 my mother came to Kingston and she said to me in an off-hand way, 'Don't you fancy going to England?' And I said, 'No, not really.' But the idea then stuck with me for a while. But in Kingston I had a cousin and a friend and we were all round about the same age. And the friend had two brothers in England, and told me he was going to England in April, which – because we were quite close – it occurred to me that if he goes off I'll have to start working out what I'm going to do, so I got back to my mother and changed my mind. The fare to England was £85 by plane, £75 by ship. At that time I was earning £5 per week. I started working in Kingston. I was encouraged to buy a sewing machine [I was a tailor] so when the thought of leaving came up, I had something that I could sell to contribute towards the fare.

Alford Gardner

The ship came and we went to sea, the roughest sea you ever could think of. It's supposed to take a day, maybe a day and a bit, from Jamaica to Cuba. It took four days. We got up on the first morning. All you could see the boys going to New York [makes sick noise] I think 75 to 80 per cent of the lads were sick. They're vomiting … 'NEW YOORK!' [laughing].

We went to Guantanamo Bay; they took water and what not, and did a bit of repair. It took another ten days to go to Newport News, Virginia.

Then we went on the train to Camp Patrick Henry in Virginia. We had a beautiful week. The first day when we got there, we got off the ship. Every man had to go into a big place, and the steam was hot, it was a fumigation place. Everybody, from the captain, everybody had to go through it. They fumigated the whole ship, and it was red hot. You put your clothes in one place, and that was going to some other fumigation place. I can still feel it, and when you through it there's a man with a spray. Bend over! Anyway, everybody got fumigated. The ship was that crowded you know.

We get on a train and the rumour is that we going on the *Queen Mary*. We come into New York and everybody come off the train on to a platform, and it moved; it was a barge, but it was like a platform, nobody knows, you didn't feel it. Someone asked are we going on the *Queen Mary*? And we're climbing on this little rusty ship. We missed the *Queen Mary* because the train was late. We went on the *Chesapeake Bay* to England, in a right big convoy, massive convoy, and the next morning we wake up and it's just us alone, 'What's happened to all them ships?' Then we heard that the ship was broken down. Then the rumours: we're a decoy ship [laughing] – you see men pray! Anyway we're on the way to

England. We hear the command, 'Sleep as you are.' But it's getting colder and colder; you go up and everything's frozen solid.

Donald Hinds
Journey to an Illusion, 1966
Towards the end of the journey, the ship stank. The stairs smelled of vomit and urine, and each day reminded us of the horrors our forebears must have suffered during the terrible Middle Passage ... Others appeared on deck with their heads wrapped in brightly coloured towels looking like Bedouin and reeking of Bay Rum ... On the twentieth morning of the voyage I awoke to the sound of bells and came to the conclusion that we were in Plymouth harbour.

Reginald Davis
When I was about seventeen, and, at that time we start to have personal ambitions – and in those era you have a drink, you could buy a beer, a smoke, you feel like you are a man then. I didn't have no family around, they went away, so we start to have a beer and drink and some of the boys we were talking and someone said, 'Oh, I am a builder' and that one said, 'My father is a mason' and so on. So we want to show off, and I said, 'Yes, my father is a policeman.' You know. Well I didn't know him; I hear about his name and his occupation. I think back; I wrote to the Central Police Station at Kingston, 'Have you ever hear about the existence of Mr Cedric Osborne Davis?' Fortunate for me, he wrote me back and say, 'I'm your father.' And he said, 'You must come to Kingston.' Because he hadn't known me, it must be fifteen years. So, when I went there, he said to me ... Well, he hugged me and embrace me and I felt wanted, it was really nice, and normally in his situation he might get promoted to a sergeant or something; my ambition was being filled. And so I said, 'I'm going to England.' At that time, I'd got twenty chickens from the farming association; they give us that. And I raised them, and when the twenty of them reached a certain stage,

they started to lay, and they started cannibalising each other because I wasn't there to look after them. I was working at Vere Royal, and when I realised I couldn't manage them I sell the twenty for £20. And then I saving some money, and I got some money from Vere Royal, and when I add it all up, all I have, I have £75. And that was my fare to England. I don't even know Kingston; straight on the bus. And when I go there and I see my father for the first time, and I said I want to come to Kingston; he say, 'Don't come to Kingston.' Because, being a policeman, he understand the condition, he say, 'Go to England, do engineering, go to England, and do engineering.' So that is what I did.

My sisters are religious so sometimes they get clothes from America to distribute [from Caribbean workers living in the USA who'd established charities to send clothing back home for their impoverished compatriots]. So when I was leaving, my sister say, 'Oh, you going to be cold out there.' So she get a lovely coat and give it to me and it have fur round the neck – and I don't know man coat different from woman, but it have fur round the neck, real woman coat. Me so chuffed, me walk about like . . . is when me get to England me know it was a woman coat they gave me, they don't know much difference, but when I go to it keep me warm. But most of them laugh at me because I was really showing off.

George Lamming
The Pleasures of Exile, 1960

There was no going back now. All the gaiety of reprieve which we felt on our departure had now turned to apprehension. Like one of the many characters which he has since created, Sam [Selvon] said on the deck, 'Is who send we up in dis place?' For it was a punishing wind which drove us from looking at the landscape. An English voice said it was the worst spring he had known in fifty years. We believed him but it seemed very cold comfort for people in our circumstances.[9]

Before You Go to Britain

What precautions might a West Indian take before embarking on a 4,000-mile trip from the Caribbean to Britain? One idea might be to check on the weather.

Ethlyn used to recount the cautionary tale of a flamboyantly stubborn Jamaican nicknamed Summer Wear who hadn't taken sufficient care when he arrived in the winter of 1959. He insisted on wearing tropical suits and other light summer clothing, no matter the weather. Putting style before practicality, though, cost him dear; within months of coming to frosty Britain, Summer Wear caught a chill and died. I'd always thought it was an apocryphal story but, in his novel *The Lonely Londoners,* Sam Selvon has a character, Sir Galahad, with a similar disposition towards clothing. For Selvon, Galahad was emblematic of the courageous but carefree Caribbean explorer. He wears a pair of pyjamas under his old grey tropical suit, has a toothbrush in his breast pocket, but no overcoat – and not even any luggage.

Many migrants who came from the West Indies were under-dressed and under-prepared for the reception in store for them, both from the weather and the culture. George Lamming recalls how port officials in Plymouth, meeting Caribbean migrants off the ship in the 1950s, were astounded by their lack of preparation: 'The officials asked what would happen after they reached Paddington, but no one answered with conviction.' The British Customs and Immigration authorities had never come across such cavalier attitudes, remembered Lamming, and were 'bewildered by this exhibition of adventure, or ignorance, or plain suicide.'[1]

This optimism – or naivety – would extend to the difficulty of finding their place in society and getting along with the British.

Before the West Indians got to England, there were clues about their likely reception from the treatment meted out to those, like Learie Constantine, who'd preceded them. A highly regarded and much loved cricketer, Constantine was considered a kind of unofficial ambassador from Trinidad to Britain, and yet in 1943, newspaper readers in the Caribbean – if they had been paying attention – would have been alarmed by the headline that Constantine had sued a respectable hotel in central London for its naked racial discrimination against him.

In 1949 the Central Office of Information had drawn up a list of names for consideration, including Constantine, before eventually commissioning H. D. Carberry and Dudley Thompson, two Jamaican law students at Oxford University, to write 'A West Indian in England', a pamphlet offering 'a fair and frank picture' of what emigrants should expect in 'unknown and darkest England'.

Ten thousand copies of the pamphlet were distributed throughout the West Indies. The subjects ranged from 'The English Reserve' (e.g. train carriages in which travellers do not 'exchange a single word for the whole period'), 'The English Climate and its Functions', 'Queuing', 'The English Pub' (a 'Poor man's night-club') and 'The Colour Problem'.

In all of my more than fifty interviews, I never met anyone who'd set eyes on one of these pamphlets. This was also true of the warnings compiled by British civil servants in the Migrant Services Division in another handy little pamphlet called 'Before You Go to Britain', which gave advice to West Indians on how to behave, what to pack and what to expect when their ships docked in Britain.

A Kensington local, Mae Marven, would argue that it might also have been a good idea to issue a comparable pamphlet to English people for them to better understand the 'familiar strangers' who'd soon be in their midst. 'We used to celebrate Empire Day and it was usual for children to be dressed in costumes of the countries that were part of the Empire,' says Mae. '[But] on reflection it seemed to me when we were having difficulties with West Indians in the forties and fifties it was because, as a community, we hadn't really been prepared for their arrival.'

In 1939, researchers with the Mass Observation project conducted a survey into race that uncovered deep-seated prejudices. It showed that English people had no intimate knowledge of West Indians; at best they were indifferent to them. And on arrival in Britain, West Indians would discover that the notion of one big Commonwealth family in an existential fight with Hitler that the Mother Country had propagandised during the Second World War was no longer fit for purpose.

The 'A West Indian in England' booklet concluded: 'You will have practically no one to fall back on if you suddenly need help ... If you can face your difficulties and come out on top good luck to you.'

*

E. R. Braithwaite
To Sir, With Love, 1959

To many in Britain a Negro is a 'darky' or a 'nigger' or a 'black'; he is identified, in their minds, with inexhaustible brute strength; and often I would hear the remark 'working like a nigger' or 'labouring like a black' used to emphasise some occasion of sustained effort. They expect of him a courteous subservience and contentment with a lowly state of menial employment and slum accommodation. It is true that here and there one sees Negroes as doctors, lawyers or talented entertainers, but they are somehow considered 'different' and not to be confused with the mass.[2]

Victor Williams

I've got an uncle who travelled to this country before I came and he said, 'When you come over here to England, when you've got a job, go to your work regular and don't talk too much.' He said, 'Do as you're told, and if a white bloke is social with you, social with him, if he doesn't care for you, don't care for him, just take no notice, and one of the last words I'm telling you, and remember what your uncle tells you. When you go in England, try your endeavour best to remember your father.'

Miss Patricia Jones
Mass Observation project, 1939
I have never known a Negro personally, but have casually met them, and once danced with one. I cannot say, therefore, that I have any personal feeling about them, either good or bad. I think they are a very fine race, and admire their physique, and still more their imaginative qualities, particularly their singing and carving. I strongly deplore the racial prejudice against them. I have no particular personal feelings about Negroes. I think they seem to be an imaginative rather than intellectual race, essentially religious, with great creative gifts, but a certain childishness of outlook. I don't think they would ever fit in successfully into the commercial world of present-day Western life.

Ms Theresa Creek
Mass Observation project, 1939
One cannot compare them with whites. Couldn't pal with them. Different rules should apply. Brought up in hot country, should be left there and missionaries not allowed to preach religion only train educationally.

Mrs B. F. Harwood
Mass Observation project, 1939
I don't know much about Negroes. I think of them as big religious children. I am not particularly interested in [them]. I think of them as tall black naked individuals with wide nose, thick lips and black frizzy hair.

R. Westgate

Mass Observation project, 1939

How do I feel about Negroes? I always feel I have to be especially polite to them, as I am conscious of the rudeness with which the average person treats them. I should not mind in the least being seen in public with a negro. [They're] a race who have never had a square deal either from the British or any other nation who have had any dealings with them.

Mrs Nella Last

Mass Observation project, 1939

Perfectly neutral – just ordinary people but different colour. Don't like any kind who smell though. I only know the 'Western' Negro who either is a stupid, blundering labourer or an entertainer with an astonishing sense of rhythm, good and bad as in the 'white' folks. Don't really know any [Negroes] and should class them as little removed from animals.

Anne Partridge

Mass Observation project, 1939

On the whole I like [Negroes] but I don't really think much about them at the moment. The schools here are often sprinkled and sometimes one-third full of Negroes and discrimination is definitely taboo in the schools. I have seen working Negroes who have been much more gentlemanly than so-called middle-class English men.

Some people – teachers in dock area schools included, find Negro children repulsive but I do not. They have the rare charm of all childhood. I do dislike the film, especially American film, habit of making a Negro seem about one-third intelligent.

As a race I like them, at any rate in school. Some folks here deride their efforts to succeed but I say good luck to them. Their taste for bright colours persists here for the young men buy very many suits and cock their hats in a dandified fashion. As I said before, I find them very courteous.

Edie White
Mass Observation project, 1939
Fine people in their own country. All right when not interfering with English people. They only imitate our worst fault ie drinking too much, eating unwholesome food, immorality and wearing too many clothes.

Bert Williams
In Jamaica if you have a dog and it doesn't bark and bite, you sell it. If you have a cat and it doesn't catch a rat it's no good to you, so what they used to do, they'd ask children to tease the dog for them. We going to school, the man would leave a stick out there for you to tease the dog, then at night when you're going home he'd let the dog go, so you'd have to walk round the other way – because the dog would chase you, because you teased it.

So, when I first came to England, my brother used to warn us; he'd say, 'Whatever you do, don't mess with the white man dog.' He said, 'You can beat up the child, their children, but,' he said, 'if you beat up the dog, he'll kill you.' Straight up.

Extracts from 'Before You Go To Britain' pamphlet[3]
With high hopes and with the right visions of work and prosperity, you are considering counting your fare and applying to the Travel Agent for a passage to Britain; but before you make up your mind, read this pamphlet.

Consider the problem of arranging for accommodation for yourself in Britain, the problem of finding employment, the difficulty of living and working in a cold and wet climate which is as different as it could possibly be from the one to which you are accustomed, the long separation from family with little hope of raising enough money to either send for them or to return, the great risks in making a success of the brave venture – consider all these things carefully before you invest such a large amount of money in a passage to Britain.

BEFORE YOU LEAVE HOME

The greatest problem about living in Britain is not so much how, as WHERE. Because of the dense population and the immense amount of damage done during the war, this is a difficulty that still faces hundreds of thousands of the native inhabitants of Great Britain.

WRITE a friend or relation in Britain, and ask them to seek an address, to book a room, or to arrange a lodging; and wait until you have received a reply from this friend saying that he has been successful in arranging accommodation, before you consider leaving home.

A reasonable price for a single room with two meals a day in London would be £3 15s a week; or bed and breakfast £2 15s; or room only £2 5s. You may pay less for wretched accommodation, but don't expect to find decent lodgings anywhere for much less than that.

Find out from the landlady what are the rules of the house: what hours meals are served, what hour of night she expects you to be indoors, when is the most convenient time to have a bath, what are the rules for inviting guests.

Gas or Electricity for heating is usually an extra charge in boarding-houses and lodgings, and you pay for it by means of a meter in which shillings, sixpences or pennies are inserted.

EXPENDITURE

You must not forget that it costs more to live in Britain than in Jamaica. Rents are more expensive, food in cafes, warm clothing, heat in your room, fare to work, entertainment – all these things you might forget to reckon with, and therefore you have little left if any to save or to send home for dependents. Here is an example of the BUDGET of a Jamaican from St Anns, who now lives in Brixton, London, and works for the British Railways as a labourer.

INCOME		EXPENDITURE	
Gross Wage	£5. 16s.0d		
Nat. Insurance	£0. 5s.5d		
Net Wage	£5. 5s.9d	Income Tax	£0. 5s.5d
		Rent	£1. 15s.0d
		Meals	£1. 5s.0d
		Lunches	£0. 9s.0d
		Fuel & Light	£0. 7s.9d
		Laundry	£0. 3s.6d
		Cigarettes (@3/7 for 20)	£0. 10s.9d
			£5. 1s.0d

4/9d is left over to buy clothes, pay fares, provide entertainment and buy toilet articles. He can neither send back money to his mother, nor save to accumulate his return passage money. There are many who are not in any job, nor have they had one since they arrived months ago.

UNEMPLOYMENT

The number of persons registered as unemployed at Local Offices of the Ministry of Labour in Great Britain in March 1954 was nearly half a million. This will give you some idea of the chance you stand for employment in competition with long standing residents of Britain. Further, there is no shortage of unskilled labour, not even for the rough, coarse, outdoor, dirty and menial jobs. There are vacancies for skilled workers; that is, men who have done a qualifying period of apprenticeship, and afterwards satisfactory service in their trades. Men who are first class fitter, riggers, lath-operators, motor engineers, tool-setters, and the like.

It is no use claiming that you are skilled in Trades, if you cannot produce satisfactory evidence of your apprenticeship, PREVIOUS EMPLOYMENT, TRADE UNION MEMBERSHIP, CHARACTER REFERENCES well as your TOOLS KITS.

CLOTHES

These are the clothes you will need to cope with the climate in Britain, which is quite different from Jamaica's.

  1 heavy winter overcoat
  1 raincoat
  1 pair woollen gloves
  FOR MEN
  1 woollen pullover or sweater
  thick woollen vests
  pairs woollen pants
  4 pairs woollen socks

Extract from 'How To Live in Britain'[4]

When British people are introduced they give a faint smile and say: 'How do you do?' The answer to this question is also: 'How do you do?' The British seldom talk to strangers in trains or on buses; they prefer to read their newspapers. It will not be long before you recognise the police. The ordinary constable is familiarly known as a 'bobby' though he likes to be addressed as 'officer' unless he has three stripes in which case you call him 'sergeant'. The police force is a public service; they can give you advice about lost property, and any person without a room for the night may call upon their help in finding a bed, though it may be a humble one ...

Provided you see that your clothes are warm and weather proof and your feet are well-shod and dry you're likely to come to little harm.

Take Courage

Most Saturday mornings in our three-bedroomed council house in 1960s Luton, Ethlyn would sweep and sing hymns as she cleaned. Occasionally I'd overhear her talking to herself: 'I'm just not used to this kind of life. Stop puke around. This is no kind of life. You thought you were really something, didn't you? Look at you now, glamour gal.'

My mother believed a great trick had been played on her. This was not the life she'd imagined for herself when she'd arrived in Britain. In excited letters home, like many of her fellow West Indian adventurers, she'd at first been thrilled to see snow for the first time or the famed British politeness, which they'd all read in text books or seen in newsreels. They'd arrived in Plymouth, the very spot from which the Armada had been vanquished. They'd sipped tea in the famous Lyons tea rooms and bantered with revellers under Eros at Piccadilly Circus. Oh, the sheer delight in just being able to say 'I walked down Oxford Circus.'

There were wonderful surprises too. Would you believe that Sheffield Steel was actually named after a city? Almost everyone I interviewed was puzzled by the factories with billowing smoke that turned out to be people's homes!

Many confessed that they were daunted by the future. If they'd had the money for the return fare, they'd have turned on their heels and headed home. With Plymouth in sight towards the end of the two-week ship's passage to England in 1952, Sam Selvon, having second thoughts about the wisdom of the enterprise, turned to George Lamming and said ruefully 'Who send we here?' My mother said the same thing. Whenever Ethlyn felt slighted by the English, her thoughts would return to the long journey she'd made to get here in 1959; and she would berate herself, saying: 'Is who tell me to come to this kiss-me-arse place?'

Ethlyn bristled when people assumed she must have lived in a mud hut in Jamaica and would be grateful to have stepped into modernity. 'But,' she would complain, 'I never carry basket 'pon my head go market.'

My mother, like many West Indians, was effectively bilingual. She reserved her best speaky-spokey Queen's English when conversing with white people. She'd only break out into patois in the company of Caribbean friends. But a decade after arrival she was often exasperated that English people still seemed wilfully, to her mind, not to understand her when speaking on the phone. Ethlyn would hand the receiver to me, her seven-year-old son, as if I were her interpreter.

Cultural differences – real and imagined – created a barrier between local people and West Indians, at least in the first years of their arrival. Bert Williams says he grew to hate the word 'Pardon?', the regular response any time he spoke to a stranger.

There are as many accounts of the generosity of the British population as there were of insincerity. Bageye was especially suspicious and wary of the overly polite attention he received from shopkeepers – the 'Yes, sir', 'Will that be all, sir?' he considered veiled insults. As we left the shop, my father would turn to me in a rage: 'Listen to the way the man speak to me! You don't hear the slur?'

Had they been aware of Civil Service briefings, the West Indians would have learned that the hypocrisy extended to Her Majesty's government. The new migrants were both welcome and unwelcome.

Two days after the arrival of the *Empire Windrush*, with cheery newspaper headlines like the *Evening Standard*'s 'Welcome Home', Prime Minister Clement Attlee received a letter from eleven Labour MPs warning that: 'An influx of coloured people domiciled here is likely to impair the harmony, strength and cohesion of our public and social life and to cause discord and unhappiness among all concerned.'[1]

Five years later, a Working Party report to the Secretary of State concluded that, even though there had been government propaganda and the imposition of restrictions on the issue of passports it was insufficient: 'Effective steps to reduce the number of coloured people seeking employment must be directed to reducing the number entering the United Kingdom for that purpose.'

Many West Indians would not have been surprised to learn that this kind of sentiment was expressed behind closed doors. They suspected all along that the Englishman's antipathy towards them was disguised by a faux politeness that couldn't be challenged.

*

Donald Hinds
Journey to an Illusion, 1966
This was Plymouth! From here Drake sailed ravaging the Spanish colonies ... from here the English fleet sailed to repel the Armada, and later the Pilgrim Fathers set sail in the Mayflower. To Plymouth 1,300 of us had come towards a future.[2]

George Lamming
The Emigrants, 1954
Some of the men had just enough to pay the fare from Plymouth to Paddington. The officials asked what would happen after they reached Paddington, but no one answered with conviction. It seemed a tragic farce. England of all places, they seemed to say. They were bewildered by this exhibition of adventure, or ignorance, or plain suicide. For a while the movies seemed truer than they had vouched for, the story of men taking ship with their last resources and sailing into unknown lands in search of adventure and fortune and mystery. England had none of these things as far as they knew. Caged within

their white collars like healthy watchdogs, they studied the emigrants as thought they were to be written off as lunatics.[3]

Donald Hinds
Journey to an Illusion, 1966
From the deck could be seen knots of white people staring back at us. I had hardly ever seen more than twelve white people together before. The occupants of Cabin 94 said goodbye without much ceremony. Buses were provided to take us to the railway station. There we found our cases were smashed beyond recognition. After some delay we boarded the boat train for Paddington. Yet another blow to romance: at the London end of the line I saw white porters asking for our bags. They actually said, 'Thank you, sir,' and accepted tips. That was a turning of the tables.[4]

Waveney Bushell
When I arrived in Plymouth there was a feeling of a sort of wonderment. So this is Britain, and it was a disappointing feeling: it was dark, unfriendly, it was an odd feeling, not a friendly and inviting place. The weather affects me personally; if there's no sun it affects what sort of day I'll have. This was sixty years ago and the place was dirty, damp and dark in July, not nice at all. Noisy. Beryl and her husband met me at Paddington station and that was very nice. There were a lot of people from Guiana, some of whom had come to meet their friends and I heard things like, 'Waveney', there were four or five people that I knew, shouting, 'Hello' and 'How are you?' and so on.

Archippus Joseph
I came on the SS *Colombie*, a French passenger ship. A lot of English people later on would say, 'Go back on your banana boat', but, if you see the ship we come on, it was something you could only dream of, so we used to laugh at them when they told us to get

back on your banana boat – they looked down on you as if you're nothing. The ship arrived in Plymouth eight and a half days later. You got the cinema, you go swimming, the food was good, plenty of wine – we weren't used to the wine, jugs of wine on the table – and whole chicken sticks; we loved it.

[The ship] arrived on 4 September [1954]. We landed and then we had a boat train and came to Paddington. When we stepped off the boat a lot of people cried because you'd formed friendships; you're living with other people you didn't know before, and from other countries as well, you formed this bond, and naturally enough you feel sorry that the boat has stopped. At Paddington we stood there and thought, 'Where are we? What happens now?' Believe it or not, we had no one to come to, and we land on that platform – and in those days a lot of West Indians who came over before used to go down to welcome ... or to see what's going on, probably just nosing around. It was nice to see them, but they can't help you.

But I had a cousin; Joe West, who came over on the boat before us, and he was standing there and it was really lucky that he saw me; I was in heaven. He had no idea I was coming – what a joy, what a relief. He said, 'There's a vacant room in the house where I'm staying, come with me.' I had two other friends and they come with me and we share.

He took us to Hackney. There was a double room, a big ten-room house, the landlord was a black man from St Kitts married to a German woman named Woodley. It was a pound a week for rent.

I cried after a while not straight away. When you're on your own and you have to look after yourself, more or less, washing and cooking and so on, a few tears shed, until you get used to your surroundings.

Shirley Williams

Because my aunty lived here in Kentish Town, who now lives in Leicester, so I stayed with her for a little while, but not for long because, once you were admitted, you got a date [to start working at the hospital]. When I arrived it was a lovely sunny day, which was lovely. The train was scary to Kentish Town and when you get into the house, 'Oh God, is this where we're going to have to sit? Live?' Little tiny rooms, shared a toilet. I said, 'Oh aunty, is this England?' She said, 'Yeah.' 'Oh my God,' I said. No shower – a bucket and a cup, and all the lodgers in the place all using the same area. I said, 'Oh no, I'm going back to Guiana.' She said, 'You don't have to go back to Guiana, you don't have to be here forever; you're going to Brighton, you'll have all the facilities there. You miss home because you miss all your family.'

Peter John Nelson

I came to England from Jamaica in 1960 at the age of ten. My parents came the year before. I stayed with some relatives for a year, and then we joined them the year after, here in Manchester. My mum was a nurse and my dad worked for the Post Office for a while and then ended up working for a cable company in Trafford Park. When I came it was very, very cold and I thought – when my dad pulled up in the row of terraced houses in Old Trafford, saw all these chimneys. Now, in Jamaica, the only building you see with a chimney was a factory, so when he pulled up in front of these houses and the smoke's coming out of all these chimneys, I thought this is where he worked. Then I realised that all the houses had these chimneys. I were ten year old, it's like an adventure. But the only disappointment was every picture I saw of England ... have you ever seen these postcards with houses covered in snow, with a robin and a beautiful little cottage? And that was my mental picture of England.

Viv Adams

We flew in to Gatwick Airport and I was imbued with a sense of otherness. I remember being grateful that we were leaving, relieved.

I just felt that some miracle had caused us to escape; that's the way I felt at the airport.

All the experiences that I encountered that afternoon was just a reprisal of those sentiments. It wasn't like I was an immigrant. I felt like I was home, because we had been used to England through images from the Ealing movies; all those comedians we used to watch in the cinema in Jamaica, this was what we thought England was like.

So when I arrive [in 1961] at Gatwick nothing surprise me. When I saw the district nurse on her pushbike I said to Percy, 'This was Hattie Jacques.' It was reassuring to see that, because I didn't feel we were coming to something alien. When the pilot came over we were standing in the vestibule waiting for Eldon [my brother who was already in England] and Ian Lesley [his friend] to go and fetch the car, which was going to take us back to Luton. Percy and I were standing with our little cardboard suitcase and our borrowed top coats, but I didn't feel like an immigrant, but like we were about to embark on a wonderful adventure that was going to close off a chapter. Suddenly I saw this white man, BOAC in his uniform, he had three gold rings on his sleeve, so I knew he had some kind of rank, and he walked across the whole concourse and came up to us. He looked just like what I had come to expect that an English man would look like – tall, fair hair, florid complexion – and he put his travel case down on the floor. I remember looking down at his travel case, beside his shoe, and I remember that his shoe was well polished, and he says, 'Have you guys just come off that flight from Kingston?' And I said, 'Yeah.' I was suspicious why he was asking, and he stepped forward and held out his hand and said, 'Well then, let me be the first to welcome you to this country, and I sincerely hope you have a successful and happy time here,' and I took his hand and shook it. He stared into my face with his washed-out blue eyes, shook our hands and did an about-turn, almost military fashion, and walked away.

For years after this, I used to think of this man with fondness and would invoke memory of our encounter as proof of the kind-hearted, welcoming nature of the English. It was such an impressive thing to happen on your first day, and I thought, 'Only good things can happen now to us.'

The music that was playing [when we got to the house] was Acker Bilk, 'Stranger on the Shore'. And then Ian Lesley started playing Ray Charles, 'I Can't Stop Loving You', and that song resonated in my chest, made me feel that we were embarked upon something of glamour that lay beyond tomorrow, and that we had achieved what we had hoped would happen – we had left the island, we were no longer on the island, we were not entrapped by the island.

Linette May Simms

When I get off I stood there and I have my baggage, and I didn't know what to do. It was February, and I asked the policeman who was walking along, I say, 'Could you tell me where I could find the YWCA?' I learned that in school before I leave, that every town will have this. I had no more than about 16 shillings [around £15 in 2019]. He said, 'Why do you want to know?' I said, 'Because I have nowhere to go sir.' He said, 'I beg your pardon?' And a Jamaican lady named Florrie, from the same ship, was walking past and she said, 'Linette, What is wrong?' I said, 'Nothing is wrong, I'm just asking him for the association.' The policeman said, 'It's alright, it's my duty to find it for her.' Florrie said, 'But you could come with me.' Policeman turned to her and asked, 'Where are you going?' She said she was going to 1 Geneva Road. 'And who get the place for you?' The policeman asked. She said her uncle. She said I could come with her. The policeman turned to me now and said, 'Would you like that?'

At Geneva Road, we went in and she took me upstairs to her aunty; her uncle was working away. She looked at me and said, 'You have a little girl with you?' And Florrie said, 'Yes; she doesn't have anywhere to stay.' And the aunty said, 'That's fine, she can stay here.'

The policeman came the next day with a policewoman to make sure I was OK, and he checked the accommodation and asked if I was OK, and when I nodded, he said, 'Welcome to England.'

Wallace Collins
Jamaican Migrant, 1965
As I stood beside the fountain in Trafalgar Square a pigeon came and perched on top of my head and shit on it and I was undaunted and proud and wrote home to my mother that ... I am making history.[5]

Bernice Smith
The Colony, BBC TV, 1964
I thought I was going to travel and that England would be a beautiful place. But when we got on the train we saw some of the smoky buildings, you know, as if they were frowning. The sun wasn't very bright; it was sort of hazy. I thought I wouldn't be able to stay in England. I wanted to cry but I was ashamed to do so. A lot of other girls were horrified. One girl held on to me as we got on the train and we had to pass through one or two tunnels, and this woman held on, she grasped me and said that she doesn't want to go into such a dark place any more, and we sort of laughed. Coming to the meadows and so on, my heart began to feel good, seeing all these beautiful flowers, but still I didn't feel too comfortable. I thought it was because I was tired and so on, but coming into Birmingham I can't quite remember what happened, but as I came in and saw where we had to live, my heart sank and most of the time I cried.

Lucile Harris
When I came to England I live in Brixton, near the market. I tell you, when I came here there were hardly any buildings standing and far as you can look it bomb and burn outright through and

through. My husband sorted out a place to live before he sent for me. When I was in Jamaica, they said this is a very dark country, so it was different, the houses were all smashed because of the war, it was 1948 and war had finished in 1945.

V. S. Naipaul

I went directly to the boarding house in Earl's Court, where a room had been reserved for me ... After the warm, rubbery smell of the ship, the smell of the air-conditioning in enclosed cabins and corridors, there were new smells in the morning. A cloying smell of milk and condensed milk. That thick, sweet smell of milk was mixed with the smell of soot; and that smell was overlaid with the airless cockroachy smell of old dirt ... I had never been in a basement before. It was not a style of building we had at home; but I had read of basements in books; and this room with an electric light burning on a bright sunny day seemed to me romantic. I was like a man entering the world of a novel, a book; entering the real world.

[But] I grew to feel that grandeur belonged to the past; that I had come to England at the wrong time; that I had come too late to find the England, the heart of empire, which (like a provincial, from a far corner of the empire) I had created in my fantasy.[6]

Louise Smith

My brother was living at a place, Claremont Road, Hartley and, when I was coming, the house was big, and the room was big – no heating; black lamp [paraffin heater]. When my brother said, 'There's no bath, we have to get a public bath.'

Public bath wicked. I wouldn't like tell you what it is like. Nasty, dirty. Not even your dog you wouldn't put inna that public bath. No. It was terrible. You have to clean that bath before you use it. My brother went and brought me a big tub, so we got hot water and look after myself; and him put bed in the bathroom for me – that's my brother – and when he come up I had a little bed in the bathroom. Tell the truth when I came, and had that experience, if I could walk back to Jamaica, I would walk, stop, rest and go. True!

Don Letts

My parents, Valerie and St Leger, came over in 1954, and when they had me and my brothers, we used to go to the local baths, public baths, on a Friday night we'd go – Camberwell. You'd go to the public bath, you'd sit in this room waiting in a queue, you'd go in the bath, they'd fill it up with water and me and my younger brother would have to share – my older brother, he'd be in the bath on his own – and I've forgotten how long you got, but I remember knocking on the door, 'More hot in number four', you'd get them to top up the hot water. When we were growing up it wasn't like, 'Oh my God, this is really bad', it's just the way it was.

Alford Gardner

My brother and I went down to Coventry Place in Leeds. We didn't have a bath in the house. We had to go to the public baths. You paid a shilling for them. It was up to you the amount of times you bathe per week. In England the norm was one shower each week. We had many more than that. For the average English family, bath night was Thursday or Friday, and they all used the same water. Our landlady couldn't understand why, when me and my brother came from work, we had to get washed before we sat down to eat.

Maizie Pinnock

When I came to Leeds, I did not know anything, but I asked questions. I took a taxi early in the morning to Harehills Terrace. The taxi driver came out and took my case out and I said, 'What do I do?' He said, 'You have to ring the bell.' I asked him, 'Where is the bell?' He rang the bell for me. Somebody came down and opened the door. Anyway, I wanted to go to the toilet and I asked, 'Where is the toilet?' I was told the toilets were outside; I was so shocked

– believe you me! I know back home you have toilets outside, but when I left Jamaica I was in town in Kingston, so I was used to indoor toilets. It was horrendous!

Olive Gordon

My husband had died. I had my brother-in-law living in England, and he told me fascinating stories about London, and it caught me, and I sold what I had and I came over. I didn't bring them [the children], I left them home; they were going to British Guiana Educational Trust. So I had three children and a mother [in Guiana] and I found it difficult.

I arrived at Plymouth and the train took me to Paddington. When I got there I had no money to get transport and I borrowed a pound and came. When I came to London my brother-in-law was working out of London, and when I got here, I rang the bell, and Mr Reynold George Gordon came down and he said, 'I told your brother-in-law you're going to be here.' When I got here it was ten o'clock so I couldn't see anything. But the next morning my brother-in-law asked Mr Reynold to take me and to go and sign up for something, and when I got downstairs, I looked. All the houses and the windows were closed, the trees were bare, everything was foggy and it was cold. And I got downstairs, and when I looked I said, 'Is this London? My God!' All the windows closed, the people gone out! If I had money I'd go back home, it was horrible.

Phyllis Hines

My sister greeted me warmly and I was glad to see her. I was up early the next morning. My sister asked me to go to the shop just across the street in front of her house. Whilst I was in the shop, the sky started to get dark all of a sudden, until it became pitch black. I could not see anything. I was afraid, I started fretting and crying. I said to myself, 'I want to go back to Jamaica if this is how England is going to be.' Then I heard my sister calling me. She had a lamp in her hand and came to take me over to the house.

Bert Williams

We came over from Jamaica and we were very respectful; we were brought up with manners. You see a white person coming towards you and you say, 'Good morning sir.' That's one of the things that my brother told me, 'Don't call him sir, nobody calls sir over here. They won't talk to you; you've got to talk to them first.' In Jamaica, if you see someone older than you or a friend of your parents, you have to nod your head and say, 'Morning sir.' But these are not things you can drop overnight.

The picture you have inside, it's not exactly what you see when you come. I had pictures of big buildings with beautiful roads and trees lining, like you see in the pictures; the same picture I would see in Jamaica of London. You see Buckingham Palace, you see all like Royal [Parks], you see the parks and everything. When you come and see the real world, and you're walking in Shepherd's Bush your second day, and there's not a blade of grass around, it's like a concrete jungle. Course, I come from the country; you want to know the time; you look up in the sky. The thing I notice as well was how low the sky was, feel like you could jump and touch it. In Jamaica it looks miles above, just that blue sky, looks miles above, and then you come here. And then the winter, that was awful; and the smells and the different sounds you're hearing. Smell of tarmac, smell of greens, smell of different fruits when you walk through Shepherd's Bush Market and look at the different fruits you never seen in your life, that sort of thing. Eating things like Brussels sprouts, cauliflower – the food was insipid. My brother used to buy English mustard to heat up the food.

George Mangar

When we got to Dover we got a train to Victoria station. I arrived about three o'clock in the afternoon and the British Council officials were there, so I went towards them, they said, 'Yes, you're here to study, OK fine you need to get a train to Ipswich.' I was told to get the Circle Line and go to Liverpool Street. In Guiana we have two trains, you go straight and come back straight. That's all I knew. We didn't have a Circle Line, District Line; nothing like that. So I got on the Circle Line, and in Guiana they call out the name of the stations as you go, and I was expecting that. The train went and I went round and round and round. I was about two hours on the train; until five o'clock I was on the train! So I said to this lady sitting next to me, 'Excuse me, where's Liverpool Street?' She said, 'You just passed it!' She said, 'You get off at the next stop and cross over.' I got on another train and eventually I came out at Liverpool Street.

So I got off at Liverpool Street and then was when I had the surprise of my life; the running men. In Guiana the only time you run is if you steal something or you're running from the rain to hide in a shop; this was five o'clock in the afternoon, all these guys running like hell, I said, 'My God! How many thieves you have in this country?' That was my first impression, I said, 'My God, I'll have to be careful here.'

I got a train at 7:20 p.m. from Liverpool Street to go to Ipswich. Now, on English trains, they've got these compartments, and this train stops everywhere, and it's getting darker and darker, and then the compartment emptied; there's only me in it, and it's two o'clock in the morning now. I'm thinking, 'My God, when will we get to Ipswich?' And I saw some boards on the side of the tracks, it said, 'Take Courage'. I thought that was meant for us! Take courage when you first come to England! I didn't know it was a bloody beer. Courage beer! When I got to Ipswich at half past two in the morning, I saw my brother and met his wife for the first time. I said, 'There are a lot of thieves in London, you know?' He said, 'What do you mean?' I told him and he said, 'Don't be silly, they're catching their trains to go home from work!'

The Sunday after, I was with my sister-in-law, she says, 'George, it's a lovely warm day, let's go for a walk.' I said, 'OK.' We went across this huge bridge, she says, 'George, this is our river.' I said, 'River? What we call this is a canal, a trench.' She says, 'No no no; this is a river.' I said, 'Our river; ferry boats take you across it.' So we go on the other side and there's an English lady and a child, and the child says, 'Mummy, look a black man!' And she says, 'No darling, that's a nigger.' I started to laugh and the boy was laughing. My sister-in-law is really angry. When we got back she told my brother Harold and he said, 'You know, George, that happens all the time.' It's alright with me, just don't touch me; you touch me, it's a different thing.

Arthur France

I got the train from Dover to London. I had a suit made by a man, name Saljo, I think he was Arab or Indian. I came to my sister in Chapeltown. I remember the first Saturday night. We sat there and some friends came in and one guy say he been here for two years, and I thought, 'He must be crazy.' Then another guy say he been here for four years and I thought, 'Bloody hell, he is mad, four years!' One of the guys said, 'England is like an open prison, you can't get out.'

Stuart Hall

Personally Speaking, 2009[7]

I will never forget landing [in England]. My mother brought me, in my felt hat, in my overcoat, with my steamer trunk. She brought me, as she thought, 'home', on a banana boat, and delivered me to Oxford. She gave me to the astonished college scout and said, 'There is my son, his trunk, his belongings. Look after him.' She delivered me, signed and sealed, to where she thought a son of hers had always belonged – Oxford.

Franklin Jackson

Manchester airport. Fill with snow. I never seen snow in my life before and as soon as we get off the plane this girl in front of me, she just sprawled out on the snow; she flat out on her face. So when I saw her did that, you should have see me in that snow, brother, I was like, just stepping like a chicken.

My mother and my father and one of their friend that drove them in the car ... it was cold, it was in January, it was cold. I would go outside, and I couldn't get my hands in my pockets because it was too cold. Once we got in the house and the big fire was on it wasn't too bad. But the house was still dark; not like ours, which is all full of light and air in Jamaica, so it was very, very different.

I couldn't stand the food. I didn't like the English bread to start with. The only thing I liked was the baked beans, but I couldn't stand the rest of the food. The eggs didn't smell the same, the meat didn't smell the same, because we used to have it fresh right off where it's come from. Over here you're getting it in all different sort of ways. They delivering it in different ways. It took me a while to get used to the food.

When I started going to school, I would come home, and because I'm not used to the names of the street, I wouldn't even know where to look for the names of the street or even the numbering of the house. I remember once, I came home from school the first week I went to school, my friend walked me halfway up the road and say, 'You just live up there.' I say, 'OK', but I didn't even know to look for the numbers on the door, never seen it before in my life. How do I know where 11 Bland Street is? And I'm looking up and down and I ask these white people, 'Do you know where 11 Bland Street is?' 'No I don't know.' And I'm a couple doors away and I don't even know.

I remember my first encounter really with white people. There was a white woman who lived in the house where my dad used to live. With her being there it gives me a little bit of time to get used to what white people look like; the way they built, but they used to all look the same to me. 'How come these people look so much alike?' Which, of course – they think the same of us, don't they? And I think, 'Jesus Christ', I couldn't understand how they speak. It was very difficult. And they found the same thing with me too, they couldn't understand me.

Joyce Estelle Trotman

When you got to Newcastle you realised there were different accents. Because when we were in the Bishops High School [in Guiana], in those days everybody, all the staff, had the Received Pronunciation [from] the south-east of England. So when you came here you realised there were different accents; there was the Geordie accent, they say, 'Ee,' and you say, 'What?'

Because that summer [of 1955] it was the best summer they had had, we were in sandals until end of September. But boy, one October morning, that north-east wind hit you, and it was the worst winter they said they had had since 1947; snow ploughs out and, of course, no central heating. And in those days it was continuous showing in the cinemas. So I sat through *The Red Shoes*, round and round and round, psyching myself to back out into the cold. But having done that, I could face any winter.

Viv Adams

The guy who was driving us, Ian Lesley, I didn't know at the time, but he was … he had a drink problem. He was an alcoholic, but I was too young to know what being an alcoholic meant, and I remember – it was a little car, we were driving through one of these towns beyond Gatwick, little English village – and he stopped the car and said, 'I'm just going to go over there and buy something.' Those days you didn't have off licences, so he had to go into this shop, where the man would sell him a pint of liquor, probably illegally, and it came back in a brown paper bag, and as he came back into the car he unzipped it and took a great big slug, licked his lips and said, 'Yeah man, let's go!'

I remember driving along this, what you'd now call an A road, and we had to stop to ask someone directions – an English man driving a car – and Ian got out and spoke to him to get the directions, and as he came back he said, 'Damn fool man,' and just zipped past the man. He saw the man as part of that image where the English man was always seen as comical; he wouldn't have done it if the man was American. There was a kind of patronising attitude that Jamaicans had about the English at that time, they saw them as not quite serious people, although they had power and all the rest of it, they weren't cool. They were people who wore funny clothes and would be funny in a kind of way, so it was legitimate to laugh at them, in a way.

The first real English family I came to know was an English family my brother Ramon had been boarding with when he was a merchant seaman. They lived in Leyton in east London, and the woman of the family was very fond of him and she used to call him her little ray of sunshine. The first time he took us there for dinner one night, a number of things became obvious to me almost immediately. They were very refined, but I felt they were poor at the same time, because the music that was being played for the supper was the Home Service, on this little radio perched on a thing in the dining room-cum-kitchen, and we had to sit down at the table, and then I'm thinking, 'Yes, we're going to have some business.' And I remember; she brought me this plate with two slivers of ham on it and, I think, half a tomato on the side. I remember looking at the ham and thought how pathetic it was because you could virtually see through to the design on the plate, and I thought, 'These people don't have a lot.' As a side order she brought another plate and it was slices of white buttered bread; that was it. I remember being conscious that they were in need.

Rena Khublall

I arrived at Gatwick and was met by my brother. It was lovely to see him, it was really lovely to see him but, when I arrived, my husband David was hiding, he didn't come out. The first thing I said, 'Where is David?' My brother said, 'He couldn't make it, he's not here.' My heart was broken, I thought, 'If he didn't have the time to come and see me, what's the point of coming, I might as well go back.' That's how I felt and then, all of a sudden, while I was talking to my brother, tears in my eyes, David jumped out. He was all dressed up – he's always dressed up, he's always well presented.

David Khublall

My heart was empty before, it was filled now. My companion is with me now! When I saw her at the terminal I couldn't let go.

Tin Baths and Paraffin Heaters

The famed West Indian cricketer, Learie Constantine, was a pioneer, one of the first black cricketers invited in 1928 to play in the Lancashire League. Constantine was widely revered. An able and erudite Trinidadian who'd served as a Welfare Officer during the Second World War, he had been responsible for West Indians working in munitions factories; he was knighted in 1962 and made a life peer soon after. So, it was shocking to learn that he'd once been turned away from a glamorous hotel in central London in the 1940s. Shocking, embarrassing (I felt embarrassed for him), but also sobering and revelatory. If such a thing could happen to the eminent West Indian cricketer, it could surely happen to the son of a Jamaican factory worker in Luton.

It has been said that the arrival in 1940s Britain of American soldiers, with their Jim Crow sensibilities intact, exacerbated the problems of race relations in this country. But the seeds of anti-black attitudes had long been planted and embedded in British soil.

This was a time of conscious bias. That which might be said unapologetically at a hotel's front desk could also be displayed without censure in the windows of guest-houses and rooms-to-let. The signs saying 'No Blacks, No Irish, No Dogs' have almost become a historical cliché now to which we are inured. But to West Indians trudging through the streets in the 1950s looking for accommodation this was a raw experience – one which, decades later for some like Waveney Bushell, still burns.

Bigoted landlords were not breaking the law in discriminating against black people, as there was no law to be broken. Up and down the country landlords disingenuously turned away the immigrants with the mantra, 'I'm sorry, but if I let you in, my other tenants would move out.' Others were more blunt, like the estate agent who complained in a 1960s BBC interview: 'How would you like it if the house next door to you was taken by a coloured person and became filled at bursting point with all of his relations and his friends and so on and so forth?'

Peter Rachman was not so 'discerning'; he was notorious for renting out flats at extortionate rates to the newly arrived immigrants in west London. But it was better to have a slum room than no room at all.

Debating the housing crisis in parliament and the deplorable 'extortion, evictions and property profiteering' which resulted from the Rent Act 1957, the Leader of the Labour Party, Harold Wilson, complained: 'Sometimes one turns over a stone in a garden or field and sees the slimy creatures which live under its protection ... But the photophobic animal world has nothing to compare with the revolting creatures of London's underworld, living there, shunning the light, growing fat by battening on human misery.'[1]

Britain was meant to be a wealthy country but the newcomers were shocked to discover that, even in flats which were not rat-infested Rachman hovels, the heating facilities were poor, toilets were outside and hygiene did not seem to be a priority.

The West Indians who'd come to England were, as Viv Adams recalls, strategic. 'If landlords wouldn't rent them accommodation they'd buy their own; if the banks didn't want to lend them money for deposits for mortgages, they'd set up their own informal and effective community savings schemes to be able to do so: the "pardner".'

A pardner system could comprise a variable number of people who made a commitment to each contribute an agreed weekly amount to be saved by an elected banker. They would then take it in turns to draw the full amount of a week's takings from the banker. So if, for instance, there were twenty savers in the scheme contributing £5 per week, then once every twenty weeks an individual could draw £100 from the banker.

And, as Don Sydney remembers, not only was the pardner system empowering, it was a way of saving face: 'Sometimes the reason the bank manager give you [for refusal] is not genuine and you know that but you can't prove it. [So] we take part in pardner because we find it less offensive and disheartening.'

★

Bodelyn

I was eight months pregnant ... and where I was living, they didn't want any baby to born there so I had to leave. I couldn't get nowhere to live so my husband ended taking me down to the police station ... and they let me sleep there for the night. The next morning, we got a room where we could only sleep but there was no cooking facilities, nothing.

Michael McMillan

There were cockroaches and mice. We were living in three rooms, six of us, in a big tenement house owned by a landlord with five other families. I think my father had a nervous breakdown. My mum had to work as well. She was a cleaner, Post Office, various things, anything to make ends meet whilst also looking after us. But my father really did suffer mentally from that moment, he started to take sleeping tablets which he became addicted to for the rest of his life. Everything stress, pressure. My parents' relationship was hard.

Edwin Hilton Hall

The coloured lads didn't like the hostel. They want to get somewhere to decent to live. They used to go to the white people's place that was advertising rooms to let. They used to close the door. I've experienced that. My skin isn't all that black, but I'm mixed – Indian, black and Chinese. And still, they used to tear me down and insult me and slam the door. 'We don't have you people, we don't have you people here.' I've experienced it ... even now talking, my temple has risen remembering what used to happen to me but, thank God, today is different.

Roy Mitchell

When I came to Leeds I went to the YMCA which was on Albion Street. I remember I was trying to find somewhere to live and I travelled around Leeds trying to find lodging in any area. It was one of the most difficult time of my life because every one of them said: 'Rooms to Let' – when I knocked they would say, 'Sorry we are filled up.' Now there would be a telephone box ten yards from the place where you had knocked and if you go to the telephone box and make a call, they would say, 'Oh yes, we have got a vacancy.' You would knock again and they would say, 'Sorry it has just been taken.'

Finally, bless her, there was one lady from Ireland, Mrs McCrum, and when I knocked on the door, she said, 'Father of God, is not another one of you again!' Anyway, we had a little chat and she said she had a room but I had to share it with someone. I said, 'I don't mind.' Funnily enough, I went into this place and she showed me the room and it was the half size of a toilet with two bedsits. I was happy to get it because at the time that was how the situation was. Now you wake up in the morning and one of you want to change, one of you had to get out of the room, because it was that small, and you couldn't be in the room together.

Learie Constantine

BBC Third Programme, 1943

When we arrived [at the hotel in 1943] they said, 'We're very sorry, we don't take foreigners.' And of course [my daughter] Gloria was at the counter and she came back to me and said, 'We are in the wrong place, Daddy. They don't take coloured people.'

They accepted the English section of our party and rejected the coloured section although we had booked the rooms for all. They told me they were full up and so on ... I produced my receipt and they made excuses but eventually we had to leave the hotel and in order to set the example that the law wouldn't discriminate I took action against the hotel.

I argued that the law of England had no room for discrimination and that if I proved my contract and a breach of it by the company judgement is almost automatic. So when I got judgement and the hotel people had to pay my costs, hundreds of letters came to me congratulating me on the step I had taken. Hotel proprietors became a little more amenable to coloured people coming in.[2]

Waveney Bushell

There was a teachers' magazine that was published then, with certain pages devoted to advertising homes. I saw this advertisement for this maisonette and I replied, and I said to the woman in my letter, 'Look I'm a West Indian, so if you feel that you can't ... '. By then I knew what life was like here ... I'd spent two years here by then, I said if you feel it's alright – in other words, don't let me come from West Kensington for you to say no politely, just write and say, 'No thank you'. And I got that place and lived there for years. She was very open about people from other countries and so on, she was quite good, and I was surprised, she was very pleasant. My expectation was that they would look you up and down.

There were all these little cards in shops that said, 'No blacks', so you knew that. Up to now, after fifty odd years in this country, I would be apprehensive going up to anybody's step in case the person who owns that house is white – up to now – and that's because when I first came here, that's what I saw in every shop.

James Berry

When I came to England in 1948, I realised that the politeness of the people wasn't a rumour, it was actually true. Alongside the other white people I had known, the British came off best. They didn't have this need to express a sense of superiority, [but] you got to know about their racial prejudice if you were looking for a job or for a room. The room would be advertised, I would go to the house, a man would come to the door, and as soon as he saw me standing there he would slam it in my face. I come after the room. 'It's gone, it's gone.' Bang. When people behave like this, you feel you could shoot down the whole place.

Mavis Stewart

It was pretty difficult at times but people managed because they knew that it was part of the journey, as it were, and it wouldn't be for ever. Here we are thousands of miles away from home. Many of us have never left before. Many of us with no relatives. We need a base – somewhere – you might even call it, I believe the word is anchorage.

I said I'm telephoning about house. 'Oh, yes, dear.' 'Can you please tell me about it, what's it like?' She told me, 'Three bedrooms, near the shops, near the parks, near the schools . . .'. And I said, 'That sounds like what we're looking for.' And she said, 'And by the way dear, you'll be glad to know there isn't a black for miles around.'

On the first week we were there, Saturday morning, we did the washing and I said to my husband, 'Can you please hang the washing out?' And he went outside with the basket full of washing and the neighbour was hanging out her washing. She looked over the fence, took one look at him, dropped her basket of washing and ran into the house.

Deen Bacchus

I had a Polish landlord and he was very very strict. If I'm going out, I had to tell him what day I'm going out – whether Friday, Saturday or Sunday. And I had to be in by 9 p.m. or else he used to lock the front door from the inside. Many nights I left and I sat on the step, 'cause you know when you ring the bell he wouldn't open – but he isn't asleep. You could see his shadow. He's peeping.

George Clark

To say 'furnished' is to disgrace the vocabulary. I mean … bare boards and a chair which had seen the better part of its life and an iron bedstead with a rather filthy mattress and perhaps sometimes generously a blanket or a pillow, but that was it.

[One] example is of two West Indian families in one single back room on the fifth floor with no washing or toilet facility at all. No cooking facility. So they would share the cooking facilities with the next landing and obviously had to take their slops down five flights of stairs each morning. That was five adults and, I think, seven children from memory – young children.

Agnes DeAbreu

What got me was the rooms that people [in the UK] live in, just one little room; that really got me. I thought you'd have a bigger area. They said you rent a room, but you couldn't imagine these small little rooms: a little wardrobe, two chairs, a little bed – and the beds were horrible.

My brother Peter was here before me. He took me and I shared a room with a friend from St Vincent and it was a little bed and it was horrible, with those old-fashioned spring. Cooking facilities and washing facilities were shared. It was difficult, a source of tension and arguments. And you could always hear other people in the house and the landlord was an African man and he wasn't friendly and welcoming. My brother and his friend had a room and the landlord had a flat. The rent was about a pound.

We moved with my brother and his friends to another place in Stamford Hill and had a big room, but no heating. We had a paraffin heater, and that's another thing I used to hate. You used to have to put it outside the door for the smell. We used to share the food and the cooking. One was an older guy with a wife and children back home and he used to like cooking.

Louise Smith

When you put on your pot of fire, you clap on pinny for cook your food and when you gone upstairs or leave it there, when you come back, sometimes people come and burn out the penny cook for them food; and sometime me have to take up the pot with the rice, it not finish cook, near, carry it in my room, put it 'pon me black lamp [paraffin heater] to finish cook. And then sometime in the building when you cook your food you cannot leave it down there, because when you come they eat out your food.

Allen Ebanks

Before leaving Jamaica, I had arranged to stay with a friend in Nottingham. On arrival at the house, I found out that my friend was already sharing a room with three other men. I joined them in the same room because there was no alternative. All five of us were from the same district back in Jamaica, so we knew each other very well, one was even my first cousin. The house was vastly over-crowded but we all got along with each other. The landlord was one of the most unscrupulous men I have ever met. One night we were in the room talking and he knocked on the door and his words were, 'Fellows it is ten o'clock, it's time you were going to bed, you are burning too much electricity.' The room only had one light bulb! Also in those days the only means of heating the house was by coal fire. All of us would put together to buy our own coal. What I shall never forget is, while we were out to work, the landlord and his family were stealing our coal. He was getting so much rent, it was not long before he could buy another house and he and his family moved out of the house.

Donald Chesworth, Policy Committee, London County Council, 1957–1963

[In the 1950s and early 1960s] the rent was protected by law and could only be marginally increased. There were, however, enormous profits to be made by translating unfurnished accommodation into furnished accommodation. There were people who specialised in getting rid of existing tenants – old people, all kinds of people. Replacing them substantially by newcomers to Britain who were in desperate need for themselves and their family's accommodation and who were therefore willing, scarcely able, but certainly willing in the circumstances to pay very substantial rents. The greater the desperation that people had for accommodation the more they were willing to meet [Peter] Rachman's terms. To that extent, he was a provider of accommodation for black people.[3]

Edward Pilkington

On the one hand West Indians suited Rachman's purposes perfectly because they couldn't find any other accommodation in London. Accommodations were extremely limited over time because of the overt colour bar that operated. So West Indians, because of the scarcity of housing open to them, were forced to pay exorbitant rents. Now, Rachman was prepared to house them, unlike many other landlords, because they were paying such high rents.

He was extremely ruthless and he wasn't prepared to stop at anything – and getting protected tenants out bringing in new tenants and then charging the earth for hovels.

People [would] come back from work in the evening. They'd find their furniture and possessions all strewn all over the road, they'd find rubbish bins dumped on their living room carpets. Some cases itching powder or even dead rats were put under their sheets. In one famous case it's said the Rachman employed a firm of builders to lift off a roof of one of his properties where tenants were being particularly stubborn ... And so for the West Indian community there is a love–hate relationship with Rachman: hate because of the exorbitant rents he was charging and the violent tactics that he employed against anyone who didn't pay the rent on time; but love because, unlike respectable and gentlemanly English landlords,

Rachman was actually prepared to give them a roof over their head – however poor the condition of that roof was.

Mr Hazel

I found the native people living was not something that you envy, because they were just as badly off when it comes to living accommodation. The term 'Rachmanism' came into being because of the problem many of us had renting accommodation and only to find if you complain that something was wrong – maybe the sink did not function properly or the furniture – the next thing you had to do was to get out as quickly as you could, because they had people going around with dogs to put you out. You end up having to rush out 'cause your life was more valuable than the money.

Viv Adams

Rachman was no angel, don't get me wrong. People talk about him as if he was the personification of evil, but there were plenty of other candidates for that title. Lots of guys running dodgy deals, mixing up family tenants with prostitutes, running scams. Rachman got the rep but he wasn't alone.

Bibs

Don't tell me about Rachman. It wasn't Rachman, so it was that Trinidadian bad man Michael X[4] who went around hassling the people.

Shirley Green
Rachman's Biographer

[Rachman] didn't need to get tenants out by rough methods. Once he started letting to black immigrants there was a colossal collision of cultures and many of the white tenants just went. But Rachman was earning such good rents from his black tenants he really could afford to let them subsidise the white controlled tenants. He had another way of getting good rents, but it was typical of the area. Most landlords in the area did what's called 'bending the basement'. He always had one prostitute in a house. Never had more than one because that counted as a brothel. But you always had one. And so there again you get a very high rent. On this basis, with the high rents from the blacks and the high rents from the prostitutes, he didn't need to go harassing out the few control tenants he had.

Jessie

quoted in *Picture Post*, 30 October 1954

I've never really had much bother over digs because we've always lived in Negro houses. Me and my friend downstairs (she's just had twins) are the only two white people in the house. I did try once to get a flat, but they said that as neither of the children has to sleep in our bed we don't get priority. The only priority I've got is that we have to go downstairs for water.

Albert

Journey to an Illusion, 1966

Six of us was sleeping on one big bed in one room … There was another room in the basement that some whores had. It seems the rightful landlord did not know what was happening. He drop in one day and find two of the black boys in bed with the prostitutes. Well, he tossed those guys out [and] that night I come from work and find my things scatter in the little alley.

I walk this town one night from the time I finish work till it was time to start work the following morning. In those days police did'n even bother to pick up a black man, because the jail would be a night shelter out of the rain and the cold. That day when I finish work I was feeling so rusty and tired that I drag myself to Charing Cross an' pay a penny an' got into the toilet, determined to have a roof over my head that night. I remember that it was a small island man cleaning up the lavatory, I think he was a Bajan. I did'n pay him no mind, I decided that I would curl up on the toilet seat and go off to sleep. I was jus' droppin' off into a sweet sleep when I hear the door breaking down, bam, bam! When I look up, the black man climb over the top and see me sleeping on the seat. Man, that Bajan man carry on, you hear. 'Get outta there, man! Is guys like you come to the white people them country and spoil it up. You should be ashamed of you'self, man. You lettin' the race down, man!' So I come out and just look him over from head to toe and back again and said to him: 'Is not me carrying down the race, boy! You see me come to England goin' around cleaning up people's shit?'[5]

Arthur France

It was very hard. There was a house in Chapeltown [in Leeds], and it was knocked down to build some flats and I felt very sad and thought they should have kept it as a museum. 144 Chapeltown Road. A Jamaican man bought that house. You had a cellar and three floors, and an attic room, and rent out rooms, and you'd have about six people living in one room. And when you arrived, when you came in a taxi, before you tell him where you want to go, that's where he used to drop you, because that was the only one. And some people lived in Grange Avenue or somewhere else and when they come, the landlady or landlord wouldn't let you in, and so you have to get up and walk around to 144 Chapeltown Road, because they will find accommodation there. And then you had 10 Grange Avenue, an African doctor bought it, so you could find accommodation, because otherwise you'd be struggling for a place to keep.

Peter John Nelson

I was twenty-three when I left home. I got married to my first wife when I was twenty-three. I bought a house in Old Trafford when I was twenty-three. One of the very few West Indians in 1973 in my age group who had his own house. I was getting good money as a welder, you see, and I did other jobs to get a deposit for a house.

I remember in the sixties, if a white guy bought a car he paid 6 per cent interest, you buy the same car you have to pay 2 per cent extra interest. Same with the houses: white guy was paying 6 per cent interest on his house, you had to pay eight. With the banks or the loan company, if you were black you were charged more interest.

Viv Adams

Accommodation ... you know we had the problem of renting rooms and living in appalling conditions in one room etc. The only way out of that was to buy your own home, but they couldn't get loans, for instance from banks or building societies. So, they set up a kind of mutual trust between each other, whereby they would operate what they knew and still know today as a pardner system. This is a way of investing money in a pool resourced by a number of people who belonged to that pool. You would put money into that pool and it would allow you to draw out a lump sum on a monthly basis as and when you may need it. It equipped them with the means to find things like deposits for homes.

Linda Small

There may be six or seven of you and every week or every month you 'throw' a pound or whatever the group decide they can afford and when. One person called the 'banker' collects the money from everyone in the group and every week or month they give each person in the group that 'hand' collected from everyone. You would get your 'draw' and it would rotate like that for maybe six or seven weeks or months, until everybody in the group got a hand or their draw and then it would start all over again.

We called it 'pardner hand' or 'Susu' or 'Club'. That's how West Indians were able to buy houses, because you would lend a friend or relative your draw and then they use that to put down a deposit, which was only a couple of hundred pounds in those days. And when they got the house you would then rent a room from them.

Sam King

When I did apply to Camberwell Council for the mortgage, they send me a letter thanking me and recommend I go back to Jamaica. I took the letter to the seller of the property and he was so shocked and disgusted, he said: 'If you swear on this Bible that you will repay the mortgage in ten years at 5 per cent, I will give you the mortgage.' We did that. He gave us the mortgage and we repaid the mortgage in five years.

We were the second black family to buy a house in Camberwell, this was 1950. Over the next twelve years my family played a part in buying about half of all the property owned by blacks in Camberwell. Because we couldn't get mortgages we pooled all our money together to help others. We called it a 'pardner' which is the same in Jamaica, and it worked very well.

Don Sydney

We take part in Susu [pardner] because we find it less offensive and disheartening to go to your bank manager to borrow money, so people collect together as a group they contribute every so often – a week a month – and they saved their money. Now, if it's four people they take it in turn to collect a certain sum every week and when they've finished and everyone has received their quota, they then use it to buy whatever furniture or housing or whatever it is they want. But it saved them going and ask their bank manager for money and being insulted and that is it.

Refusal – you could regard it if you're very sensitive and they turn you down and you felt you were being offended, because sometimes the reason they give you is not genuine and you know that, but you can't prove it and you have no authority to argue or disagree with the manager.

Robert Young

Well, you have got to accept something; the first immigrants of West Indians background might not have been all that educated, but they knew what they wanted. They wanted a house so they could rent, they bought a house, it was two up and two down, but there were three families living in it, because they only lived in one room, and they would rent the rooms off to accommodate the other people, which was excellent. People didn't like living in a house where there is white people, they liked to live with black people and I think they accommodated each other by that – and you would get two putting together to buy a house.

What happened, these houses [in Manchester] were pretty long in the tooth, old, and when they bought them, so come the time they were not going to refurbish them, they were going to knock them down to rebuild – and that is what they did, they did not see it. I mean, when you lost your house on Guildhall Street – that was an old street opposite Denmark Road – and those were the first houses that they knocked down, they only got £150 for them or £200. I mean, the houses were only a small amount when they buy them you know, they only put down like £40 and then paid them off, because most of them you couldn't get a mortgage, so the person who owned them would give you a private mortgage, so you could build up your stake. Or there was the pardner [money] . . . would be normally £2 or £5 a week because £5 a week was the most that you could get at that time, so two people would join to throw in £5 a week and when you would get a draw for £60 or £100 and this phenomenal amount of money – and people then use it as a deposit for their house, deposit for their car or bought it outright and then moved on.

Ethlyn Adams

Pardner? You have to pay up – and on time. No man, the pardner can't work if one man don't pay; someone have to pay for him or else it break down, you mad! You have to pay the pardner – even if it mean no food inna the house for the pickney nyam [eat]. Is so plenty people pay buy big house when they get them draw from the pardner. But my husband? That man, the evil wretch, just take him draw, find poker gamble out the money. Time him finish, couldn't buy no house; can't even buy toilet paper.

Alford Gardner

You couldn't get to live in accommodation unless you had a special family who would take you in. Nearly all of us had to share for a period.

A special firm, a solicitor's firm, one special man decided that his firm would get houses for West Indians and they started buying houses and did them up and rented them to West Indians. And, anyway, I got to know him and he got to know me and we talked about buying house and he said if he buy some houses in my name and do them up and ... I said to my wife ... and she said, 'Oh, no, not in our name.'

We were living in a house in Clarendon Place [in Leeds], about eight or nine of us – there were two of us in each room. Then we met up with this man, we had just started up the cricket club, and we decided to buy a house, so five of us bought this house and each of us had our own room and we were nicely settled by then.

This gentleman ... we had no agreement. All we talked about was that you bought the house and it's your house and you owe 'X' amount of money. At that time I paid 400-odd pounds for my house and it took me about eighteen months or two years to pay it but I never had anything on paper, nothing, as far as I know ... Every week you go to the office and you pay. When you finish pay ... here are your title deeds and [he said], 'What do you want to do with your title deeds? You can leave them here.'

That man was just interested in helping West Indians – an Englishman, a man that should have been knighted! We bought this house in Regent Terrace and we started a cricket club. We got married here ... a few of us got married and started our families. We each had our own room and the time come for us to buy house and this man really helped for each of us to buy our own house. I wanted a house near a school, so I moved from the house that we bought to where I bought my house; and each boy bought his house and sold that other one to one other boy.

We bought the house in my name and all you had to do was to go down and every week and pay. That's all I did, I mean you bought the house and put in my furniture. I can even remember going into the house; a big man, six foot odd, and jumping up and he said, 'Solid, solid.' Oh, he was a lovely man.

Viv Adams

Because a lot of West Indians were able to, through that method ... to actually do things which a lot of working people in England could not do, which is namely become house owners. That sort of ... in a way triggered a lot of later resentment.

Karihzma Delpratt

We were living in a rented house when I was three, four years old; my dad always said he bought his first house because I wasn't allowed to make noise in the house. So obviously my mum would be worried about me making noise and upsetting the landlords, so that's why he bought his first house in Balham. So I could run up and down and my mum would say, 'Stop your noise,' and I'd be sliding down the bannisters and she'd say, 'If you break your neck, I kill you!' And my dad would say, 'Leave the pickney!'

Reginald Davis

White people in Jamaica, you don't interact with them because, in a sense, they were better than you, financially, intellectually and socially, so you don't mix with them. When I go to England, I find, I didn't know that poor people were in England. When I go there, I find there are more deteriorating in values than black people, because black people are trying to go up but they are to be content with what they are. They have this little white thing. They lose the ambition of striving to be anything other than white.

The good thing in English people, they're not prejudice. When I say so I know, when you are in a stage like them, they respect you without no prejudice, but if you have certain qualities that is degrading to them, they choose you as what you are. And because I improve myself to such a way, I buy a house in a nice area, I've got lovely cars and I send my son to university, 'Oh, Mr Davis, How're you man?' And so on. I feel more comfortable with them, because black people covet you, when you're ambitious. I'm not speaking racist, but a black person they waste what they have, and if you try to leave hope they say, 'What you play now?'

Michael McMillan

My dad was in High Wycombe at the train station and he saw this woman that he knew, which was my mother. They'd known each other because they were from different villages back home. Back home he'd seen a girl; now he'd seen a woman, and she looked fine and he chirpsed [St Vincent word for 'flirted with'] her; asked for her number. I think she was living in London at the time. So weeks later, he tracked her down, where she was living. She was living in a house with other women. The landlady did not want any male visitors. My dad apparently went and visited the house; the landlady, when my mother came home from work, said that there was a male visitor so you can't stay here any more. She was really strict. Not only did she not want any hanky panky in her house, no suggestion of it. So my mum had to leave. So my mum was now homeless, which probably pleased my dad, so now she had to move in with him. So that's when they got together. Then they moved to High Wycombe, bought a house and got married. I think, soon after they were married, in 1961.

If You Can't Get a Job

It was always difficult to reconcile Ethlyn's happy tales of a privileged life in Jamaica – looked after by servants such that she left home not even knowing how to boil an egg – with her eventual job on the production line of Vauxhall Motors. But she would tell the story of her servant who struggled to find a dressmaker's job when she left her family's employment. Ethlyn's mother would chastise the crying servant, saying, 'If you can't get a job to cut the cloth, get a job to wash it.' That phlegmatic and practical approach was typical of West Indian migrants who were forced to settle for unskilled work in Britain.

A government report of 1953 into 'The Employment of Coloured People in the UK' displayed the kind of prejudice that West Indian workers would meet on the factory floor: 'The unskilled workers who form the majority, are difficult to place, because they are on the whole physically unsuited for heavy manual work, particularly outdoors in winter or in hot conditions underground and appear to be generally lacking in stamina. There is also some indication that they are more volatile in temperament than white workers and more easily provoked to violence.'

Ethlyn, who worked as much overtime as was humanly possible, would have been amused to learn, according to the same report, that: 'Coloured women are said to be slow mentally, and the speed of work in modern factories is said to be quite beyond their capacity.'

Some employers, driven by the practical need for workers, were more enlightened. The transport industry became a big employer. A number of tailors I interviewed for the book, a dozen or so, ended up on the buses, often gratefully so, even though they were not initially welcomed in cities such as Bristol. The successful Bristol

Bus Boycott, organised by West Indians in 1963 after applicants were barred from becoming drivers and conductors, was a landmark in breaking down prejudicial practices that were found everywhere in Britain, from bus companies to hairdressing salons and schools.

Of course, such prejudice also made some more determined. Without it E. R. Braithwaite, the former engineer who was turned down continuously for work commensurate with his skills and qualification, might never have written *To Sir, With Love*; and Linette Richards-Lord, the nurse who was stymied at every turn and nicknamed 'The Bedpan Queen', might never have become the Director of Nursing in the UK. What was lovely to see, as I grew up in 1960s Luton, was West Indians' vicarious pleasure, singing to the rafters, any time one of their group was elevated to a position above the ranks Britain had tried to keep them from. Years before Trevor McDonald surfaced, West Indians were already celebrating the achievements of Clyde Alleyne, who secured a position as a broadcaster on British television news, working for Tyne Tees. Alleyne would later play a pivotal role in establishing the Leeds West Indian Carnival.

Whether presenting on the TV, clipping tickets on the buses or cleaning toilets, these visible pioneers were introducing ordinary white working-class people like David Wheeler to the notion that, but for the colour of their skin, there was not much difference between them. He knew 'one or two smashing fellas, they were all right really, yeah, not much different from the fellas down the pub, not that you'd ever see one in a pub.'

But it would be some years yet before West Indians were pulling pints behind the bar or even cutting 'white' hair in salons.

★

Hilary Alderson

There was one West Indian I met in Leeds. She came for a job at the Co-operative hairdressers' salon where I worked. We had a really long counter and desk where the receptionist sat. She walked all the way down. She was really pretty and all the girls were abuzz because she looked quite exotic. She came for an interview and Mr Raymond, the manager, didn't give her a job, and we had a protest and wanted to know why, and he said he would have given her a job but the customers wouldn't have liked her doing their hair. He was quite a meek and mild bloke. He said he had to think about his clients! Things were so much different in those days.

Memo from D. J. Stewart to Mr Goldberg and Mr Hariman
12 March 1949
There is relatively little objection to the importation of women, for example, for domestic employment, where their living conditions would be controlled, since the worst troubles concern men who settle in unsatisfactory districts and get into street fights owing to quarrels about coloured men associating with white women etc.

Mr Johnson
After the first week at the Labour Exchange I kind of got tired of the clerk telling me: 'Sorry, Mr Johnson, but we have nothing for you today.' All through those weeks the Exchange never sen' me to one job. I started to walk on me own, looking out for big black buildings which I use' to take as markers for factories. All those days I never come across any colour discrimination from anybody. They were all nice when they told me that they had nothing for me. Sometimes they would have taken me on, but as it was I was just a few hours too late. Boy, the Englishman can be the nicest man out when he is telling you no. It is just like he wants to cry when he tell you he can't help you. Trouble is that he keep on tellin' you no almost every time. You know, boy, when you out of a job and all the while coming up on the brick wall, you feel like you would just sit on the sidewalk and let the dustman sweep you up.

Francis Williams

I heard about this job in the Leeds Infirmary kitchen, I went out and got the job. That's where I started my catering, because one day I went in and the kitchen superintendent asked me, 'Would you like to be a chef?' I said, 'Of course, that will help me out a bit.' So, he put me in a room working with these white men and one white woman. I was glad and not glad. The white chefs were calling me all sorts of names. They were calling me a monkey, they were calling me a baboon and all sorts of names. The white lady chef, her name was Amy, she said to me, 'Francis, don't take notice of those idiots.' I didn't, I ignored them. [But] many times, I went down to the toilets and I cried, and I said, 'Father I'm just asking you to give me courage.' I prayed and I cried.

E. R. Braithwaite

To Sir, With Love, 1959

I tried everything – labour exchanges, employment agencies, news-paper ads – all with the same results. I even advertised myself mentioning my qualifications and the colour of my skin, but there were no takers. Then I tried applying for jobs without mentioning my colour, but when they saw me the reasons given for turning me down were all variations of the same theme: too black ... I had now been jobless for nearly eighteen months ... I had been sitting beside the lake in St James's Park ... near me was seated a thin, bespectacled old gentleman.

'Talking helps, you know [...]; if you can talk with someone you're not lonely any more, don't you think?'

Soon we were chatting away, unreservedly, like old friends, and I had told him everything.

'Teaching,' he said presently. 'That's the thing. Why not get a job as a teacher?'

'That's rather unlikely,' I replied. 'I have had no training as a teacher.'

'Oh, that's absolutely not necessary. Your degrees would be considered in lieu of training, and I feel sure that with your experience and obvious ability you could do well.'

'Look here, Sir, if these people would not let me near ordinary inanimate equipment about which I understand quite a bit, is it reasonable to expect them to entrust the education of their children to me?'[1]

Joyce Estelle Trotman

I turned up and, besides myself, there was only one other woman on the staff at the boys' comprehensive school. You're black, you're a woman, you're expatriate. When I left Guiana I was acting Principal of a training college, but here in a run-down Bermondsey school I'm now a teacher being patronised by young men still wet behind the ears, straight out of training school.

On one of the first days, I went into the class and there were a lot of Bibles in the room, and they were pelting each other with them, half of them with their backs to me. And I said, 'If you want to learn come in the front, and if you want to do that get on with it' – because I can't fight them, they're boys, they're taller than me. And Michael Stacy, that morning, he say, 'You fucking black cunt.' I mean, in those days, I couldn't say those words, my mouth couldn't form them – and I swallowed hard and said, 'Pens down.' I said, 'Michael, I know I'm black, and I'm beautiful and I've come to teach you your English and I'm not going anywhere.' I said 'Michael, you see that eff and that cee? Don't you dare call me that again.' I didn't ask for an apology, what you want an apology for?

It came again with Peter Crow, he called me a monkey. I sent him out. 'Oh, Miss, can I come back in?' I said, 'No Peter, monkeys do not teach, and I'm a teacher; monkeys do not teach.' I said, 'No, you can't come.' So eventually he came and said, 'Oh Miss, sorry Miss, you're not a monkey Miss.'

Later they were singing 'I'm dreaming of a white Christmas just like before the niggers came' and another boy swore. And when the headmaster summoned his mother, we had to rescue the boy from the mother. Because she was using the same language that he was using at me, and then you realise that he knows no other. That was the culture in England at that time.

Yvonne Connolly

I was twenty-three and had taught at a boarding school in Jamaica. I planned to study for a degree in education in Britain and return home. Of course, I ended up staying. I was a supply teacher, living in Camden, but I was assigned to teach in Greenwich.

I remember somebody at the office asking: 'Who are you?' I replied, 'I am a supply teacher, allocated to this division.' They said, 'Oh, but you are black.' I said, 'Well, obviously, yes.'

I got the second job I applied for, at Ringcross. I was flabbergasted ... People cut out photos of me from the newspapers and wrote to the school, telling me to go back to where I came from and that I looked like a monkey ... Somebody even threatened to burn the school down. On my first day, I was escorted into the school by one of the senior inspectors from Inner London's Education Authority because they took some of the threats seriously.

Agnes DeAbreu

One time he [my husband, Jim] got a job in a factory and the boss went in to show him what to do. He pick up a piece of old cloth, threw a cloth at him and said, 'Clean the oil,' on the machine and Jim took it up and he said, 'You do it,' and he walked out. He came home and I said, 'What happened?' and he said this is what happened and in the end he said, 'You know what, I think I'll go on the railways,' and he applied, and then he got the job as a guard on the railways. It was equal pay [on the railways], but in the factories you get what they decide and they pay you less than if you're white.

Horace Halliburton writing in *Birmingham Gazette*

10 August 1949

To put it bluntly, the coloured man is not wanted in British industry. My compatriots – like myself – have tried times without number to find work in the Midlands. Some have got work, but not the type of employment their qualifications entitle them to.

As a result, there are many coloured men in the hostel who spend their days journeying backwards and forwards to employment exchanges and factories for interviews. You can usually find several of them sitting about waiting for work.

This, of course, gives rise to the impression that the Jamaican is lazy and does not want to work. Nothing could be further from the truth. Most of the hostel's coloured men served in the Forces during the war and were given vocational training for industry. They came to Great Britain because, back at home, we look to this country as the land of opportunity and enterprise. We came here to work, and work we will – if we can get the opportunity.

In my own case, I am most anxious to find work. Educationally I am suited for administrative work in engineering. As a vocation I trained myself to become a skilled metal turner, but I can name twelve firms whom I have visited for the purpose of finding employment.

The only work that Great Britain can offer me is navvying – or sweeping the roads. I am not afraid to tackle either, but I have tried to make something of my life and I do not think it is fair to expect me to settle to work with no prospects and no future. Would you do it – or would you go on looking for the job you are qualified to undertake?

Many of my countrymen have already given up all hope of finding this and are doing unskilled jobs to save up the passage money to go back home.

[At] a recent interview an Employment Exchange manager [...] told me: 'I am sorry for you. It is talent wasted, but the factories will not employ coloured men. Do not blame us. Blame the managements

– and they in turn will blame their employees. British workmen do not like sharing their benches with a coloured man and that's an end to it.'

I ask you, is it fair? Is there some deep inherent feeling in the British character that labels a coloured man as a savage or a head-hunter with a boiling pot up his sleeve?

Donald Hinds
Journey to an Illusion, 1966

Laziness is not a West Indian peculiarity. Except for a few hundred West Indians from Barbados, the rest of us paid our own fares to come to Britain. Do you really think that a young man of twenty-two or -three who has worked for eight or perhaps nine years would spend a hundred pounds on fares and perhaps another sixty or seventy pounds on overhead costs just to come to London to walk the streets in thin clothes, being insulted right, left and centre, so that he may get National Assistance[2]?[3]

Louise Smith

I was one of the cleaners in a hospital. We get on alright but the patient, them white, they was funny with us. Some of them didn't want us to touch them because we are monkey, they say when you climb the tree, make me look if you have tail. That time you have a little job, you're trying to keep it, you have to pay rent, you have to look after yourself, and me grunt many day for what they do, some of these white say, 'Don't touch me.' Sometimes when we clean, me feel me going to use a broomstick on them patient, them they're super clean. My brother warn me, 'Don't say anything to them 'cause you know better. Don't say a word. They don't know what they're saying.' I just walk away. Zip me mouth.

Maizie Pinnock

I worked as an auxiliary nurse doing every earthly thing except giving an injection. Everything you can think of. When I went to

Ward 49 this particular patient came in. One night, I was looking after another patient – you know they were like babies, they couldn't do anything for themselves, you had to do everything. Some of them were very dirty, so you had to bathe them. Oh! Hospital work is a very dirty job! Anyway, this man, he had some dirty clothes on, so I gave him a bath and I put his dirty clothes in the side of the locker. I was doing another patient and his visitors came in and they said to him, 'Oh, you look nice, you got nice clean clothes on. Where's the clothes you came with?' He said to them, 'Oh, I don't know. That nigger bathe me, you can ask that nigger.' I'm telling you, I just put what I was doing down and I said to him, 'Let me tell you something, I have a name. My name is Maizie,' and I said, 'I don't want you ever call me a nigger again!'[4]

Louise Lange

[In Nottingham in 1957] you were treated like animal at work, they never treat us good at work. They claim that we've got no sense, we can't do sums and we hard to learn. I say how good are these people to learn, but we never get the chance. I says to one of the foremen one day, 'Why you treat the black men like that?' 'Well, they coming and taking our women. So this is how we get our own back.'

Waveney Bushell

I applied from home, my friend wrote me saying, apply here, it was the LCC [London County Council] which was very liberal-minded, I think.[5] My husband was a civil servant at home, he had certificates in accountancy and so on; it never got him anywhere. You should hear the answers he got from people when he turned up, his name being Bushell, they thought he was white. The manager said things like, 'Look around and what do you see there?'; and he didn't know what to say, there were people working and so on. And the man would say, 'Do you see anybody like yourself here?' You know, they were very rude to our men. That's why a lot of our men went on buses. I had to say to our professor when I was at university, 'A lot of the men on buses were teachers at home, but they couldn't get in anywhere.' But London was one of the first places that did employ [black] men in an office. He [my husband] had to go to university first.

Alford Gardner

I went for work at Barnbow [munitions factory near Leeds], where they made tanks. But getting a job, I especially had problems with the union. This old man, little Fred, the vice-president of the union, says the best thing to do is join the union. I tuned up and the man who was president said, 'What the bloody hell are you doing here?'

Old Fred told him I come to join the union.[6]

Skilled men get a green card, semi-skilled men get a red card. So, to get a job you have to get a red card from the union, the union wouldn't give me a card.

The president claimed I couldn't join the union because I didn't have a job and they had a right row, the two of them.

So later I was talking with some men, and they said the best thing to do is just go up to Barnbow and see if you can sort something out. So I got the bus and went up there, wait at the gate, and said, 'I'd like to apply for a job.' The gate man said, 'Oh no you can't'; and another gate man come up and I told him, 'I've come to see the labour officer,' and he said, 'Oh yes man, I'll tell you what, I'll phone.' He phone and the labour officer say, 'Send him in'; and I went in and saw the labour officer and he say, 'I'm not supposed to do this, but I'm an ex-RAF man myself,' and it was him that gave me the booklet that have printed in it: 'Unless you born in the UK or the Dominions of UK stock you're not eligible to work in this factory.'

Jamaica [was a] colony. Canada, Australia, they were Dominions. Of UK stock; you have to be white. These things, a lot of people don't know. The ex-RAF man said, 'What you have to do is to write to the Colonial Office.' I did that. Anyway, they took time out, checking me out, they even checked my family in Jamaica to see if I was a communist or some damn thing.

John M. Darragh,

'Coloured Workers', *Picture Post*, 12 February 1955

As a member of a Social Survey Team dealing with the employment of coloured workers in Birmingham, I cannot agree with Mr Woodrow Wyatt (12 Jan.) when he says, 'At present there is no more prejudice over Jamaicans, Africans, Indians, or Pakistanis than there might be about groups of Welsh, Scottish or Irish or even Londoners going to Birmingham.' I know from experience that Welsh, Scots, Irish and Londoners have already deep roots in the city. They can be found in every walk of life, even to serving as Councillors and Members of Parliament. There is an antagonism purely to 'coloured strangers', perhaps not so apparent when they were few and the possibility of them creating additional problems of overcrowding and Trade Union administration was not a factor.

The position has now been changed, however, by the sudden influx of West Indians and by many people who claim to act in the interests of the coloured workers, and who have created a dangerous situation by attempting to intimidate Trade Unions and Managements into overthrowing existing Industrial machinery. The progress in this country of Joint Consultative and Negotiating Machinery is now threatened by the cry of 'Colour Bar'[7] on the smallest issue, and the issue has completely lost its true perspective.

Shirley Williams

You didn't have much in your head about what's going on. You had to get on with nursing, following the rules. You just did it. If there was a derogatory remark made to you, it had to go over your head, you could not report it. Who do you report it to? I heard of people that had situations where they've cried about the way they were spoken to or spoken about and they were the ones got into trouble.

Bert Williams

When I left, I was sixteen, but I was already working in Jamaica. I had a sense of responsibility, I knew right from wrong and when I came here, I didn't want to mix with the boys and girls because I thought they were stupid, they were childish, man. I was hanging about with big Jamaican guys who were drinking and had cars and so on. I hung around in London and first got a job as a plumber's mate; I lasted two days. I carried this guy's bag for him and we went into this school, and all the toilets were blocked, and he said I had to put my hand down. I was sixteen and I said, 'No, I'm not going to do that.' So he said, 'Well, you can eff off then,' and he went and that was it.

You soon learn fast. Later, I worked in a factory and there were comments made, you know, about your colour or 'chalky', they used to call me or 'curly' or 'coon'. One thing I used to hate was the television programme, 'Love Thy Neighbour' [popular 1970s programme with a black couple and a white couple, where the men feuded while the women sought to foster good relations]; you can guarantee that you go into work the next day and you're going to get a new name called, what they pick up from the show. And even today when I'm doing my talks I try to avoid those terms, all those old-fashioned terms, I try to avoid using them, because I don't want to be putting ideas in people's heads. I don't want to give them arms to go and call somebody else it, because I know how hurtful it is.

Especially when I served in the Royal Air Force; I mean, you definitely had to pretend you were badder than you were. They like to challenge you. They're all seventeen, eighteen, nineteen, twenty-year-old boys and you're in a billet; there's got to be some smart guy's going to challenge you. So you've got to put your foot down. If somebody says something, you've got to attack them straight away, you can't let it rest otherwise you feel the next person is doing it. So you used to pretend you're badder than you are, going up to them in their face, and you're shaking, but they don't know you're shaking, right in their face, and I used to use lots of Jamaican language so they didn't understand what I say, 'What the bloodseed you t'ink you're talking about?' So it sounded worse, I sound madder than I am. They don't know what you're saying and it sounds vicious to them, and to you as well, but they don't know you're shaking in your boots. But that's something that I learned from Jamaica. You've got to look after yourself, you've got to nip it in the bud otherwise you're going to let the next person do the same.

Stanley Crooke
The Colony, BBC TV, 1964

Seeing me working here [in a railway signal box], you would look and say, 'Well, that chap looks perfectly happy. He's working amongst English people. How come they say there is no integration in this country?' I may have a different story to tell. I know quite a few men working in the same job as I, we work together, we may travel on the same train together; on the train we discuss things appertaining to the job. We get into the station and the moment we arrive at the station, all contact ends. We don't even walk ten yards together on the station platform. So this matter of integration is very very difficult. Apparently both of us, in this case my fellow work mate and myself, are finding it difficult to bridge a gap which apparently doesn't exist.

Wallace Collins
Jamaican Migrant, 1965

One day the foreman said to me, 'I don't care what they say about your fucking black race, you're all the same to me; Wallace you're making a good job here and you know it, you will be the last to leave if there's a slacking off of work.' And with that he walked off.

I walked up to a group of men standing up to their ankles in mud and enquired for the foreman. They indicated that I should go around the corner. I duly skirted the dry ground against the fence to a rather muddy purplish looking Irishman looking up at me with his wan blue eyes. 'Yes Tosh.' I showed him my job card, which stated clearly that I was a carpenter. He looked at the card in my hand then at me and pointed down in the hole. 'I want somebody to finish off this hole, can you handle a pick and shovel?' I said no, to which he replied, 'Sorry mate.' I turned about and walked from the scene feeling bad, but as I passed the men standing in the pool of mud one of them grunted sarcastically, loud enough for me to hear, 'A perfect city gentleman.'[8]

Peter John Nelson

I was fifteen when I left school and I started an apprenticeship, because I was lucky enough to get an apprenticeship at Massey Fergusson; I think I was the first black apprentice they had there. They had black welders there but I was the first apprentice. I was sent to college, to Stretford Tech, one day a week for my City and Guilds. I worked there eleven years and then I left and I went in the army, came out, went back in, got redundancy and did other jobs, security and all that and then I ended up at the brewery. I worked at the brewery in Moss Side for eleven years and then from there I got this present job. My best wage packet was £3.50, my mum kept the three quid and gave me the fifty pence, I didn't sleep for three days. I didn't know what to do with it. There were six of us brothers and sisters and my mum used it to pay for those who were still at college, to buy the books and that.

In the sixties, if you were a black worker and you turn up in a car, you won't be working the next day, you'd be sacked – especially if the foreman turned up to work on a bicycle – until we had the Industrial Relations Act. That was the most important act, I think, because it not only affected the black workers, it affected everybody. Before that a foreman could sack you and didn't have to give a reason. Or if you were a skilled man and earning five pound an hour, he'd take you off that job and give you two pound jobs or three pound, and there was nothing you could do. As a member of the trade union, the Boilermakers, we went on marches and campaigned and then we got the Industrial Relations Act, out of that came ACAS – if you get sacked, they have to tell you why, you have to have warnings and the foreman couldn't just make decisions just like that. Before that Act, we had no say, the foreman came in and he'd had a bad night, he could just sack you like that. We (the black workers) benefitted but the white guys did it too, because the white guy could get sacked as well.

We worked forty hours a week, I used to work ten hour shifts; when I did nights – I loved nights – I did four ten-hour shifts and then I'd have three days off, so when I was a young man that was great, because you can go out Friday night, Saturday night, you know what I mean?

Owen Townsend

There were so many jobs going; they tended to be building, factory work. The worst job I did in England was working in Rochdale digging a toilet pit, and the water board went on strike, and all the toilets in Rochdale backed up into my pit; it was unbelievable. I laugh now but it wasn't funny at the time. It was cold, in the middle of winter.

The next one, I was working at Liverpool docks, roofing in the middle of winter. I'd never done anything like that in my life but whatever was available you'd do, good experience still. I remember when I first went up on this building, the containers looked like little toys, that's how high up we were, and the roof was white with ice, and I stood by this scaffolding pole and hold on for about a whole hour and they couldn't move me! I refused to budge until the sun came up and melt the ice.

Guy Bailey

Coming to England and seeing these wonderful buses, which I had never seen before, and I thought how nice it would be to drive a bus. And I did apply for a job as a bus conductor and an interview was arranged for me to come to the bus station for an interview, and I came to the bus station, which is here, and when I actually got to the reception area, the receptionist said to the manager, 'Oh, Mr Bailey is here; he's black.' And the manager then spoke with me and explained that in a sense he wasn't prepared to offer me an interview because if he did he would 'displease his bus crew.'

Cyril Buckley, traffic manager, Bristol Omnibus Company

Round Up, BBC Home Service, 1963

Well, we are as such at the present time [operating a colour bar] simply because, whilst we can within this city, we shall go on engaging white labour before coloured labour. This is the policy of the company in light of the experience in other cities and towns where they have engaged coloured labour and their labour situation has deteriorated – because then it is regarded no longer as the white man's job and the white people start leaving and they find themselves more short of staff than they were before.[9]

Paul Stephenson

There were no rights. Black people had no rights [in the early sixties]. I was arrested and thrown in jail for refusing to leave a public house. Couldn't work on the buses. Couldn't be a policeman. Couldn't be a fireman.

It was a time when [Martin] Luther King was marching and the students down south [in the USA] were marching for freedom and against discrimination and racism that I felt something had to be done in Bristol.

There were streets I couldn't go down because I was black. They were saying, 'Go home monkey!' They'd throw stones bottles, bricks. I was the only black child in the school. It was a very hard time. Apart from not being able to get a job, you couldn't get a house, you couldn't get lodgings: 'No blacks, no Irish, no dogs, no children'. You couldn't go into a pub without the say-so of the manager; it was a de facto segregation.

I was very angry about the way discrimination was working and the open hostility that some Bristolians had towards black people and, to me, the bus company was giving a clear signal to any employer if you don't want blacks, don't have them! So I decided to make it a symbol of a fight for black justice. Then I thought, yes, we'll boycott the buses.

Ron Nethercott, Transport and General Workers' Union

Round Up, BBC Home Service, 1963

I didn't hear one bus man say, 'I don't want to work with a black person'; what he says was, 'I don't want to lose my overtime!' The problem really was that the great resentment wasn't particularly about coloured people. I mean, I had three coloured people sitting where we are only last week in this house and I have many friends who are coloured – it was about overtime. The bus men were earning a lot of overtime to make up their very poor wages; it wasn't just about race. I'm not saying there wasn't something about it but ... I can't put my finger on anything about race and my dealings with the bus men ... There were some people who were prejudiced. I'm not saying that there weren't ... I'd be a fool to make that sort of comment. The majority of people would agree that it was really about their standard of living; they saw it as black people threatening their standards of living. But they would have been the same had they been Martians.

Paul Stephenson

I went and saw the bus manager, Ian Painty. But he was quite adamant that having black people on the buses would infuriate the crews and the women wouldn't want to be seen with black people. I just went to the more radically minded black members of the community and sought their support and said, 'Listen, I'm going to call a boycott of the buses.' They said, 'That's great,' and some said, 'Don't, because we won't win and it will only make more trouble for us.' I believe it woke up the city to racism in a way – the *Evening Post* admitted they had never had so much letters to the editor.

Norman Samuels

An inspector came to me and said, 'Your conductor said he don't want to work with you again so we have to find you another conductor.' You know, even passenger-wise, anybody that boarded my bus, they don't look in the cab, [but] as soon as they see black people – no matter how much they want to go to work – they look up in the cab they draw back. You know, it get worse before it get better. They sometimes fight in the canteen; they would come up and say nasty things to you and partly want to pass it off as a joke.

Roy Hackett

I called a meeting. Talk to our black members and they bring their family out and their friends and companions and work mates and that's it. But having said that, we had a lot of white people joined us voluntarily. People were going about their business and they asked what is this all about and when we told them, they joined us – like people going shopping with their children, you know; people coming from school, after they take their children to school, they joined us as well. They just stopped there and they kept piling up behind each other. I mean, you have gangs of people coming down and telling us all kinds of rude words but they didn't throw any stones. However, one came up to me and said to me, 'Anytime one of your chaps come up these buses my wife will stop working on these buses.' And I said, 'Let me tell you something now. Well you can start making arrangements because we are going to go on these buses.'

Bus conductor
Journey to an Illusion, 1966

I think the best thing about coloured conductors working on the buses up and down the country was that it gave the ordinary Englishman the chance of meeting a black man. Ten years ago when you gave a passenger his change and ticket, besides marvelling at the fact that you actually spoke English and that you gave him the correct change, he would also grab hold of your hand and then shout to all the bus that your hands are warm. Some, of course, gave your hands a vigorous rub to see whether it was dirt which made you black. All these things sound incredible, but they are all true. So many people put their hands on my hair for good luck in the first year of my working on London buses that I was in fear of going bald prematurely.[10]

Rum, Coke and Molotov Cocktails

Before the West Indians came to Britain, the Poles arrived –
300,000 of them – and before the Poles there were the Irish. But
no matter the order of their arrival and their imagined place in
the affections of the British public, all three shared a number
of needs: food, work, shelter and companionship. For largely
single men, often billeted together in austere hostels, there was
a premium placed on the company of women – and that's where
the trouble began, in 1948 and again a decade later (with the rise
of Teddy boys) culminating in vicious fights and rioting.

West Indian men, even when earning meagre wages, always
dressed to a point beyond distinction, and they were well-mannered
and attentive towards women. And, as if that wasn't enough to
make Irish or Polish or English blood boil, they were really good
dancers! Throw in a pint or three on a Saturday night, some rough
baiting, and you had a recipe for mayhem. The fighting in all-male
hostels in 1948 was a rehearsal for the riots in Nottingham and
Notting Hill a decade later.

Though the authorities framed the Notting Hill disturbances as
the unfortunate consequence of black and white hooliganism, Don
Letts argues that that assessment naively or cynically failed to take
into account the sinister atmosphere that pervaded the streets at
the time: 'The cultural climate back then, it was very polarised, it
was very racially tense. This thing was all-pervasive, you couldn't
escape it. It would be in your face. When I was growing up: graffiti, Banksy? Fuck that! Graffiti was like six feet letters: KBW, Keep
Britain White. That was graffiti back in my day.'

The Notting Hill riots weren't simply the result of petty jealousies;
they were grounded in the naked, racist sentiment of Keep Britain

White mobs. Up to 400 youths, mainly Teddy boys, tooled up 'with iron bars, butcher's knives and weighted leather belts', descended on Notting Hill on the August bank holiday in 1958 bent on 'nigger-hunting'. On the first night of the 'racial riots', five West Indians lay blooded and beaten unconscious in the streets.

Both Bageye and Ethlyn, who came to Britain the following year, were scandalised by the news when it reached Jamaica. They remember all over Kingston the passionate and determined talk of raising a posse of men who would sail to England to side with their compatriots under attack. That ship never sailed, but the Chief Minister, Norman Manley, did rush to Britain to investigate for himself the unprovoked assaults on West Indians.

In London, if you were a West Indian living in the East End on 29 August 1958, you didn't venture west; you kept your head down and waited for the violence to blow over. But there were scores of young men – mostly Jamaicans – who headed over from Brixton to patrol the streets of Notting Hill and face down the Teddy boys.

In the past there had been inter-island rivalries, with Jamaicans often accused of arrogance. Jamaicans, who were from one of the biggest and most populous islands in the region, had a reputation for talking disparagingly of other West Indians from the smaller islands whom they described pejoratively as 'smallees'. But Rena Khublall recalls that, at this moment of crisis, the fearless Jamaicans were appreciated by all of the islanders: 'I would love to see the Jamaicans fight the Teddy boys because it would make the place safer for people to walk around and go about.'

And Carlton Gaskin agrees: 'All the West Indians thought the Jamaicans were aggressive but that was the only means of changing things.'

My parents rarely spoke of the incidents in Notting Hill. I think they were embarrassed by them and by the growing suspicion that the sentiments expressed by the Teddy boys were widely held among the English (never the Irish, Scottish or Welsh).

The hostility shown towards West Indians was shocking. Decades earlier, the Mass Observation survey of 1939 had shown the prevalence of white antipathy towards black people. In the months after the arrival of the *Windrush*, there had been numerous outbreaks of disturbances and some brawls between black and white men (mostly Poles and Irish), who were temporarily housed cheek-by-jowl in hostels. There the disputes had centred on jealousies over women. The same initially might have been true of Nottingham and later Notting Hill in 1958, though the violence was fundamentally a manifestation of the nativist and racist sentiments of thuggish Teddy boys. But, even so, the suddenness and viciousness of the Notting Hill riots took the authorities by surprise.

In some ways, Notting Hill was the clash of youth between the Teddy boys, the first manifestation of a new teenage culture in Britain, and young West Indian men, who also prided themselves on their individualism and style. Both squared off on the streets of Notting Hill's volatile neighbourhoods. It is clear, though, that attempts by the authorities to brand the events as the result of both black and white hooligans, who were equally to blame for the violence, was untrue. The West Indians fought back against white mobs intent on throwing bricks and Molotov cocktails wherever they heard the sound of the West Indian Bluebeat music.

*

D. G. Ednie

Regional Controller, National Service Hostels, 3 August 1948
Jamaicans were involved in a fracas [at Castle Donnington Hostel, a government-run hostel for migrant workers from the West Indies and Europe] with some of the Irish and EVW residents [European Voluntary Workers, part of the European influx displaced by World War Two seeking jobs in the UK]. Cutlery, crockery, chairs and other articles had been thrown about with considerable breakages, and

a number of the Jamaicans armed with iron piping and bricks had injured a Pole and three Irish who had to be taken to the hospital for treatment. Once again it would appear to have been caused by trouble over a local prostitute on Saturday night in a public house.

At the time of our arrival the Jamaicans were in their own sleeping site, and on the roadway to it and in adjoining sleeping sites and the communal site, gangs of Irish and EVWs were hanging about. I also visited the Jamaicans and found them in a very excited state, still armed and ready for trouble ... These Jamaicans are childish, insolent and arrogant, and a large number of this gang are undoubtedly looking for trouble.

Internal memorandum
W. H. Hardman, Ministry of Labour, 7 August 1948

We must be realistic and face the fact that however charming they may be individually, these West Indians do tend to get cross, and then to start fighting with other residents, in particular the Irish and the Poles. I should not be surprised, however, if the next report we get is from Weston-on-Trent, particularly if they are foolish enough to organise a dance there, as it is invariably in connection with women that these troubles seem to arise. On my recent tours round the regions, I heard several times that the Poles in particular intensely resent seeing black men dancing with white girls, whereas the white girls all too frequently seem to prefer dancing with the black men. My Personal Assistant suggests that they are probably better dancers!

Internal memorandum
S. D. Morton, Ministry of Labour, 9 August 1948

The Jamaicans, thirty-three of whom were engaged by the Stanton Ironworks at Ilkeston, have been something of a problem from the time of their arrival. They have the reputation of being good workers, but in the hostel at Castle Donnington and in the village, they showed a childish pride in their British citizenship and arrogantly claimed all sorts of privileges on the strength of it … With reference to the NSHC's [National Service Hostels Corporation] suggestion that the number of Jamaicans in any one hostel should be limited to three, I can only say that this would result in the loss of good workers to essential iron and steel production.

Birmingham Gazette
9 August 1949
About fifty police were rushed to Causeway Green Hostel, near Oldbury, last night when racial rioting broke out [...]. Three Poles and one Jamaican were badly hurt. They were taken to the hostel sick-bay. Several rooms were wrecked and corridors were littered with broken glass and bricks.

Poles, armed with sticks, stones, razors and chairs, surrounded the Jamaican quarters. Then they rushed with yells and threats and broke windows to get inside. One Jamaican was attacked in bed and badly beaten up with bricks.

The police managed to restore order. But they had to escort individual residents returning to the camp to their quarters. Some Jamaicans, however, decided to leave. They packed their bags and demanded police escort. As they walked through the main gates of the camp they were followed by catcalls and jeering from other residents.

Girl residents, who number 120, ran from their rooms when the fighting began and sought refuge outside the camp. Local residents, behind barred doors, watched Jamaicans, pursued by Poles armed with sticks and bottles, hiding in a nearby cornfield.

Charles Noel
'The coloured men in the Midlands say make life better for all of us', *Birmingham Gazette*, 17 August 1949
There have been so many different opinions regarding the racial disputes in the Causeway Green Hostel that I think it necessary to state a few stark facts.

Many English people grossly underestimate their coloured brothers. They seem to forget that evolution takes place and regard the coloured peoples, especially Negroes, as antediluvians.

We are quite aware of English psychology and it is no use practising British diplomacy on us. We have been so often deceived that we become alert and even sceptical, and rightly so.

It is useless some white people mixing with us indoors and ignoring us when they are amongst their white companions. This is very often done by people who, only a few minutes ago, ate and danced with us, and also by workmates.

Edwin Hilton Hall

We thought that people will accept us, but it was very hostile to us. We couldn't go quietly in a shop without them abusing us: 'Blackie, Nigger, Moonshine!' One chap said to me, 'Why don't you go back to your country?' I remember this clearly, I said, 'Well I belongs to England. I solve England and I come here to build England. So, don't tell me to go back to my country.' Of course, I was young, and I had a terrible temper. I wouldn't stand no abuse from these people.

Some of the lads used to go out and when they come back to the hostel, a couple used to come in with their eyes swollen and they used to say they were beaten in the street. So, when we go out shopping, we used to go in a gang. If we go to the pub for a drink, we all used to congregate together, and we leave. Six, seven, eight of us used to go to the pub together. We couldn't risk going back to the hostel on our own.

Horace Halliburton

'I Protest Against the Colour Bar', *Birmingham Gazette*,
11 August 1949
The problem of Causeway Green is by no means unique in this country. It is an example of Great Britain's colour bar. Similar instances are constantly arising in other parts of the country.

My sixty fellow West Indians in the hostel know only too well that the ill-feeling and fighting of the past week cannot be blamed on individual differences of opinion and local domestic arguments.

The story of Causeway Green riot really started at the beginning of the year when management suddenly decided to segregate the coloured inhabitants from the Polish and British.

This created considerable resentment amongst the West Indians. They felt that they had been singled out and herded together because other people had found them unsuitable to live with. Nevertheless, their protests had no result and a special section of the hostel was allocated to coloured men.

Many Birmingham people have automatically placed the cause on the question of women friends but, although minor arguments and petty jealousies may have arisen over girls coming to dances at the hostel, I would like to point out that this is only a very minor cause of dissension.

What really annoys my countrymen is the constant baiting and jeering which is directed at the coloured man. Although educated and trained in social standards and industrial work, the Jamaican is coloured, and he is not allowed to forget it. At mealtimes, he is shunned by white men. Although a British subject, he is made to feel an interloper in English life, in this case by non-British subjects.

Viv Adams

It was startling how, within a decade of the *Windrush* arriving, attitudes against the presence of so many black people hardened, especially in places like London and Nottingham, in the presence of West Indians in their midst, seemed to have rubbed rather uneasily certain members of the population and this percolated, as we now know ... into these civic disturbances that occurred in Notting Hill, in the so-called famous Notting Hill riots in the late 1950s and earlier which I think occurred in Nottingham [on 23 August 1958 a serious disturbance broke out between locals and West Indians, starting in a pub in the St Ann's district; the *Nottingham Evening Post*, taken aback by its severity, reported 'the whole place was like a slaughterhouse.'].

Eric Irons

It started at the St Ann's Inn [Nottingham]. There were two accounts. One was that a West Indian was in there chatting up a young lady and as soon as he left the premises he was assaulted. The other account is that someone insulted a West Indian's white companion. I think the police and everybody was shocked by the speed and ferocity of the West Indian response. Only one black person was in the area that night [23 August 1958]. He was among the milling crowd of white people fighting among themselves. The Assistant Chief Constable was telling me, 'When my men saw this one black man coming through the crowd, they shadowed him until he got to his address in [...] Street.'

Chris Stredder

I was trying to get through the crowd of people and I couldn't and I was being pushed towards the side of the road. I was pushed against a shop window and all of a sudden this man's head hit the window and he fell on to the floor and, because I was pushed against the window, the blood from his head spattered across the front of my dress and I could not move. I actually wet myself; I couldn't move, I was that terrified. He was black and he was on the floor at the side of me and I wanted to run but I couldn't; I was just totally traumatised by it.

Charles Coyne

There was a couple of coloured lads getting on to this lad and his wife, a white couple, I went to intervene and finished up with the two coloured lads coming for me. I got stabbed five times, I finished up in hospital. I was off work a month.

White people used to stand in groups and they used to chant 'black beasts' and all sorts because they'd done summat wrong to the local community, I mean, they put five or six on us in hospital; they cut one bloke's throat, stabbed me five times, after that they just stood in groups and they used to, every now and then, they used to have a fight; there used to be fifty or sixty or seventy on the corner of the streets. They were families; in a sense it was everybody, the average person come down on the streets to see if there's owt going off, like nosy bleeders.

George Leigh

The police came to tell us, 'Scram!' Which we did. I was ever so frightened because everybody had left the street, we couldn't see anybody! I said, something wrong. So I ran and caught the bus to get out of town, Nottingham.

Sylvie Kershaw

I was born in St Ann's on Plantagenet Street. I was married on August 23 1958 at the old St Ann's Church in Robin Hood Chase at three o'clock and the riot started that day. We didn't really know anything about it until we went on our honeymoon and we went to Ilfracombe and we were in the guest house and people were calling Nottingham 'the pits', so we said we came from just outside Nottingham.

Teddy boy

BBC News, 1 September 1958

They shouldn't be allowed in. They should be kept out. They shouldn't be let in in the first place. I don't like them with white girls. I don't like them at all; they're too filthy. I don't mind Irish, Scotch, they all belong to the same country, don't they? We don't need a load of foreigners in here, especially black anyway. I think they ought to be shot; the whole lot of them.

Franklin Jackson

It was frightening because, as a young boy I wasn't used to white people, and I wasn't used to all this type of treatment. Daddy used to tell me about them. He used to say, 'When I'm going down the street, if I see a group of white people or Teddy boys, I would cross to the other side because they would spit on me and all that.' I saw many likkle things to do with that as well. It was a total shock.

Bert Williams

In the summertime they'd stand outside the pub with a glass in their hand, like they do today, and if you were just one black guy walking along, you were in trouble, but if there were two or three of you, you've got no fear because they're not going to challenge you, unless there's a bunch of them. But if they were like twenty-nine, thirty years old they wouldn't bother you; but if they were youngsters, sixteen, seventeen years old, they'd have a chase. You know where they are. For instance you'd be, 'Oh God', you've got to pass this pub; you don't know who is there, but you know that Teddy boys normally hang out there, so you try and avoid it and you go the long way round to avoid it. But some guys would go straight through it just for a laugh; some guys are wicked, you know, or some guys like a good fight.

Orville Burrowes

An individual would be walking down the road and a group of white boys would set upon him, beat him up. I heard a crowd outside of my premises and I looked through the window and I saw a white woman in front of a black guy. And she was shouting, 'If you're going to kill him, you'll have to kill me first,' and she sort of stretched out her arms, sort of protect the guy. The boy was standing with his back against the wall and she prevented him from getting a hiding.

Rudy Braithwaite

The atmosphere was bad. People would come into the corner shop and they would be served before me, you know, and I would stand there, of course too reserved to say anything about it. I remember one blonde woman with a basket in hand, she said: 'These niggers are everywhere, everywhere. I mean you can't get rid of them. Everywhere. We went through them with the war, and now we have them here, everywhere.'

Velma Davis

Those were very frightening days for me. I just got here the year before [from Trinidad], and knowing at the time in Ladbroke Grove you could've count the amount of blacks on one hand, because it wasn't many. I remember coming in from work. First thing as I came up, I get to find about black and white, which is something I did not know at all at home. I didn't remember the colour of my skin. Right. And when I got here it was like this: 'Golliwog, nigger, black. Go back where you came from.' And it was I was thinking, 'My God at home it was like the haves and the have nots. You could be black like hell and you have it and you up there,' you know? But to come here now and meet people telling you you black and you thinking, 'My God, I never notice I was black before. I didn't know it was a problem.'

I remember the house I lived in – it was one of Rachman's houses – and one of the girls who was downstairs, English girl, blonde English, she used to love the black men, and I remember few times some guys passing and saying, 'Nigger lover house, we gwan get them.' But I didn't think it was going to be a riot.

BBC News, 31 August 1958

Something new and ugly raises its head in Britain – in Notting Hill Gate, only a mile or two from London's West End – racial violence. An angry crowd of youths chases a Negro into a greengrocers shop while police reinforcements are called up to check the riot, one of many that have broken out in a few days.[1]

David Wheeler

A coloured bloke came out of Latimer Road station. And he looked, to my memory, very well-dressed and he had a briefcase. I would say he looked like a doctor of something like that. He walked from Latimer Road station, down past us. And there was a crowd of blokes outside the York pub and they literally chased him up the road to try and beat him up. And a local greengrocer named Freddie Bloomfield grabbed hold of him; and he was an ex-boxer, Freddie. And he took him into his greengrocers and he told these blokes to bugger off.

Things started snowballing from there, you'd get lorryloads of young white blokes going round and looking for West Indians, and it got to the stage where a lot of West Indians would not come out.

Orville Burrowes

One night we were accompanying some people crossing to the other side of the bridge. And a crowd of Teddy boys was coming this side. The leader of that crowd was a butcher. And the leader of our crowd was a chef, from the Montparnasse. So they had a confrontation at the top of the steps to the bridge, and the white fella, the butcher, got cut from the chef. And the guy collapsed on the ground and the whole crowd dispersed.

Police Inspector Sydney Vass

On 31 August 1958, I was posted to duty at Notting Hill Station. On parading for duty at 2 p.m., I was informed that on the previous night and early morning there had been a number of incidents which indicated that racial prejudices were leading to serious disturbances between white and coloured people and that there was a liability that many assaults might take place.

I instructed the officers serving under me to be alert to detect any signs of racial disturbances and to report immediately the fullest details.

At about 8:30 p.m., information was received that a man of colour was being attacked by white men near Latimer Road station W11, and that police in the vicinity needed assistance. Officers were at once sent to the scene by police motor vehicle and it was found that the coloured man had been able to make good his escape and that the men who had attacked him had disappeared in the crowds that had begun to assemble.

From that moment until about 3 a.m. on 1 September, there was a continuous stream of messages and information from callers at the police station to say that disturbances were taking place in the vicinity of Bramley Road W11, and the adjacent streets. I attended with other officers and the position as I saw it was as follows. Hundreds of people, probably about 800, had gathered in groups in Bramley Road etc, and were lining the pavement and roadway. From remarks I overheard, it seemed that by far the greater majority of the people were assembled to watch, what they called 'nigger baiting'. Most of these people would not themselves have taken any active part in any violence but appeared to be willing to enjoy.

George Lamming
The Pleasures of Exile, 1960

I am walking up the street, and three men are walking towards me. I do not think that they are the enemy from Notting Hill; nor do I think that they are not. I simply do not know, for there is no way of telling. It is my particular way of seeing which creates this doubt, in spite of all I have read about what was happening. And it is in this moment of doubt that my life is endangered, for while I wonder and watch and wait, the men and I are actually getting nearer. I begin with the grave disadvantage that if they are the enemy, then they have seen their target long ago. While I am working out the possibilities, they have already chosen unanimously the result. There it is. I am completely in their power by the fact that the experience has not trained me to strike without the certainty of the enemy's presence. I am completely immobilised by all my social and racial education as a West Indian.[2]

Ainsley Grant

One night we saw about three white chaps who worked in the garage where I used to work. They were fellows we'd talked to, had tea with them, we even used to go to work on the same bus. As we passed we saw them waving and shouting, 'Nigger', 'black bastard', 'boo'. One of them eventually get a glimpse of me and he shift to the back of the crowd ... Another night, me and my brother were with three other chaps coming home from the pictures. As soon as we passed a crowd of white people the booing and cursing started. We boys used to walk in groups of four. I used to carry a long knife ... Those were terrible time. Every evening when the crowd gather around, we say to ourselves, 'Tonight is going to be the night.' Some of us used to go to bed with bricks and milk bottles piled up on the floor.

PC Dennis Clifford

On Tuesday 2 September, 1958, at 10:35 p.m., in St Lukes Road, Notting Hill, I saw Miguel Defreitas of 10 Kensal Road W10, with other coloured men surrounded by a large hostile crowd. I said to the accused, 'Get out of the area quickly.' He replied, 'I don't need you to fucking protect me.' He walked slowly up the road, and stopped to talk to a white woman. I again asked him to keep moving, and he said, 'I'll go when I'm ready.' The crowd became very menacing, so I arrested him, taken to Notting Hill Police Station, where he was charged. When cautioned he said, 'I suppose I'm to blame.'

Rena Khublall

I would love to see the Jamaicans fight the Teddy boys because it would make the place safer for people to walk around and go about. And it was good because there were Teddy boys and the skinheads – you don't feel safe. For a black woman walking down the street on a Sunday afternoon or on a Saturday evening, you would not have felt safe at all. Someone would have said something or do something. I wouldn't go out on my own in the evening.

Carlton 'Stanley' Gaskin

Thank God for the Jamaicans. Jamaicans didn't always accept things as they were. I must say that. They did a hell of a lot to improve conditions for West Indians. All the West Indians thought they were aggressive but that was the only means of changing things.

Mrs Werner, Manager of the Calypso Club

Racial Problems in England, BBC Home Service, 1958

We were slightly on edge because we realised the Teddy boys were not going to stay in Ladbroke Grove but they were going to start to travel. And, naturally, being there was only two very well-known coloured clubs round here – which was the Calypso and the Blues – we were expecting them to arrive there. Then I had a telephone call at seven-thirty from a friend of ours, because we had quite a lot of white friends that didn't want to see this happen and were trying to avoid a lot of trouble that was going on here by warning us beforehand. The person phoned me up and said the best thing for me to do was to make sure that I had plenty people in the club to protect me, because they were definitely out to bomb the Calypso Club and to come in and wreck the place – because it was known as a coloured club, you see. Naturally, when you're warned like that, you try to defend yourself the best way possible. Not by as they were doing, throwing bombs. But by having enough water around the place or enough implements to stop fires should they start.

Police Inspector Vincent Coventry

On 1 September, 1958, I was the Duty Officer at Notting Hill Station from 2 p.m. to 10 p.m., and responsible with the officers under my command for the prevention of crime and the protection of life and property of this sub-division.

I was well aware, following the incidents of the previous nights and early mornings, of the number of incidents involving disturbances between white and coloured persons, and that there was a liability that many other assaults could be expected.

I instructed the officers serving under me to be on the alert to detect any anticipated racial disturbances, and posted the men in the vicinity of Bramley Road, as far as possible to report immediately, in order that any possible disturbance could receive attention.

Latimer Road station situated in Bramley Road W10, is used by the local coloured population to travel to and from work, and as far as I am aware, no untoward incident occurred until about 8:30 p.m. when a message was received that white and coloured men were fighting in the vicinity of this station. With other officers I went to the scene and found that, on our arrival, the disturbance, if any, had terminated. There was a crowd of about 150 persons of both sexes and varying ages present in Bramley Road, these included a number of adolescents. From my conversation with these people in moving them out of the area, they were sightseeing following previous press publicity given to that area. Numbers of them expressed their personal fears and deplored the violence that had previously occurred. The younger element appeared to be present for the purpose of witnessing any disorder or violence.

The crowds in this area appeared to increase, and police constantly kept them on the move, round the surrounding streets bounded by Latimer Road, Blenheim Crescent, Lancaster Road.

Wilbert Augustus Campbell
aka Count Suckle, the sound system king
About ten o'clock there was petrol bomb coming through the house, the house was on fire. So we tried to run to the door but there was about 5,000 people out there, white people. 'Burn the niggers, kill the niggers! Send them back to their country.' The house is on fire. We can't go through the front door; they were out to kill we. And we stay on the roof till the police come.

Mrs Werner
So we prepared the place [the Calypso Club] and a few of the boys were down there sitting around in case they did charge the place. And we just kept out our customers – much to their distress – and left the place as free as possible, so if they wanted to do damage then that's all they would do is damage to the place and not to the people ... Now I have a friend up on Portland Road. She had three children in the house and there was also a pregnant woman on the premises. They were sitting down watching television and a bomb was thrown into their place. Now, if it wasn't for the fact that these boys were very ignorant and very amateurish about their methods and not all their bombs go off, where would we be?

Velma Davis
At the Tube station you meet this group of guys, they were not locals, I don't know where they came from, black guys. Group of guys just saying, 'Go home and pray for your brothers. Go home and don't come out. Go home and lock up. Hide!' So we walk home fast. When we get in I remember my friend, she had this thing about putting a wardrobe to the door, every night ... to keep pushing this wardrobe to keep them off. She just felt safe. Once the wardrobe was at the door she felt nobody could come in and get us. I really didn't know what was happening. I couldn't understand it.

Hubert 'Baron' Baker

They [Teddy boys] dropped one of these [threatening] cards through the letter box at 9 Blenheim Crescent. We had the lights all turned off. No movement inside, and I distinctly hear, 'Let's burn the niggers! Let's lynch the niggers!' And from those spoken words I says, 'Start bomb them' and then you see the Molotov cocktail bombs coming out from number 9. And they say, 'Oh they are bombing us too.' I says, 'Open the gate and throw them back where they are coming from.' It was a very serious bit of fighting that night because we were very, very angry.

PC Dennis Feist

On Tuesday 2 September, 1958 at Talbot Road W2, at 10:55 p.m. I saw Thomas Williams leave the Bluey's Club and saw that his right-hand side-pocket was bulging. He was stopped and searched, down his left trouser leg was found a piece of iron curved at the end. In his right-hand side-pocket a bottle containing petrol with a piece of cotton wool protruding from the neck. In his left-hand inside pocket a comb case containing an open razor blade. He was arrested and he said, 'I have got to protect myself.' He was taken to Notting Hill Police Station. He was charged and cautioned. He made no reply.

Rene Webb

We had clashes, even with the police themselves out of that riot – without any question. It was quite plain that there was nobody protecting us so we had to protect ourselves. We did not see them as upholders of law. They took sides, and they didn't take sides with us. We see them as a part of the enemy because that was their behaviour.

PC Norman Fraser

Further to my statement of 2 September, 1958 concerning the arrest of JOHN ANDREWS and five other men of colour, by myself and other officers, from a Ford Consul Saloon motor car. I wish to state that this car, index no. VLR 595, had been watched by myself and the other officers at several other trouble spots during that same evening. On each occasion the car stopped with the engine running behind the white section of the crowd. At 10:30 p.m. I was with PC Furneaux and the crew of three x R/T car at a disturbance at Westbourne Park Road junction with Ledbury Road. This car again drove up behind a group of white people and decided to stop it. As previously recorded I arrested JOHN ANDREWS, whom I found sitting by the rear nearside door holding an iron bar in his hand. The other five occupants of the car were similarly armed and were arrested at the same time.

Hubert 'Baron' Baker

We were determined to use any means, any weapon, anything at our disposal. I never forget at that time I was an ex-serviceman. I knew guerrilla warfare. I knew all about their game and it was very, very effective; because it was not just me alone, you had servicemen there too. It was a surprise, because the whole of that area we had men on the housetop, all of the top of the houses, waiting for them. Then when they saw the Molotov cocktail bombs come, they start to panic and run ... There were iron bars, there were machetes, there were all kind of weapons, we had guns, we had hand grenades; because, don't ever forget, you had Americans here during that period who were well prepared to give us all the necessary equipment we needed ... When the police saw the amount of people that was in number 9, they drove the Black Maria and rammed the gates and said, 'Not one of you black bastards coming out.' And I was arrested immediately, but we gave Oswald Mosley and his Teddy boys such a whipping in Blenheim Crescent that I think even now they have lost all desire of wanting to come back.

George Mangar

When we got here [to Britain in 1959], I was told the Teddy boys are racists and they've got bicycle chains and razor blades and that kind of thing. I said, 'I'm not afraid of people like that because I can take care of myself.' Harold [my older brother] said to me, 'Be careful, these guys with these drainpipe trousers and long coats.' I was told that, if you walk in fear, fear follows you. I fear nothing, I don't go with fear in my heart.

After the riots people were wary. They would never have a go at people from Jamaica, because those guys stood up for their rights. Most Jamaicans had big cars, they used to buy American cars, small guys with big cars, wonderful to see them in the summertime, wonderful: Chevrolets, Pontiacs, big huge cars. They were feared because they stopped them, they took no nonsense – they stood up for their own. I thought that was fair, right thing to do, stand up for themselves.

Waveney Bushell

My head teacher was very anxious and used to write to me, I think the first weekend when there was a riot. Because black people used to be waylaid when they came out of the Tube station. Now I never read the local paper, so I don't think I was aware that that was happening until I met my friends and they would say, 'Did you know what happened? Did you read or did you hear?' My first reaction was, thank heavens I'm not living in that area, because I wouldn't like to come out of the Tube station and be hit by anybody and … my head teacher wrote to me and said, 'I hope you're not in that area, where this is happening.'

It made us concentrate our safety, my friends, who are not fighting people. And again, I'm not saying this is a virtue, we were apprehensive; but in my area, when this was happening in Notting Hill, I went to register with a doctor and he deliberately changed the words he said. He couldn't say to me, 'I don't want you on my list,' so he said, 'You're not on my list, so I can't be your doctor,' or something crazy like that. So I, living outside of Notting Hill, didn't get the physical things but there was I, being insulted and degraded and everything else by the local GP. I just walked out, but I remember saying, 'Oh my God, what am I doing here,' you know, which I've asked myself a lot, 'What am I doing in this country?'

Viv Adams

But you see, I sometimes think that can be exaggerated; because I do not think it was principally the whole population of even in the Notting Hill area that this was happening. It was an element, as it is today with certain kind of right-wing parties. It was an element of youthful exuberance by what we now know – The Teddy boys' element. Maybe they were giving a voice to sentiments that were felt generally in the population; but it was not every Englishman stepping out of his house and hurling bricks and bottles at every black person they saw.

George Lamming

One of the paradoxes of Notting Hill was that the vast majority of the people in this country felt a deep sense of outrage. They genuinely felt it was wrong and beastly that such a thing should happen. It's one of the reasons why those English kids were so severely sentenced [for the riots], a decision which I thought at the time, and still do now, was not altogether sound. It was not altogether sound because it was done as a way of informing the world how this country felt about Notting Hill. But a large number of the people who felt so bitterly about the events in Notting Hill feel no less bitterly about the presence of black men in this overcrowded country.

Eddie Adams

I can remember an open-air meeting in Kensington Park Rd, and Mosley was on the back of a lorry speaking to the crowd.[3] He was very theatrical and what he'd do, he'd stop speaking and pose to allow people to take photographs of him and then he'd speak again a little bit later and I was heckling him ... in my mind I associated him with Hitler, the way he was performing was more like a 1930s event, stage-managed with lights coming on, all that sort of thing.

Hubert 'Baron' Baker

I spoke right before the town hall in Railington Rd and I was technically opposing him because I knew he couldn't be right; he couldn't win. He was fighting a losing battle and the striking point is when he said, 'If you want to see the West Indians work give them some Kitty Cat and pig feet.' So I shook him off. I said, 'Oh no, Oswald, when I came here in 1944 I wasn't eating that; I was eating a slice of bacon and some egg powder.'

Velma Davis

I know [Mosley] came down to Ladbroke Grove to have some meetings, but at the time I was so scared of being out because of the Teddy boys, you wouldn't go to the meeting because you knew he was speaking against you, so you stayed away ... [The riots] fuelled a coming together of local black organisations into bigger ones that said we have to fight nationally, and one of the people who did that from Notting Hill was Claudia Jones.

Nobody was killed during the riots, but in May the following year a young Antiguan carpenter, Kelso Cochrane, was set upon in the Notting Hill area by a group of white youths, who stabbed him to death.

Rudy Braithwaite

Everybody turned up for that funeral [Kelso Cochrane's], black and white, people were crying all over the place. There were white folks who from their windows were hailing the procession when they passed. They were moved. Many of them were quite angry during the funeral and they were accusing Mosley for it, they were openly shouting that this was a Mosley thing.

Ben Bousquet

I was one of the people who was angry, and I wanted to go to his funeral to show solidarity and so on. So I was going, but when I got there and I saw so many white people ... there's a time in your life as a young person where you're right; you're always right, no matter how wrong you are, you think you're right, and I thought I was right. And I thought, 'No, I'm not going to this funeral with all these white people there. Where were they when we wanted help? They weren't there and I'm not going to play that game.' So I went home. And for a long while I would have nothing to do with white people.

Viv Adams

Not everybody was so welcoming. No scratch that. Hardly anybody else was as welcoming. The truth is it was a virulent time. Something was happening in the country. Something was causing a souring of the way in which people generally felt. The headlines were pretty vociferous so that you couldn't ignore it. The establishment coarsened the way in which race was viewed, and gave licence to ordinary people's assumptions that black people were pariahs.

Wallace Collins

Jamaican Migrant, 1965

The ordinary man in the street was bellowing against the migrant like cantankerous fishwives ... Everything seemed hopeless, panic was everywhere whenever a black face showed ... It seemed to me that the English had dropped their politeness, their sympathy for the dark ignoramus, and came to terms with themselves that the migrant was a potential challenge to their security and social standing, and they reacted with bold belligerence.[4]

Paul Stephenson

My grandmother was born in Britain and we, as a black family, go back about 200 years. I was born just before the war so I spent most of my time in north Essex during the war. I was well accepted. I remember I was doing my National Service in the Royal Air Force, living in Germany when the riots broke out in Notting Hill, and when I got back to England I saw large numbers of Caribbean people arriving by train. It was the largest crowd of black people I had ever seen in my life; it was about 200 or 300, but it made me look and become aware of the transformation that was happening in England and that I would be seen to be an immigrant and no longer a Black English boy, as I was perceived in those days; and I then knew there was going to be a real challenge to Britain as to how black people were going to be received in this country.

Rudy Braithwaite

There was a turning point. You could sense a change. People were more friendly. People were beginning to react and respond in a different way. Carnival is the most endearing legacy of that troubling period.

Glue Gun Revolutionaries

What could be done to take away the bad taste and ill-feeling of the Notting Hill riots? The answer was Carnival.

The Caribbean Carnival is a hybrid, with roots in Africa, Europe and South Asia. In eighteenth-century Trinidad masquerade, a fore-runner of Carnival, was brought to the island by French settlers in masked balls and street parades, premised on a notion of an inversion, of a world turned upside-down. On the slave plantations, that masquerade became fused with African traditions and the enslaved's own role reversals, mocking the dress sense and behaviour of their 'owners'. These traditions merged after emancipation in the ritual celebration of Canne Burleys (Canboulay), putting out the cane fires after the crop had been harvested. Carnival, then, was not a sombre remembrance of punishing plantation life. Rather it was a wild, bacchanalian affair. For one weekend in the year the enslaved and, later, the newly emancipated, lived out a fantasy; with the existing order turned upside-down, they became masters and mistresses, rulers of the land. With road marches, calypso bands and outlandishly costumed Kings and Queens, Carnival was an intoxicating celebration, a counter to the harsh realities of slavery.

Could such an overt display of exuberance be transplanted to buttoned-up Britain? Hilary Alderson remembers life in late fifties Leeds being drab and dreary: 'Excitement was frowned upon. *Rock Around the Clock* had come out a few years earlier and that caused riots. I saw it at the local cinema and there were police there in case we got up and started jiving about in the aisles. It was quite oppressive.' If jiving in the aisles was discouraged, how would jiving in the streets be viewed?

And then there was the problem of black people themselves. I was always struck by the fact that almost all of the West Indians I encountered growing up in Luton were a strange mix; they were both courageous and timid. They'd been brave enough to take a chance on a new life 4,000 miles away from home, but they were nervous of the authorities and of attracting attention to themselves. The last thing they wanted, after all of the negativity of the riots, was to prance up and down Notting Hill or Chapeltown in Leeds.

The key people behind Carnival were revolutionary figures. In Chapeltown, the energetic educationalist Arthur France saw himself as a Black Power advocate who'd need to swap his black beret and leather jacket for sequins, glitter and feathers. In Notting Hill, separately, there were two women whose admirers claim were the driving force behind Carnival. One was Claudia Jones, a chain-smoking communist who'd been kicked out of the USA; and the other was Rhaune Laslett who, inconveniently for some, had no West Indian connection, but was a local activist born to Russian and Native American parents.

Carnival was welcoming and inclusive, and after all the shameful and divisive talk of 'Keep Britain White', it was just what this multicultural country needed. The Old World monochrome streets would be transformed with a vibrant, New World Caribbean Technicolor; so that a corner of Britain (specifically Notting Hill and the Chapeltown district of Leeds), on one weekend at least, would be forever West Indian.

*

Donald Hinds

Claudia [Jones] asked for suggestions which would wash the taste of Notting Hill and Nottingham out of our mouths. It was then that someone, most likely a Trinidadian, suggested that we should have a Carnival – in winter? It was December of 1958. Everybody laughed, and then Claudia called us to order. 'Why not?' she asked. 'Could it not be held in a hall somewhere?'

Carlton 'Stanley' Gaskin

Rhaune Laslett was the person who decide to hold a little carnival. No Trinidadian or Jamaican. She organised this little carnival where you had the Scottish doing their little thing, Welsh doing their thing and West Indians doing their little thing. All different members of the community. There was no carnival as such as it is now. All the different ethnic groups did something in our little carnival.

Mae Marven

Before the West Indians arrived, there were obviously street parties. We used to celebrate Empire Day and it was usual for children to be dressed in costumes of the countries that were part of the Empire.

Now the English way of life certainly did have a more restrained way of expressing oneself. People coming from the West Indies were, perhaps, freer in their self-expression, perhaps in public with different people.

I went to a prayer meeting one evening and the leader said, 'Well, now in the hall below, Carnival costumes are being made for the children and if anyone is interested to call in on their way out, you're very welcome.'

A lady named Lee said that they were having a little difficulty with the headdress and I said, 'Headdress, well I did a millinery course some years back; maybe I could lend a hand,' and that was my being a Carnivalist.

Mandy Phillips

Mrs Laslett had an open truck and she was sitting down on a big chair like a throne, with all the children around her. Some had bonnets, some had powder in their face, some had little aprons on them. That was the first time I saw them. They didn't really have big music, I think just a little something like a little radio to make some music. There were around six of us from Dominica and we heard there was going to be a Carnival, so we each threw on some fancy dresses and we went out looking for the Carnival.

Mike Laslett O'Brien

My mother's thing was pretty much that she was going to be just here … spilling out of the houses into the street – just like a party for the Queen's Jubilee or something.

The reason there is this controversy is that all historians rely on documentary evidence. They want something written down somewhere. When my mother did this thing there was no sense of it being an historic moment; there was no sense that we've got to write this down, we've got to record this.

Ishmahil Blagrove

It was like, 'Rhaune Laslett, a white woman, what does she know about Carnival?' The reality was you had these people from Trinidad who weren't small-time Carnivalists … they were big players. They would have turned any little street jump-up into a Carnival. So that's why people try to push Rhaune Laslett out by saying that Rhaune 'staged the event', but 'we were the ones that made it!'

Ansel Wong, former Carnival Chair

The Carnival has a number of origins, all of them contested. There is certainly a notion that the mother of Carnival, Claudia Jones, started the first Carnival at St Pancras Town Hall. She agreed that the proceeds from the sale of tickets for the carnival shall be used to pay for the legal fees of those people arrested during the Notting Hill riots in the year before.

Chris Mullard, former Carnival Chair

It came out of this cauldron, if you like, of hate which was expressed by white people towards black people in the 1950s in this country. I remember walking down the street, just down here where I live ... you know, being spat at, being bullied, being attacked by the British Fascist Movement, who had their offices up the end of the street.

Colin Jordan, White Defence League[1]

The trouble was here long before we set up our headquarters in this area. The fact is the people, not having previously a constitutional political outlet for their indignation at the evils of the coloured invasion, resorted to blind violence. We now offer them a constitutional political outlet.

There are many immediate evils of the coloured invasion ... But in our opinion the most important is the long-term one of mass inter-breeding ... that must lead ultimately to a mulatto Britain. Insofar as we believe the civilisation and culture of our country is a product of our race, we feel that if we have a mulatto population in the future that must mean the downfall of the civilisation and culture of our country, which we hold so dear.

We believe in preventing the evils which must result from coloured immigration by removing the problem completely ... by stopping all further coloured immigration into our country and repatriating, with every humane consideration, the coloured immigrants already here.

Chris Mullard, former Carnival Chair

There was a feeling, I think, in this country then that something should be done, seriously done, in terms of community relations, in terms of race relations, and Carnival was always seen as part of that. Carnival's rootage was still that, because there are many political people involved in Carnival, it isn't just people dressing up and dancing on streets, this is about community action.

Corinne Skinner-Carter[2]

[Claudia Jones] was so full of energy, she exhausted everyone, including herself. She used to chain-smoke but I never saw her actually finish a cigarette. And she talked liked she smoked.

I thought it would be a very severe, austere person that I was going to meet. I was invited to go there to meet her, to press her hair ... Today they use chemicals to straighten. In those days we used what they call an iron comb, and we straightened the hair in the fire – and the grease ... I was presented with this rather handsome, elegant lady, and I was shocked, because communists were supposed to have two heads.

In addition to the costume displays, the song and dance performances and the jump-up that provided the main entertainments of the Carnival, a central feature of all the early Carnivals, and the one borrowed from the popular festival in the Caribbean, was the Carnival Queen beauty contest. The crowning of the Carnival Queen was a highlight of the evening.

She [Claudia] also started – I know that the women nowadays would drop their hands in horror – started beauty contests, a black beauty contest. And this was before Black Power days. This was before we all knew that we were beautiful. We might not have known it but she knew that we were beautiful and she started this beauty contest. And the first year there was a girl called Fay Craig that won this beauty contest, and I'm telling you, Fay Craig was black, I mean really black. But pretty. But without Claudia we would not have known that, because then we used to judge everybody's beauty by the European standard.

Of course, in the late 1950s and early 1960s most people, including radicals, would have accepted female beauty contests, largely uncritically. But, for Claudia, the idea of installing real, dark black, black, as beautiful, using a low-culture institution like the beauty contest, was a brilliant move in its time – and knowing black audiences delighted in this insertion of African features into the aesthetics of standards of physical beauty. The contests were a very popular feature of the Carnival, attracting business sponsorship, as well as providing a career vehicle for some of the contestants.

Viv Adams

The organisers were very wily and exploited their connections. They weren't messing around. If you look at the original brochure for that 1959 Caribbean Carnival in the acknowledgements, it lists Dr Bor of Kew Gardens, 'for his help in facilitating our securing of palms for our tropical décor'. I love that.

Donald Hinds

[The first Carnival] was held in St Pancras town hall in January 1959. The BBC televised it. The London papers were not pleased to see and hear hundreds of blacks doing the jump-up in a hall near you, or them. Five more Carnivals followed annually, up to 1964 [before the first street festival].

Russ Henderson

I'll tell you what happen. There is a woman called Mrs Laslett, I used to live in the Grove, you see, and she used to do community work and put on things for the kids you know, fetes. And she, knowing that I had this steel band, which was a real novelty then, and saying, 'Could I come and play for the kids in a street carnival?'

So they put up some buntings and they block off the street, you see. They had a donkey ride and these children taking the donkey ride up and down the street with a clown. So after half an hour playing this band, I found it was getting boring. So I turned to the boys in the band, all of us were used to Carnival back home like we was taking a march. So I went to the chap with the donkey and I say, 'Look, follow us, because we taking a march and we making a block out of the streets.' So we started, and the kids started following us and they had their little donkey cart, with the clown and carrying the kids; and as we started to make this round, the crowds just started gathering on the streets, you know. This was a novelty to them – 1965 – a steel band on the road.

So it was really only the kids who were dressed up and the three of us in our pretty shirts, that was all, and the crowd just followed us. Well, that was the biggest route we ever took in a Carnival because it just snowballed and we went all the way to Whiteley's, right over the Bayswater Road and came right up. The police were just helping us with the traffic, helping people to move out of the way, because they didn't know what it was. Nobody knew if we had permission, nobody knew.

People would ask, 'How far are you going?' and we'd say, 'Just back to Acklam Road,' and they would come a little way with their shopping, then peel off and someone else would join in. There was no route, really – if you saw a bus coming, you just went another way.

Rhaune Laslett was a good woman ... I'd hate to think people have left her out of the history because of her colour. I never went on the streets playing for anyone before I did it for her ... I had the only steel band at the time. The first time I did that rounds through Notting Hill was the day that I did it for Mrs Laslett. Carnival started with Mrs Laslett.

Corinne Skinner-Carter

We disrobed ourselves of our urban, cosmopolitan, adopted English ways and robed ourselves in our own visible cultural mantle. It was our way of saying to the dominant culture, 'Here we come – look, we here.'

Mandy Phillips

The very first big band I saw come up was a Trinidadian band. It was an orchestral jazz band, there was no steel band. And then people started following them. They just started to play and people followed them. And then the other year now a steel band came out.

That ship that come in with the banana, they decided to sponsor us, so we each had the Dominica costume, with a big skirt and head ties, and we all had a bunch of banana.

Darcus Howe
Open University, 2011
The first Carnival I was in England, I cried with tears, because all they had was a Carnival dance at Porchester Hall around Notting Hill, and some people wore costumes, but haltingly. I contest with a lot of people that Carnival did not begin in those dances; it began on the street, because Carnival is the development of concealed practice into the open.

We came out of the bottom of this road, Great Western Road, and then I look up and saw a bus, 28 bus, and I thought, 'My God, these white people are going to think we are crazy.' So, every step was taken haltingly … but then, you know, the rhythm is there but a little quietude … you know, and that's how it began.[3]

Arthur France
The first Carnival masquerade I ever saw as a little boy in the Caribbean was David and Goliath, based on the Bible story, and that captured me. It was magic. I can see it in front of me now. All that colour and drama is in complete contrast to what we find when we come to the Motherland. When I came here it was cold, not just physically, but people were cold and unfriendly towards you. There was an association for African, Caribbean and Asian people that organised dances at Christmas and Easter Whitsun. That was about it. It's a funny thing. Here we were – all these people from the Caribbean islands – but we'd never met each other over there. Back then you couldn't just go from island to island, even though some of them were only fifty miles away. It wasn't until we travel over 3,000 miles that we meet.

I was living in a bedsit at 15 Grange Avenue [in Leeds] with one bed and one chair, and I get together with a few friend and we call a meeting to discuss forming an association. That was a founding members' meeting on the last Sunday in November in 1964 and we invite twenty-seven people. I never forget, it was packed; some have to sit on the bed and on the floor in the bedsit. We just get together and talk some shit and form the United Caribbean Association. Imagine that! All of us coming together in England and things falling apart in the West Indies.

We wanted to look smart so we got this company who made school blazers [the uniform shop on Bow Lane] to make some for us, and used the Federation logo for a badge on the breast pocket. It cost £7 each to make them.

I did some research on Carnival and put together a document and brought the idea to the committee. They chucked me out of the meeting saying I was crazy. Black guys on the committee! Black people back then – and some of us still – we feel a kind of inferiority. Some of them were 'fraid that if we go on the street we would get arrested.

Yes, and church people weren't happy either. To them Carnival is devil work. You have to realise the history of Carnival. The steel band was termed the devil instrument.

Ruben McTair

Steel band in the Caribbean, in Trinidad; there's a [steel] pan yard down the road there, and you dare not go there as a young boy in the pan yard, because it seemed like only vagabonds played pan.

Arthur France

Remember the name of the bands then: Hell's Gate; The Devil Dodgers; None Shall Escape. They used to go out the road and fight; a steel band going down the road and one coming up, and when they clash? It's cutlass!

If you want play steel band you could never get a decent woman. And if a woman went around steel band, she is an outcast and no good for nothing. That's how it was then. And for some people it never change ... A lot of abuse I got. One time I overheard a woman say: 'Oh, we have a crazy man from Nevis want us to look fool for the white man. I wish the police could lock him up or come and drown him.' In my mind, I think the white man done think I'm crazy anyway, so frig him, I'm not worried if you're embarrassed.

Sheila Howarth, Carnival Queen

I was born in Leeds in 1957. My parents came here from St Kitts. When it came to Carnival, other people from Caribbean islands were homesick, they were alone, and they wanted to find something that was their own. They owned the Carnival and they decided to share it with the people of Leeds, to give them a little slice of their beauty, of their heritage. My father played pan, he played tenor pan with a string around his neck so he could play and march. But I don't think he wanted us lot [his children] to be part of that kind of culture. He saw it as old-fashioned and embarrassing; he didn't want to be embarrassed. We were Black British. We wasn't Black Caribbeans, so we were over here for a better life. So with them bringing the Carnival, we were going backwards, bringing his old life over here.

Clinton Cameron

When I was growing up there was no Carnival in Jamaica. They've introduced one now but it was so much more ingrained in the culture of the Eastern Caribbean. I'm not a Carnival person. I was aware of Carnival in Leeds from the very beginning, but I was never involved with it because I am not a Carnival person ... A Carnival person, in my opinion, is someone who is relentlessly cheerful and makes a lot of noise. I have never been one for all that noise.

Arthur France

The committee chucked me out of the meeting that Sunday afternoon, but I ain't taking no for an answer. So I went around and canvassed different members individually and, eventually, the committee half-heartedly say, 'OK, go ahead.' And so we had a friend named Sam LalSingh from Trinidad and he said, 'Don't worry, I'll give you a hand' – and that for me ring bells. Because once he say he giving you a hand, he's serious. Another friend, Kent Thomas, meself and Mrs Gordon turned up – because she's a seamstress, she wanted to do some sewing, turn up with she scissors ready to work. We took off from there. We made costumes for five Queens: a sub-goddess, a Hawaii dancer, a snow queen, a gondolier, a Native American.

Rashida Robinson, Carnival Queen

It was everybody coming together [in 1967] as a little unit, a family, because we all helped each other. We didn't know what we were doing because none of us made costumes in Trinidad.

I came from Trinidad in the sixties to work as a nurse. Arthur France used to follow all the nurses, when they came to England, up in Knaresborough. He'd come and collect us to go to parties in Leeds, ferry us backwards and forwards. When Carnival started, we didn't know what we were doing because none of us made costumes in Trinidad; well, I never had. I'd been to Carnival but never knew what sequins to put on ... because it wasn't allowed. My parents are Muslim, I am Muslim; we went to see Carnival Mas in Trinidad, but weren't allowed to play.

Because of the culture, the Muslims didn't play Carnival in those days. My father sort of ran the mosque in the village we came from. In those days you didn't wear the skimpy bikinis and so ... but it was just something he wouldn't allow us to do. I was coming to England to do my nursing ... I got my independence in England, being away from home. Not that I was controlled at home, but at home I never made decisions. I came here when I was eighteen/nineteen. So I grew up; I learned to do things.

There of course was opposition. Because even when we had gatherings and you made a lot of noise, the local people were very wary of what was going on, they always think we're something different until they got to realise that it's West Indian people, that's how they live, as people who enjoy themselves.

Arthur France

Now this thing had never been done before. All kind of permission was needed. Closing off the roads, you name it, dealing with the police ... They brought in Inspector Exley from Barnsley to oversee it. Now Exley, the first black man he met was me. Because in Barnsley no other black people lived down there except Charlie Williams [a black 1970s comedian who mostly toured working men's clubs]. I don't even like call that man's name. Well, tell you the truth, I felt a little sorry for him because, there he was, a little black man living in Barnsley on his own and predominantly white people; and for white people, it was anything for a laugh. But they're laughing at you. Charlie Williams wasn't strong enough to say respect me as a person, not someone to lick the man's boots.

Let me tell you something. When I had to meet with the Inspector of Police, I make him come to meet me, rather than I go to him. I was living in a bedsit, as I told you. So I'm in charge when he come into my bedsit; if I go to his office he in charge. I didn't have any chairs. My bed was balanced on books and the police inspector had to sit on books. Inspector Exley, he realised I was very passionate and he was too scared to disagree, so anything I said, he said 'Yeah!'

Ruben McTair

What you have to remember is what Caribbean people were thinking. I'm not in Leeds. I'm in Chapelton [Jamaica], I'm in Basseterre, Castries, Port of Spain, Kingston. And before that I was in Accra, Lagos, Monrovia, Akan. My people are Yoruba, Ibo, Ashanti. I know my roots. And that is why ... that is exactly why we need Carnival. Carnival connect up all the dots. Yes! So we don't forget our roots.

Rashida Robinson, Carnival Queen

So the first time I wore a costume was in 1967 in Leeds. By then [when I put on my first outfit] my father would not have objected; he knew my lifestyle had changed, but he knew I would still be respectable. Even so in those days you had to be careful; you never knew if people would take your photograph and send it abroad. People could take your picture and send it back home – and Trinidad, even now, is a small place.

I remember feathers was a bigger problem, feathers for the costumes. We couldn't find them in any of the shops or markets. But you know how black people like their chicken and rice 'n' peas for Sunday dinner? Arthur saw immediately that was the answer: chickens. We went round the houses and took a big order; went up to Otley, brought back dozens of chickens, plucked them and sold them on to the people for their Sunday dinner.

Brian Phillips

I am known in the community as Bushwacker. It goes back to my time in Carnival and we jump-up: me; Shaggy who's a good friend of mine; and Godfather, who's the local DJ played the first sound on the road and plays at Jouve, the day of Carnival when you come out in pyjamas. So we was a gang together and was named the Bushwackers because we just have our fun from original back home in the Caribbean. I'm from St Kitts and as a boy I grew up knowing about Carnival with Masquerade and Bull and jump-up and have fun. I was brought here by my parents, so was my other brother as well, and the significance is it is the only connection we have to our roots. The same as when English people or white people went to the Caribbean and they had their events taken to the Caribbean, like they'll have tea at a certain time [no matter the weather], they do certain things at a certain time. We came here with the only part of our culture left, is Carnival; it's all we have left.

I got involved because there is no other memory for most of West Indian people. Carnival meant more than just jump-up and have fun and have a dance and have the reggae concert in the park today. It meant more than that. Carnival was/is a way of life. It's a part of our life and if that dies, we die as well as a people. That's how I see it anyway.

Clinton Cameron

Even though I'm not a Carnivalist, what I think Carnival has done is very good and significant. Carnival also helped to challenge local people's perception and the press's description of West Indians. In the sixties and seventies what people thought of Chapeltown is more of a reflection of what they thought of black people from the Caribbean, rather than any objective facts about violence or criminality in the area. In the sixties till even now, people thought that Chapeltown was a black area and that anything that is illegal or bad was happening here. Drugs, prostitution and any kind of lawlessness. It was hardly different from many other parts of Leeds, really. People could and did, come to Carnival and see for themselves how that was counter to the reality.

Wilmer James

This is the workshop where we do the welding; is where everything starts from; the heart of Carnival. No, more like the backbone. This is like the starting of everything, with the frame, then we move from here ...

I'm only got involved 'cause Mr France ask me. He know my expertise. I came here when I was seventeen and did a five-and-a-half year apprenticeship. I came from St Kitts I grew up at Russell village in St Kitts but I was born in Nevis. I had two sisters who came here before me.

Personally, me, I never really like Leeds, but I stayed here because my siblings was here. I always find that Yorkshire people was racist. Still is now; 60 per cent of the guys who around my age, they would tell you the same. Because the Yorkshire people didn't like black people. Up to now I don't think they really get on with black people. I would have rather live in Birmingham, the Midlands. I did like London, but London is a bit expensive to live. When you just come here, you haven't got a lot on, you know what I mean? I would have like to live in Bedford, anywhere south.

Seriously though, we have a saying that the white man puts to you ... he's not going to tell you this, but he'll say, 'If you black get back.' As longs as you this colour, you have to be extra good to achieve, to reach where you want to be; and then at the end of it all you still get knocked back. Like in America, we always knew it was a problem there with racism. But with the Americans you know where you stand; with the English you don't. Back in the sixties, they wouldn't exactly say they don't like you, but with their actions you can read the small print.

Carnival changed things a little bit. What I know a long time ago is you can have a white friend, but you not allowed to go home with them or to their house. Nowadays maybe you get as far as their sitting room, but nothing else.

Seriously, I think Carnival changed a lot of white people perception. But! But! Carnival is a black people thing. I'm telling you the truth! It's our thing. We have to watch it. We have to be very careful and watch Carnival, 'cause in the next generation, the white man be coming on like he invent it.

Hughbon Condor

I've been designing costumes since the early days of Carnival. I met this guy, Arthur France, in one of the streets in Chapeltown and he approached me and he said, 'What the Carnival needs is good designers like you.' It was funny 'cause at the time I'd never designed any Carnival costumes.

Well, that's typical Arthur, always roping in people ... Back in St Kitts, as a kid, I remember making my own stilts and walking on them and jamming in the Carnival with some big woman ... But in this country I'd never shown any flair as such. I'm not really sure why Arthur approached me. Perhaps he just had this feeling about me. I think he probably knew that I was an engineer.

It was funny 'cause I did my apprenticeship in a place called Cleckheaton, in a factory with 800 white people, and I was only one of two black persons. And for me to come back to my family and be involved with Carnival at Chapeltown was great, because it was almost like 'I'm back home again' where we were in charge – we owned the streets, we organised it. At work, as a black person, you almost seem insignificant; generally speaking, there was that view that the black man wasn't capable of anything.

For example, for the design 'Man on Horseback Nah See Dem' it was a way of celebrating the abolition of slavery. It was an expression my grandmother used to say when I was a kid. Basically she was referring to a period when the slave masters were riding the horse in the fields, and they could get away with a certain misdemeanour, providing the man on the horse didn't see them.

It was a full-sized horse and there was an effigy of a man to represent the whole colonial imperialism and the power; and he came on riding this particular horse and the Carnival Queen, a slave girl, was being dragged along by him. One side of the horse was the scenes of the beauty of the Caribbean with the palm trees and lots of wonderful flowers; and the other side was the sugar-cane plantation ... As the Queen got into the middle of the stage she got her hands free, found a cutlass and tried to mimic the other slave workers and chopped down the whole sugarcane. She stripped her slave clothes off to reveal her true African identity. She then pulled the man off the horse, took a whip and actually whipped him. She got on the horse.

That whole performance at the Carnival show took place in about three minutes, but the design took months and months, working on it most weekends to get all the mechanics right. It was inspired by her cultural awakening, and that's what Carnival was – a spiritual awakening.

Dawn Cameron (with Susan Pitter)

We're both from Jamaican families in Chapeltown. Our dads both worked on buses – ordinary working-class men but with a real commitment to education, self-empowerment and black politics. My solid commitment to Carnival arises out of that, out of the way I was brought up; my dad saying to us: 'You are not half-caste, you are black.' A real Garveyite modus operandi [followers of black nationalist leader Marcus Garvey, whose ambition was to achieve black self-sufficiency for people in the African diaspora] ... And if you look at Chapeltown Road over Carnival weekend, what you do see are black entrepreneurs who realise there are tens of thousands of people coming into the area, so they decide they will set up a Carnival village and from the start they set up jerk chicken stalls and sell sugar cane.

Susan Pitter

Carnival started off with committed people wanting it to happen, planning and delivering it. But it doesn't mean they were good at both – no fault of theirs; they were often volunteers. Its amateurishness was its charm.

Dawn Cameron

It's very rare that you see yourself in a mainstream proper, proper theatre. We don't see ourselves in British culture usually; we don't see ourselves represented in that way and we love it, we love it. Like when we were little and we'd watch any racist stuff on TV 'cause at least there were some black people in it. I loved the warmth of

Carnival; that sense of belonging and achievement. It's impossible to turn your back on that.

Arthur France

We were young radicals and we realise we wanted some people to make us look good. So Mrs Clareta Wenham – she's like a stately person that people respect – so we draft in Mrs Clareta Wenham. And then we heard about this black television announcer, Clyde Alleyne. If we can get Clyde to be the MC at the King and Queen Carnival show. Well … Clyde was on Tyne Tees Television – before Trevor McDonald. So we phoned the studio and Clyde was there! And Clyde took the call, just as if he was somebody you knew … And at the first Carnival black people didn't believe it could happen. The joke was this: I remember the night when the show start and we're backstage and the place is packed, 'cause people just came to laugh at us, and you know what surprised people, and I can hear it now, when the curtain went back and Clyde stood up. 'Ladies and Gentlemen.' That voice! People couldn't believe what they were hearing. This is the man!

Ruben McTair

I'll be honest, right up until the night before, no, even on the morning, I thought it was going to be a disaster. I had thought it impossible to achieve. But Arthur had something. I tell you, black people are hell to move. Mr Arthur France must have had something. Must have had plenty. Still has till today. Secretly, a lot of folk – and I mean black folk – had come, I'm ashamed to say, had come to jeer. But that day there was a lot of Doubting Thomases converted. Brother, they had come to jeer but stayed to cheer.

Angela Wenham

To see a group of West Indians jamming on the road, it were fantastic, it was really good fun. You dance all the way, you lead the party, you just jam. And to see all these faces looking at you in shock – the Carnival is actually going ahead – and no policemen arresting you, because that was one of the worry, it was fantastic.

Wilmer James

I liked to see people enjoying themselves. I liked mixing with some of the girls who came in and got their frames made up. To see them going up on the stage on the night, Beverley and all the gal dem wearing costumes, it give me pleasure to know that I was a part of that or I made that. I feel good to see them dancing around in my thing.

Sheila Howarth, Carnival Queen

It was only when I experienced Carnival for the first time that I realised up till then I had seen everything in black or white, grey really. The streets were grey. Leeds was grey, but suddenly there was all this colour. It was brilliant.

Rashida Robinson, Carnival Queen

The first costume I wore was Native American Indians with feathers and a beautiful headpiece. Putting a costume on was like dressing up as a little doll, it was something new. Because I couldn't sew, I'd never made anything for myself. So just doing it, seeing it on the table – someone designed it and you made it and you put it on, and I still have that special feeling, up to today. It's me in a different light, something I enjoy; and it's no fairytale, it's reality now, and I will continue to do it for as long as I can.

It's something you dream about doing; when you were in Trinidad you saw all these young people in a costume, never had the opportunity to do it although you wanted to do it. But now I can do it for real.

In the early days they started to see us as people who enjoy themselves and have this vibrant enthusiasm for what they are doing; it was just a buzz and so they just joined in. In Leeds, even outside of Carnival, we made a lot of noise and they'd wonder what was going on, and most of the time we were sober, but we just love life.

And I still have that special feeling putting on the Carnival Queen costume. Each time is like the first time, and I put it on and walk with pride.

Ian Charles

First time we used to drag the floats, actually drag them with our hands on ropes along the route all the way into the centre of Leeds and drag them back. The worse thing about it was coming back now it was uphill. So you can imagine. Hahaha ... And that was it! We change up to lorries now. We have a dozen floats on lorries.

Lord Silky, Calypsonian

Well, I'm a Calypsonian and troupe leader for the Cockspur troupe. I do both. I used to mess around as a kid in the Caribbean trying to sing, I wasn't successful because I was too young. I met Arthur France at the youth club in St Kitts and he inspire me 'cause he said they're going to have a Carnival in England if I ever want to sing. He came to the youth club and he was recruiting people and I say, 'Yeah man,' and I jump to the occasion. For that first Carnival in 1967, I start writing lyrics and I made a song. 'St Kitts is my born in land I say':

St Kitts is my born in land I say I say
England is my home in every way every way
No matter what Enoch Powell say[4]
In England I bound to stay
St Kitts is me born in land I say

The second verse now, because Arthur (France) is the one who encourage me to sing, I thought if I bring him into my song now, well ... it'll be good for the song. So the second verse went like this:

Give three cheers to Arthur France and co and co
For bringing Carnival to Great Britain, Great Britain
For he has done his very best
To make it a big success
Carnival is here let's do the rest

And when you hear that verse you know I'm gonna win with that!

Sheila Howarth, Carnival Queen

When I competed as a Carnival Queen, wow! I was a Rainbow Queen. My costume was huge, it had a pot of gold and a rainbow, and it just transformed me. Everyone was cheering for me from being this ordinary woman. And I'd never seen so many black people. You wasn't alone as you thought you were. No one had ever praised me in such a way but for once I was important. When you're wearing that costume you can pretend that it's not you. For that little time it's not you. You are that costume, you kind of morph into what it is.

It transformed me into something spectacular. And everyone wants your photo and you believe that you are somebody – and you are. And then the following day you don't care. You're back down your normal everyday Sheila Howarth. But for that day you're a Queen! I tell you what, you can get the ugliest girl you can find, and you make her queen and you have boosted her confidence a million times. For that one day, I was Queen of Chapeltown, an African Queen. As Leeds folk would say, it were brilliant.

Would You Let Your Daughter Marry a Negro?

'Would You Let Your Daughter Marry a Negro?' asked the headline in a 1954 edition of *Picture Post*.

The newspaper journalist worked himself up into a bit of a lather: 'If your daughter or mine does take to bringing a coloured boyfriend home, what shall we do or say? We shall be failing in our duty if we do not tell her how difficult a road she is preparing to tread. If we do not tell her that, there are still landladies who scream and shut the door, and some who even faint at the sight of a Negro on the doorstep after dark.'

Yet there were some foolish enough to accede to their daughter's wishes. They included Stanley Cripps. *Picture Post* had the proof: a wedding photo of 'the daughter of a former Cabinet Minister and a native'. There stood Peggy Cripps in her white wedding gown beside her husband Joseph Appiah in Ghanaian kente cloth.

But before marriage came fraternising (i.e. sex). And it was the thought of intimacy between the races that often caused most consternation. A decade before, the Duke of Buccleuch had written to the Colonial Office warning that 'loose relations between black men of totally different standards, both moral and material, and our simple country girls has unpleasant features.'

But you can't legislate for attraction. For young black men like Darcus Howe who arrived from Trinidad in 1961, the entertainment at the weekend shebeens meant dancing into the early hours with girls, girls, girls. 'The girls were Australian, Swedish, whatever – it was black men and white girls – mine was Italian. That's how it was.'

Some white people may have felt threatened, but the so-called threat was always overstated. Recalling those times, Bageye asserted that there was never much socialising with white people anyway and that, if by unhappy circumstance you found yourself near a 'decent' white woman, she'd act as if tainted by your presence: 'You couldn't even stand up at the same bus stop as a white woman.'

Those brave enough to do so were also just being practical, believes Carlton Gaskin, because of the small number of women who came over in the first years after the *Windrush*. 'Those were the days, if you wanted to get married, your wife got to be white. Because who else can you marry? But the funny thing is those girls who did decide to form any relationship with us, they suffered because even their family gave them a hard time. I mean some got married and their brothers wouldn't even accept the fact that their brother-in-law was black.'

That outcome was repeated up and down the country. The alarm bells sounded by *Picture Post* were still ringing a decade later when, appearing on BBC's *Any Questions*, the Conservative MP Sir Gerald Nabarro, echoing *Picture Post*, asked his fellow panellists: 'How would you feel if your daughter wanted to marry a big buck nigger with the prospect of coffee-coloured grandchildren?'

What is not so readily acknowledged is that often the disapproval of mixed marriages ran both ways. Had the editors of *Picture Post* dug a bit deeper they might have been surprised to learn that many black people shared similar views. The consensus among adults in black communities was that the coffee-coloured children of mixed-race marriages in Britain were to be pitied; they were unwanted and unloved.

★

Hubert 'Baron' Baker

[During World War Two] at one of the bases where we were stationed, we had social occasions which the locals would arrange. When we tried to get dances all the WAAFs [Women's Auxiliary Air

Force] would want to rest. But when an English airman approached them, they would take the floor with them ... The situation was explained to the Commanding Officer and he issued instructions that WAAFs who didn't want to dance shouldn't attend dances.

Trevor Philpott
Picture Post, 30 October 1954

In the unstirred minds of many British mothers, a black man is something out of the jungle. In taking a black man, her daughter is taking also black magic, black-heartedness, and all kinds of black evil. Purity is white, sin is black. The association is so deep that it cannot easily be shaken off. A friend of mine, who is small, tolerant and blonde, described to me a few days ago the inexplicable terror which swept through her as a Negro walked behind her up the stairs of a boarding house. The man was only going upstairs. She was terrified.

Dorothy Skinner

The Police Sergeant, the Detective Sergeant that used to chase up was called Sergeant Newton, and the policewomen were called Sgt Kippax and Sgt Foley. Sgt Kippax was a big woman, very bombastic, and one day I was talking to a black guy on Denmark Road [in Manchester] and she went right to my mother's house on the bike in police uniform, parked her bicycle outside my mother's house – don't forget they are terrace streets, terrace houses in the streets – and she went to see my mother. And she went in the house and she said to my mother, 'I have just seen your daughter talking to a man who is as black as the coal in that grate,' and pointed to my mother's fire; and my mother repeated that when I came in. She said, 'You have been talking to a bloody black man, and the bloody police woman has come and told me he is as black as the bloody grate, the hobs of hell,' she said. They didn't like it. They were dangerous, these immigrants that had just come over, it was unbelievable; white women can't go with black men, don't talk to them. I don't know what they were thinking really, you know, but don't forget it is a completely white country.

Elizabeth May Gilman

The first people that came here after the war was the Poles. Then people came from the Caribbean and that's when all the trouble started. And I think it was over them going out with the white ladies. I think that was a lot of the trouble. The white boys didn't want the black lads going with their girlfriends.

Chris Stredder

You were considered the lowest of the low if you went with a black man in the 1950s, you couldn't go any lower than that. Your life was hell, believe me.

Earl Cameron

London at that time, it was very mixed, I mean the clubs and so on, all classes, a lot of society women would come to places like the Caribbean Club, just to mix with black men, and very high-class women go there from time to time. It was all rather decadent to be honest, but that's what it was all about.

Donald Hinds

The legend of the black man as a sexual demon lives on. Some Negroes have begun to believe in their sexual prowess and are treating it as racial 'upmanship'. In 1960, in a small factory in Leeds, a white man was said to have asked a white woman why she was living with a coloured man. The woman replied with scorn: 'If you can let me have it four times each night, then I'll come and live with you.' The man, in a state of shock, wandered around the factory asking every coloured man whether he was capable of having sexual intercourse four times each night.

John Prince

I went to shower; when I turned around there were twenty white men looking to see what my sexual organs were like. They were passing remarks, you know. I was really annoyed. I said, 'I can't believe this.' This was all about that myth.

Alfred Harvey

Good sex was the thing that really attract them to us, I think sex played a great part in it, stamina, that's why they call me king dick. Well, the dick gone now but the king still remain.

Dorothy Leigh

We was dancing [at the Rialto ballroom, Longheaton] and I fell on the floor and he [George Leigh] picked me up, and that's it. [Laughs] I don't know whether it was love at first sight. He took me home. He was polite, he was a gentleman. People used to speak to me at time, but if I was with him, no, they wouldn't speak to me; they would say, 'Oh well I didn't see you.' But they did, but they used to look the other way. They wouldn't pass you, they'd stop and stay there until we passed.

When we moved into this house, a friend of mine that I'd known a long, long time, she stopped me in the street and she said, 'Don't get settled in that house, because I'm going to have you out.' I had no right to go in front of her because of him. I never made many white women friends did I really [to husband]? It's only as I've got older that I've made more white women friends. I just didn't trust them. If you had a West Indian woman as a friend, you had her for life.

Hilary Alderson

Leeds [in the 1950s and 1960s] was grim, quite grey, with days and nights of pea-soup fog. Life was a bit drab and dreary. Excitement was frowned upon. *Rock Around the Clock* had come out a few years earlier and that caused riots. I saw it at the local cinema and there were police there in case we got up and started jiving about in the aisles. It was quite oppressive. You were a young adult but not allowed to be an adult with a mind of your own.

There were two main ballrooms, the Majestic and the Mecca Locarno. We used to go to the tea dance at the Majestic on our Wednesday afternoon off – they had a proper band, crooner and glitter ball. It was all gilt and had a big balcony. But you weren't supposed to go the Mecca. It was considered common; only common girls with too much make-up went there. I started working at the Co-Op at sixteen, and we'd brave it occasionally at lunchtime in defiance of our parents. I didn't particularly like it.

Actually, there were some black students in Leeds and I danced with one of them once at the Majestic. That was uncomfortable because we didn't really encounter coloured people back then and some people are really, you know ...

The students were obviously well-off because they were studying and abroad. They were very well spoken. But some people would have thought it was infra dig, a bit beneath you – to dance with them.

We were stood up in the 'cattle market' by the ladies cloakroom, when he approached me. Sometimes you'd obviously have to turn down the requests for a dance, but I couldn't do that to him, because I thought he'd be really hurt, and I didn't want him to think it was because he was black ... I still felt awkward because it was such a new experience and I worried that everyone would think: 'God, she's dancing with a black man!'

Mary Jacobs

If you danced with a black man you were very discriminated against because people didn't like it. People would comment, 'You ought to be ashamed of yourself,' as you walked past. People like my mother, people my mother's age would be thinking, 'I wouldn't like my daughter to do what she's doing.'

Well, it was exciting because we hadn't seen anybody like that before, I'd never had close contact with anybody of a different colour. They were very different from the local boys that we'd seen and we were interested to get to know them better. They were young, they were quite dashing really ... He [Jake] was more friendly with me than the others were.

Someone had seen me in this field with a picnic with a group of people and said I was in a field with six black men, as though I was there alone, and my father went out of his mind. He said, 'I'll lock you up, you won't go out ever again.' And he did lock me up for quite some time, wouldn't let me go to college, wouldn't let me go anywhere. He was very, very much against it.

Wallace Collins
Jamaican Migrant, 1965

Jamaican men are polygamous to say the least, in fact they are 'wild', for their monumental faith in their virility would incite them to move any mountain to raise a skirt and claim its contents.

Ken and I arrived at Hammersmith Underground station half an hour early for our date, and decided to scout around. There were two English girls making as if they wanted to give us the eye, but we were shy. Ken was bolder than I so he approached them in a way that was typical of the Jamaican cat. The left side of his body was taut, his right hand caressed his chin, raising his eyebrow, his right foot shuffling forward as he jerked his right knee to vibrate his body, while in the same movement he did a quarter pirouette and swung his left arm from the shoulders like a rooster fencing in his hen; we called this movement towards the female, 'Constacklin'. One of the girls smiled, but the other stepped away and said, 'Do you mind?'

[Ken] was a real cowboy both in gait and in manner. He was always rooting, tooting, shooting his weight around and floating his fists indiscriminately free of cost. He walked as if he expected to draw a gun at any moment; squaring his shoulders, elbows open, toes in, chipping the asphalt; swinging his arm from the shoulders and glaring at anybody he suspected.[1]

Johnny Edgecombe (aka Johnny Edge)

In Leicester Square in a basement there was two little English ladies who used to run a jazz club and they used to have a lunchtime session. All the nice chicks who used to work in Dolcis and Saxone [shoe shops], they all used to come down for the lunchtime session and we didn't have any trouble, because the chicks used to like dancing the jitterbug and all that. But when you come out on the road they wouldn't be seen with you. They wouldn't walk down the road with you, because if one of these chicks decide to go out with me and one of my buddies then, if the word get back to wherever she come from, her parents become nigger lovers.

Kate Paul, diary

Birmingham, 2 October 1960

The people on this street live on their sexual instincts and fear. It's a street of brothels and men hanging about on corners. To be white is exceptional. I have just been out for cigarettes. The street was scattered with Jamaicans and Indians, standing in small groups, or wandering in and out of houses. A few old women, no longer of any interest, walk slowly up the street carrying shopping bags.

There is suspicion and fear, eyes shift from one face to another, black, bloodshot ones and pale shifting ones ... Men in cars kerbcrawl and raise their fingers, leaning forward, eager, their faces drawn with lust. I hate these, not the streetwalkers.

As for them, I think they're made to be in such a losing business. It's really terrible in the street. They have cock-fights and stabbings and the police come up here in twos or on motorbikes. At night it's really grim; men melting into doorways, beckoning. The endless crawl of cars, the slamming of doors, the women's shrill voices. Old men insulting young tarts.

The old couple upstairs, us and two of the tarts are the only whites. The old people, Leopold and his wife, are ancient, amazingly kind and straight from a Balzac novel.[2]

Agnes DeAbreu

You know what? Because my people are originally from Madeira, we have light skin. Back in 1958, if I was walking with Jim, people would assume I was a white woman. Sometimes people look on you and they just spit on the floor in front of you. You can be racist but not ... But sometimes I did find some black people who were racist too. They think I'm white and he's black and it shouldn't be. A lot of them feel like you're nobody. They think you're low class, a black man pick you up. But if a black woman is with a white man they don't get anything like that. You get it from both sides a bit, but you just ignore it.

Charles Moorcroft

One evening we were coming from an occasion. I saw someone passing by and then they just spit, you know, and I thought that was strange. So I said to him, 'Why did you have to spit like that?' He said, 'Because you're a nigger walking with a white woman.' I said, 'I beg your pardon.' I said, 'I'm not a nigger.' I said, 'I'm just a black man. Not because my pigment is black and yours is white, do you think there's any difference?' Really, that was something that really shook me up.

Mary Jacobs

My father said [to Jake], 'I've nothing against you as a person, it's not you that I'm against, it's the fact that you want to marry my daughter.' And I think that's the whole point of it. People look and think, 'I wouldn't like my daughter to marry a black man.'

He wouldn't acknowledge it. He just didn't look at me, didn't say anything. I didn't know what to do. I do remember saying, whether it was at that point or earlier, I remember him saying that, 'Now you've taken up with this young man, from Trinidad, this black man, you will never get a decent boyfriend, never.' He said, 'Don't come back here. I don't ever want to see you again.' My mother and I were both crying, and I came away thinking that that was the end, that I would never see my family again. Nobody came to my wedding.

Chris Stredder

[A friend] was walking down Smetton Dale with him [her boyfriend] and a group of white women spat at her; and this was a quite common occurrence for her, they used to call her 'black man's meat' and 'black whore'. And when she was pregnant her family didn't want to know her either. She was a nice girl and it used to break her, when these women used to gang up on her, and I used to think, 'Oh God.' I wasn't brave enough to be her friend, basically because I didn't want the same treatment. If you was a friend you get the same treatment. I didn't speak to her as much as I should.

Bet Lowe

I went to a jazz club in Nottingham and heard a saxophone chap, Joe Harriott, and it blew me away. I wasn't a modern jazz fan, but the technicality of the chap, and he put his heart and soul into it, and at the end, we had a chat with him. He always wore a three-piece suit and a white shirt. He went to Alpha Boys' School in Jamaica. I was studying music and he asked if he could be of any help. All he was really interested in was how to get his leg over as soon as possible. So he took my phone number.

A week later we went back to his place and he had a bottle of wine; things took the usual sort of route they do, but I wasn't up for any of that, so I said I was going home. 'On your way,' he said, 'Could you go to the pub next door, get me a bottle of Beaujolais and twenty cigarettes?' Which I did, out of my money, so I think I had to pay for the pleasure of his company for two or three hours.

By the 1960s, you'd see mixed couples in London. Later, when I was with Joe's cousin, Ralph, we had a ground floor flat, and there was a fire, because the man upstairs knocked a heater over and it burned a hole right through the floor and the ceiling through to our place. We had a leery chap come along and repair the damage. He was, you know, very suggestive, asking me personal questions about the set-up, how long had we been together, blah blah blah. These days I'd have been justified in punching him in the face. It was insinuated that: 'You might think you've got a nice looking boyfriend but you must be up for anything, you know must be a bit of a slag really.'

Dorothy Leigh

It wasn't only the whites. They [black women] used to say, we had the cream and they were jealous, very, very jealous, because I suppose they felt threatened when they came here.

Louise Lange

The white women, they're easy, easy like a bird. You've just got to buy them a glass of mild, or a glass of lager and that's alright for them. It was so strange to us, we couldn't believe what we were seeing happening. It was a surprise [to see black men having relationships with white women] because we didn't know that these things could happen.

John Prince

[My friend] was very clever, a brilliant natural engineer, a qualified teacher, head over heels in love with this girl who had nothing, in my view, to commend her. Physically she was not attractive, she had terribly black teeth, some missing; she didn't speak, in my view, even Standard English, but he was besotted with her. He invited my wife and I over for dinner. Someone invites you for dinner from our cultural point of view, you have to go there prepared to eat the food, and burp to show that you really enjoyed it. So I went there hungry and she proceeded to give us dinner, baked beans on toast; she wasn't even accomplished in the skills of domesticity, you know, yet he was madly in love with her, and they got married and had children. It was always a successful relationship but, you see, if he was back in the Caribbean, there's no way that he would marry a working-class girl that swept the street or who worked at the cash till. He would not have married her equivalent back in our society.

Louise Smith

The one I married, he was from Jamaica like myself, so that was why I picked him. If he's from Barbados, [because] I don't born there, when we ready to go home me say 'I don't want to go,' what going to happen to me? And he'd say he want to go Barbados, so in my mind I say I'm find a man from Jamaica, and I did. White man? No! Me hear too much 'You black bastard', me hear it too much. Not to me, but me hear it. My friend did have one and when he ready to tell her off, 'Oh you black bastard!' And the white woman tell the black man, 'You black bastard!' I hear it all over the bus stop, I hear it. Stick to your own.

Eric Irons

As you're going along, you see people on the buses turning their heads looking with their eyes popping out, and most of it was disapproval.

Nelly Irons (with Eric Irons)

I was fascinated by him. He said to me once, 'Would it be possible for you to marry me?' And I said, 'Possible, but not very probable.'

Mr James

quoted in *Picture Post*, 1954

If two people have real love then they don't notice colour. And when others, sometimes without good manners, take notice of it, it only draws the man and wife together. To me, my wife is the best human being in the world – and I'm very proud to say that. People should look into the man – not at him.

E. R. Braithwaite

To Sir, With Love

After lunch we all sat down to discuss the matter [my proposed marriage to Gillian]. Gillian's parents were very frank in expressing their opinion. Mr Blanchard said, 'We would, even now, prefer that Gillian had fallen in love with someone of her own colour; it would have made everything so much easier for her as well as for us. Before this I would have unhesitatingly asserted that I was without prejudice, racial otherwise, but now that it has reached me to become a personal, intimate issue, I know that I would do anything in my power to break this up, if I thought it would do any good. It's not just the two of you, Rick, that have to be considered. You might have children; what happens to them? They'll belong nowhere, and nobody will want them.'[3]

Alford Gardner

I went to the house, the woman who was to be my wife house, to have a word with the father, to ask for his daughter's hand, as you do, and he came in, 'What's he doing here? Get him out of here!' Just like that. I just turned and walked out. I was halfway down the road when she came running. I wasn't even in a room then; we'd bought a house by then and we had our own room. So she came. She went back home and got her clothes and whatever, and moved out [from her home] and we moved in together.

I was able to buy my own house and one day I came home and he was there [the father] and he said, 'How do, how are you?', and

I said, 'Fine, thank you.' That's the only talk me and him ever had. I never had a word with him. The mother was alright. I mean, I couldn't care less. I was the first one in the family that have their own house. The rest of the family, we all got on alright.

Dorothy Leigh

When we got married there was nobody about when we went into the registry office; when we came out there was just people everywhere [about 200] looking! It was surprising how the word got round that somebody had gone in the registry office to get married and one were black and one were white, I suppose. The police had to come and move them away so we could get out.

Bet Lowe

Joe had always said that he'd got a cousin that lived in Ilford. One day he took me and my friend, Sue, to a jazz club, which was really a drinking and gambling club called the Cubana, to meet his cousin Ralph.

Ralph and I got on really well. But my mum didn't even put herself out a little bit to find out where Jamaica was or anything about it whatsoever. She was totally blinkered; it was all what the neighbours might think. In fact, one of my aunties, my Auntie Connie – this is an indication of what they were like – when I had my son, Daniel, she came to the maternity home to see the baby. And she said to me, 'There dear, alright dear, at least he's the right colour.' Really, when my auntie said about the right colour, that was when I should have actually said something, put her straight, but I didn't.

Babs

quoted in *Picture Post*, 30 October 1954
There were objections alright. Auntie Mary – who had only seen [Johnnie's] photograph. 'Oh, it's alright for you, Barbara,' they said, 'you're big. What about the children? Remember they'll only

be little.' Well, I want children and I think I've got enough love to protect them from anybody's insults. We shall have to get out of this place first. This room has to do for bedroom, sitting room and dining room. We were going to live in the flat at Finchley with Dad, but when the man heard that Johnnie was black, he said we'd have to go.

He wouldn't mind for himself, he said, but the other tenants would complain. They were all middle-class people. They said nothing to your face, that kind don't, but they'd already been to tell him that a Negro kept calling on me. Down here, they'll shout it at you in the streets, 'Fancy marrying a nigger!' Well, I can fight against that – and make them wish they'd never opened their mouths.

When we go out we do get people staring. But when you're in love you don't notice. Sometimes, waiters and barmen will just keep Johnnie standing there waiting to be served, until he goes away. I used to flare up at them, but it only makes you feel cheap and spoils the evening. Now I give them a sly smile and walk out.

I'm not a child, and I knew what I was doing when I married him. In fact I suppose I wanted to protect him, really. We shall be alright.

Archippus Joseph

I got called up to do National Service. By then I was madly in love with Josephine, so I became a PTI [Physical Training Instructor] so I wouldn't be posted abroad. She became my wife, Josephine. We met in the dance hall, the Royal in Tottenham Court Road. She loved dancing. You look around for the girl who can dance, it was the jive then. I asked her for a dance and she was brilliant at dancing. There was only a handful of black men and no black women there.

I got called up in January 1957. I was a bit worried, you don't get paid much, just under a pound a week, so I was losing the money I wanted to save up for two years.

Josephine had a sister and some friends, some Irish chaps, and we all used to go out together. I was still in the Army and the food wasn't very palatable. Josephine worked in a grocery store and every weekend she used to send me a parcel of food. It made me think how good she was, and meeting the sister and we all got on so well, and so eventually I wrote to her parents in Dublin and said, 'I'm in love with your daughter, and I intend to marry her, but with your blessing.' And I said, 'You don't know me and with or without your permission, we'll get married, but I'd like to have you on my side.'

The father, Edward Johnson, came over, and he'd been in the Dublin Fusiliers and had fought in World War One. He said to me, 'Don't worry about colour or anything like that. I've been in the Army, with your people, I love them so well, all I'm asking you, she is my favourite daughter, take care of her.' What a family! I was so fortunate in meeting her family. Remember, there were more Irish in Montserrat before the blacks! Yes! We celebrate the same St Patrick's Day, the same as them. Montserrat is called the Emerald Isle, the same as Ireland.

The mother came over. The father died a couple of years after we were married. The mother came over with the son and daughters, and we lived in the same house in London Fields.

Personally, I've never really encountered any major racial prejudice; apart from, people used to shout at you occasionally, 'Nigger, get back home.' With my wife being white, they'd shout, 'Where are all the white men, couldn't you find a white man? Why you marry a nigger?'

Elizabeth Young

I was with the coloured child, Negro child, in the pram, which I was fostering, and a woman bumped into me and said, 'Nigger lover.' I felt a physical sense of shock. I can't describe to you how you do feel. Your knees go weak. Why, I don't really know. But when I sort of recovered my senses, I just said 'Well, the child's not mine.' And I felt awful after that. I felt really quite guilty. I felt I'd denied the child. And the awful thing was, if the child had been mine how would I have reacted? I don't know.

Dorothy Skinner

I couldn't tell my mum [about boyfriends] things like that. I had to be in for a certain time. I couldn't say I had a boyfriend, I was sixteen, seventeen, eighteen and I had an illegitimate son. I started having a baby [with] my boyfriend. I don't mean he was a sex maniac either; I had sex once with him on the Thursday night and it was I think it was 23 August and that would have been 1956 and my son was born on 19 May in 1957.

Well, during that, course he knew I was having a baby and he was in a funny position because he didn't like work and he wouldn't get a job in Trafford Park; and he used to repair a man's car and the man was called Mr Rose, he helped him in the garage, and he used to like a little bet. I think that is how he ticked over all week.

So, I was having this baby and then, I think it was over the Christmas time, I walked in a pub and he was stuck in the corner, and when he seen me go in with my friend Margaret and her cousin Marie and her husband, he run in the corner like a rat. He was with this woman and that was the minute I fell out with him.

And I had this son of his and when the son was born he was interested, he gave me money, he bought me the baby's clothes and things like that; he was a kind-hearted Pisces but I was never the same with him after.

When my son was one, I got put in an unmarried mothers' home for three months, 'cause my mother wouldn't have me in the house having a baby.

I was visited by somebody from the town hall called Mrs Pennington, a great big, stout woman, very official and she said, 'You can't have this child adopted because two white people don't want a half-caste child.' I think that was a term that I can't stand and then, 'Two black people won't want a coloured child, a half-white one.'

That was her excuse. 'So it can't go, it can't be adopted.' But the next thing that can happen is she says, 'You can send him to Dr Barnardos.' So I said, 'Oh, well where is Dr Barnardos?' 'Oh, it's right near London, down south somewhere.' When she told me that I thought, 'Well, I won't be able to see much of him down there.' So everything was stopped.

So, I thought I am not having him adopted; I am going to have him, I am going to get myself a little room somewhere, I will pay the rent because the social was giving you nothing in them days only seven [shillings] and six [pence]. And I thought I will put him in a nursery and I will go to work.

But my father stepped in and said, 'No you are not going in no room, you can come home.' Well, at the time I said, 'Come home? Well, what about the neighbours?' And my mother said, 'Well, bugger the neighbours.'

You see, that is what people worried about in them days, the neighbours. What would the neighbours think? My mother said, 'Oh bugger the bloody neighbours, who do they think they are?'

So my mother changed her tune when the child was born, and my mother brought him up really, because I then married a white guy and come living here.

And my dad said when I got married, 'I don't think you had better take him [the child] with you, you can leave him here.' And I had to do what my father said in them days and I left him there, but I was only round the corner so I was still involved with his life.

Soon Come

Of all the stories I heard when conducting these interviews, the tales of the children left behind temporarily in the West Indies were the most poignant and pitiful. They were nicknamed 'barrel children' after the fact that their parents in England would, once or twice a year, send back barrels of clothing and gifts to them in the West Indies. Growing up in Luton I'd heard such tales and been a little mystified. Who would leave a child 4,000 miles away? I asked the same question when I listened to interviewees remembering their younger selves, alone in the West Indies, staring up at airplanes crossing the sky, wondering if one of them would be bringing their parents back to them.

Claudette Crawford-Brown, a sociologist at the University of the West Indies who coined the phrase 'barrel child', argues that, 'It's not that Caribbean mothers are wicked and cruel ... [rather] they are simply forced to make a choice between satisfying their children's material needs or their emotional needs.'[1]

Crawford-Brown focused on the relationship between mother and child. But all my interviewees who'd been the parents of barrel children, both mothers and fathers, were troubled by my questions and seemed burdened, to some degree, with a sense of guilt about the past. Listening to Rena Khublall, who managed to send for her three children after five years, it was clear that, decades later, she still regretted the decision to leave the children and grieved over the loss of those five years.

There are no government statistics on the number of barrel children but every other person I interviewed had a connection with such a child.

The stories told to me were strikingly similar. The parents came to the UK in the 1950s or 1960s but could not initially afford to bring the child with them. The child was left behind with relatives, usually in the care of grandparents. After a while, years later, the parents would feel sufficiently established and could now afford to send for the child or children. But there were emotional complications.

The children left behind were often infants and, with time, forged strong attachments to their grandparents; as far as the children were concerned these elders were their real parents. When they were sent for, there was much anxiety, both for the children and grandparents, who were now bereft.

When these barrel children arrived in Britain, both they and their actual parents found it difficult to bond. The barrel children had been traumatised initially by the separation. In the intervening years before their reunion, their parents had sometimes had more children in England. The reunions were always emotional. Often the barrel children were lovingly embraced. But there were many times when they were rejected or felt ostracised. Great tensions arose in the family and some even split up as a consequence.

★

Franklin Jackson

Our parents leave us with relatives in Jamaica when they come here. There was two of us at her house, two at another house and one in somebody else's, all in the district. That was how everybody used to do it. The lady I stayed with, even though she didn't treat us right when our clothes came and things like that, she wasn't bad, she was OK. One of the chappy my brother stayed with, he didn't like him much. When my parents wrote, my aunt would read the letters to us. But when they sent parcels to us, clothes or shoes, it was so wrong; my aunt would have her children in the room sort out what they wanted first and then give what was left over. They always got the first pick, and the best.

My daddy came [to England] in 1960 and my mother came in 1962 or 1963. I went to the airport to see her off. We rode on this lorry to see my mother off and I used to cry for everything, so I cried my eyes out to see her going on this plane. It was a likkle bit like, 'When am I going to see her again? When am I going to go to England?' I just wanted to find out how quick I was going to get to England.

I was twelve when my mother came up so I was a big boy and she said she was going to send for us soon. And in 1965, at the age of fifteen, my parents sent a ticket for me and I was told I'm going to England. My cousin was bringing me up. I was the first one because I was the eldest.

When they wrote to say I had a plane ticket and would be coming to join my parents in England, I ran all around my district and tell everyone I knew, that's what I did, I don't think I stopped running. I went to every one of my friend's house. They would all have been envious or jealous of me coming to England, of course.

Because I never seen a plane before, I was scared. These bigger boys told me, 'When you go to England on that plane, if a bird shit on the plane it will crash,' and I came to England with my heart in my mouth!

It was nice to join my parents. In those days there wasn't much emotion, most of them did not deal with emotion; they did not come from a place where there was much emotion. Even my mother, she wasn't one to tell us that she love us and thing like that. We know they love us, we know. It wasn't like today where, even me on the phone with my children, it's, 'Love you, love you.' It wasn't something we did, but that's how it was in those days.

As my mother reminded me, I never let her rest a day without asking her when she's going to send for my brothers and sisters. I came up in 1965 and they got here by 1968. So it wasn't too bad, because they had to save up that money. Because I was the eldest they sent for me first, because if they leave it too long it would be harder to get me up, and it made sense because, over here, they had two children since they left me in Jamaica.

So it would make sense to have me up, because I could help look after the young ones. When my parents go to work in the morning, I used to get up in the morning, bathe them, dress them, take them to nursery, take them home, cook for their dinner, keep them at home until their mammy comes home.

Everine Shand

I was always excited when the parcels came ... it was clothes and shoes and ribbons for your hair. We received barrels too, but that was mainly with food. Because we had our own farm, we didn't need as much.

My cousins' parents were also in England, so we all used to sit on top of the hill and watch the ships coming in. We'd just sit there, saying, 'Oh my gosh, I wonder if my parents are on this ship' or 'I want to go to England on that' or 'I wonder if that's where I'm going to be travelling to England, if I do go.'

I knew [my mother, Vera] was in England because I'd hear family talking about the money coming from [there]. My mother didn't think toys were important. So my aunt used to use that against me because she didn't like my mother, saying things like, 'Look at that ugly dress your mum sent, and look at [your cousin's] beautiful dress.' I never thought my things were good enough.

When I arrive [England] was cold, miserable and dark [and I was] stuck in a house with eight people, having to share a bed with a woman that [I'd] never met in [my] life'.

At school [in West Bromwich], I didn't understand them and they didn't understand me. The teachers felt that I was cheating somehow [because] I was this little black Jamaican girl who could do the work.

My mother didn't accept me, had no maternal instincts, I don't even remember her hugging me when she saw me at the airport.

Marjorie Price

Well, I was born in Antigua, but I don't know if you know about this little Island, Barbuda. My mother came from there, so I'm a mixture of both, and I understand that I was given to my grandparents at age six months. I don't know why, my mother was married at a very young age, I'm told. I suppose my mother might have been experiencing difficulty. And I went there to live with them on the island of Barbuda.

Absolutely fantastic, blissful childhood I had. Everything organic, everybody grew their own, and you shared. If you had fish you would share it, and people would give you vegetables, whatever. And I remember as a child going along to the seaside with my uncles with a broomstick and a nail and, as a fish swim by, used to stick it. And going into the bit of wild that was there to get wild boar for food. I went along with my uncle, and when the wild boar was approaching, he would lift me up and put me in a tree. I remember those things as clear as yesterday.

I also had great-grandparents. My grandmother's mother was alive. I remember the first time I saw her was the night before she died. In those days you were buried the same day because there was no facility to keep bodies. And I remember all the men in the village came, and they got the timber and made a coffin; and something I always remember, every child would be lifted over my great-grandma's coffin. All can say is it must have been some old, ancient rituals, but I don't know what it meant.

My father, Sidney, was a merchant seaman. The marriage between my mother and father did not last but he remained devoted to her, he worshipped her. On the other hand, I don't think she ever felt the same.

My mother remarried. My father used to come to Antigua from time to time. And I remember him coming home, I think I was fourteen then, and he said, 'I'm going to take my children.' This was me and my brother.

And my brother says to him, 'Take my sister first, because she's a girl.' I think he thought I needed protection, but from what, I don't know. I don't think there was child abuse, I don't think so; people weren't going down those roads, unlike now, you would probably have to think twice.

It was sad separating from my mother but then, you didn't have a choice. It took you a while but I suppose when you are a child you don't even know what your emotions are. Sometimes I did have longings, because I looked back at Antigua and I remembered going to school and having friends.

I had to have a chaperone to bring me to England. She was a lady who he paid to bring me here, her name was Barbara and in those days it took two whole weeks by ship. I was wearing ordinary Caribbean clothes and you come to England and, wow! It was June. I remember the ship was an English ship, it was called SS *Herbert*. All the sailors on there were English and the captain, and everything was done in the English way. Everything was done to time.

S. Victor

We had a large family, but they were in Jamaica. Early in the 1960s I went home [from Britain] to see my children as well as give birth to the seventh one. I was disappointed with the way in which my children were being looked after. My husband and I worked hard over here and sent money regularly to the person who was looking after them. But I was disappointed.

From St Elizabeth I wrote a letter to my husband and told him that all of us were coming over to join him. I told him in no uncertain terms that I was not about to leave any of them behind and go anywhere. Just like how a scorpion carries all her babies on her back. I was prepared to do the same. So whether he had any money or not, he was to arrange for us to come up and find a suitable house for us to live in. He did. That was in Fallowfield [Manchester] in 1964.

Stephen Marks

When I came here in 1960 I left behind a woman who I was living with. We had six children but two had died at birth. But I also had five other girlfriends. I thought about sending for the one that I had children with so that we could perhaps get married over here. In those days you needed a wife and there was pressure to get one. I chose not to send for her. Instead I got married and settled down with another Jamaican woman who I met right here in Manchester. I forgot about the ones in Jamaica, although I still continued to support my children out there by sending money to my mother who would pass it on to them.

Pauline Clark

[My aunt] had eleven children [six have never left Jamaica, but five were born over here] and she needed her husband to play his father-figure role. But that was not to be. He showed no interest, affection or love to neither his wife nor their children. That household was the exact opposite of ours, absolutely no family atmosphere whatsoever. There was a complete lack of guidelines for the children to follow, no parental support – even the matter of talking to the children was not there … As a result, as children they grew up without having had any respect for their parents. Now that my aunt is widowed she is bearing the brunt of it. They have no manners and as far as they are concerned she is just another woman. The sad thing about it is that this behaviour has passed on to the next generation.

Viv Adams

When it came down to the last two boys in the family, because [my older brother] Bertram was the last one to go off and then become a seaman. [My brother] Percy and I were the last two and it wasn't quite clear what was supposed to happen to us. All I was conscious of was that we wouldn't be left behind. Because to be left behind was to be abandoned to a fate worse than death. We lived in dreams of the day when salvation would come. One night we went and stayed with [our other brother] Ramon, whose ship had come into port and Percy and I visited him. There reached a point when the ship had to leave Kingston harbour and go out to anchor before they could return and Ramon said, 'Just stay in the cabin, don't say anything, they're not going to know, you're just getting a little ride.' I remember being excited by the prospect that maybe Ramon had pulled a flanker and Percy and I could sail away as stowaways aboard the ship. I remember coming on deck and seeing the inky blackness of the night and hearing the chunk chunk chunk of the screws in the boat, and thinking, 'This is really happening.' I had no inkling of what would happen if Ramon had indeed arranged for some illegal transit for us. He hadn't. Eventually, later in the evening, the ship returned to port.

We were left for a year and we were anxious. But we were also kind of prepared.

My mother wrote to us, but it was just a by-product of the ongoing conscious debate that 'soon come', hang on a little more, so as a child you just put up with that.

Ramon was doing all kinds of things, saving money, the flight was quite a lot of money. You didn't need visas because we were British people. Going from Jamaica to Britain was like going from London to Manchester; you just got on the plane, you're gone. It came that he had managed to find the flights for us and he said, 'Don't bother with no clothes from Jamaica because that's just going to make you look stupid in England, just come as you are.' He had a great coat, a double-breasted trench coat, a coat for a grown man, like the actor George Sanders or someone; so Percy, a sixteen-year-old boy, had to wear this long coat down to his ankles, because we were coming in March, but it was anticipated that it was going to still be cold. I had a duffle coat. We arrived on the 24 March 1962.

Owen Townsend

I was born in 1950 in Jamaica, Westmoreland. My mother was a seamstress and my father was a carpenter and builder I came to the UK in 1965. I came to join my mother and father and my younger sister, she came a few years before me. So I was fifteen when I came to England. I have no memory of my mother in Jamaica. My father came to Jamaica in 1963 and that is the first memory I have of him, when I was thirteen. I have no clear memory of my mother and that means she must have left when I was quite young. I've never checked when she left, it's the first time I've ever thought about it really. My grandparents brought me up, my mother's parents, in the country. I love the country, I still love the countryside, and I've been living in cities since I was about thirteen when I went to Kingston to live, a couple of years before I came here. City life and country life are so different. It was a revelation when I went to Kingston, but still, I have this hankering for the countryside, still to this day really.

They decided to bring us to England to join them; like most immigrants did, you bring your children once you've settled and have somewhere for them. Typical West Indian parents bringing their kids over. Really I met my mother when I was fifteen. It's a massive gap there. I identify my grandmother and grandfather as my parents. It was strange [when I came over] because I think my mother's memory of me was as a baby. I was a child in Jamaica, and when I came as a fifteen year old. A teenager in the fifties in Jamaica, you're a man – especially in the country, because you have a lot of responsibilities. So I came here like a young adult really. I wasn't living with them very long, a couple of years, I think it was, before I started living on my own.

Rena Khublall

When I was leaving Guiana, my mother and my brothers came with me to the airport, the whole family, everybody came with me to the airport. The three boys stayed with my mum. I was thinking what a dreadful decision I made, what a decision to have to leave my young children behind and come away. I didn't think of myself, I thought what of their lives, what's it going to be like? My mum was my rock, and my brothers and my sisters, they looked after the boys for me. I cried all the way, when I got to England I was hoarse. I cried and cried and cried.

It was hard, it took me a while to get used to it, but afterwards you get used to it. We were working towards the children. I always had that in mind. Whatever I'm doing, I've got to do, and get the children as quickly as possible.

My main thoughts were with the children, only worrying about them. We got on with it and did what we had to do. It took us five years and all three came together. The eldest [David] was nine, Martin was seven, and Moses was five.

We were separated for five years. When the boys came it was touch and go to get them to ... it was five years, of course they don't know me that much. They know I'm their mum, they know me as mum – my eldest one used to write me letters – and they know that mum was here, mum and dad's here. But when the children got here it was completely different, they didn't know how to approach us or how I will be towards them. All I did was I cuddled them up, hugged them up. I've got photographs of that.

David Khublall

We were strangers to the youngest, he rebelled; when she held him he said, 'Leave me rass! Leave me rass!' Because his mother was his grandmother.

Rena Khublall

He loved his grandmother, my mum, because she spoiled him rotten because he was the baby. Over the few weeks, couple of days, they were OK. They had parties, and the only friend they had was my nephew, whereas at home they have all the other nieces and nephews, and they missed them terribly.

David Khublall

Their mum missed them for the time they were still in Guyana, very much.

Rena Khublall

I wished I was there with them. Even until now I wish it hadn't happened. I missed those years; I wish I could turn back the clock to those five years. I missed them – that emptiness is there – I wasn't with them for that growing up period of time, I really miss that. So what I do now, I try to make up.

Francis Williams

When my daughter came here to live with me, she was a bit stand-offish. She never called me mom, she called me aunty, because she said her mom was back in Jamaica. It started when she was in Jamaica. Every week I'd write to my mom to find out how my daughter was getting on, and how she was progressing in school. In every letter I always would say, 'I am your mom.' And you know, when she answered me back she would say 'My mom is here with me in Jamaica.' I said, 'Oh, what have I done?' So, I said to myself, 'OK then we'll see.' When she came to live with me here, I used to give her a lot of loving. I used to hug her up and say to her, 'I am your Mummy.' Eventually she changed and started calling me mommy.

June Wood

When I got here I just cried. When it was going into the winter and it was going to snow, I cried some more. I'd never forget that. It felt like living with a stranger, it was starting all over again. My brother and I wanted to go back to Jamaica because we missed our grandparents. They were kind to us. They were the only people I knew from when I was a child. I tried absconding from home many times, but I got into trouble for running away ... One time she got the police to find me. I didn't know how my mother felt at the time. Just looking at her I knew she was strict.

Vanley Burke

My mother left to come to England when I was about three years old. She came to study to be a nurse and I stayed behind. My family is a little complicated. My grandparents, Beulah and Mordecai Burke, who I grew up with; my grandfather was a very gentle man, but he was very strict in his own way – but he wasn't a brutal person in any shape or form. He, amongst others, prior to coming to England, would go to America to do farm working picking crops, oranges, pineapples. These contracts were normally for about six months and after that time they would return, having improved their lot with a little bit of an American twang and sometimes new American clothes and things like that. Although I didn't see him dress like that or speaking, but there were quite a few people who used the opportunity to improve their status. My grandmother she was a lovely lady; I spent a lot of time with her. She had become my mother by then so my reference to her would be 'Mamma' and my mother I would refer to as 'sister', because I spent all my time with my grandmother. She's a devoted Christian and pretty hard-working in the house there.

We shared a house – we called it a yard – with other members of the family. It was in the strictest sense of the word a compound like you would see in Africa, but it was little houses, and we would refer to each other as the top house and the bottom house and the other one would be where other family members would live, cousins and the extended family as well and, even if they might not live there, they would visit daily and so other members of the family were involved in bringing you up.

Later in 1960 my grandparents, who I was living with, came to join her in England and I moved to live with an aunt of mine a few miles away.

At that point I was an only child. I have never met my father. As a young person what would happen was that you would eavesdrop on conversations coming from abroad, because you were really never included in these conversations and so you would pick up little stories to find out what was happening and rarely did they write to you. You'd get Christmas presents and things like that in the post, but you wouldn't really get a letter to say exactly what was happening in England so you'd eavesdrop on conversations and I heard that my mother had gotten married and at a later time I saw the wedding photographs, which was the first time I sort of physically seen my mother – strangely enough, in a photograph.

Carol Sydney

I was nine and I remember going to Port Antonio [Jamaica] to see her off because so many people went to see them off and we drove down to Port Antonio and she got on this, I think it was a banana boat, as the main thing they were carrying was bananas, but there was a few passengers as well. And then she came here [England] and she went into nursing and eventually she moved to Grays [Essex], which is where I joined her. I think I understood a certain amount – that she was looking for a better life and the idea was that she would send for me as soon as she got settled, but obviously this didn't happen overnight ...

Eventually, you get this letter to say, 'Yes, I've got somewhere, I'm settled and you can come and join me.' And of course you're all excited. I don't really know [how my grandparents felt]. Think they were pleased for me. Maybe sad that I was leaving, even though another cousin of mine was there [Jamaica] – they were looking after them as well – so it wasn't that they were going to be left entirely on their own.

Don Letts

Me and my brother were born here. My father brought over his son – previous son on his side – and my mother did the same – she brought over a son from her previous relationship – and, man, they got a rough deal.

Derek came over in his early teens, so at that age, where he's turning into a teenager. Anyway, so that immediately goes fucking pear-shaped and he's vibing on American soul; he was into the mod thing, polo neck, Cuban-heeled boots and he used to go to the Ram Jam club in Brixton, but he was of the generation that was still looking to America for tips – because there was no perceived cultural depth to Jamaican culture then, they were always looking somewhere else. So he's doing the soul boy thing. He was not my parents' kid between them, and the advent of music coming into his life, fashion, style and girls – collision course; he left home about fifteen or sixteen years.

Then Desmond, the one underneath him, one day cops bring him home; he'd just been caught with his mates in the West End. Some of them had been stealing, but he wasn't, so they wanted to give him a ticking off. Mum said, 'He ain't coming in this house; take him away.' She banished him from the house for ten years; the police had come to the house and shamed her. My mum was hardcore. That was her biological son. They would have been twelve-ish when they came over.

Jennifer Campbell

I was born in Kingston, Jamaica and I arrived in the UK aged fourteen; my brother came about three years later. My parents were here since I was about two. So eventually I got the chance to come and join them. My brother and myself had been separated from them for those twelve years. We were brought up by my grandmother, she was good to us, so we just had to accept where we were. We just knew our parents were in England and we used to get barrels every year, they send clothes for us.

So that was my dad came to England when I was about two and then a year later he send for my mum. We were left with our grandmother in the St James parish in a village called Malden. I had a happy childhood. Even though my brother and I were together, up to a point we got separate because he went to his grandfather and I stayed with my grandmother, my father's mother, so we separated. Call it different grandparents. Jamaican families are difficult, complicated, let's not go into it … I was kind of sad and I was kind of happy when I heard I was coming to England, because I would miss my grandmother; she'd be on her own, she'd have no one else to help her because it was just her and me. But then I wanted to meet my parents because I only met my father once, just when he came back to sort my papers out when I was thirteen. I never met my mother at all. All I had was a picture of the marriage, and that was when I was about two or three I got that. That's the only picture I had of them …

I travelled by plane. It was the first time I'd been on a plane. It was exciting and I had a full three seats for myself, stretched out, the air hostess looked out for me … My arrival, though, was not very good. I don't know if she [my mother] knew how to show emotions, but all she did was just fling me a cardigan like this, that was it, and she just didn't appear very friendly at all, or loving or motherly, nothing like that.

I don't think it was her idea to send for me; I think it was my father's main idea. It wasn't a very good atmosphere or surroundings, it wasn't good to be in. I just wanted to go back to Jamaica because I was happy there. It was a week later I wanted to go back but I stuck it out for two years. My parents already had another child from the time they was here and he was ten. I used to do most things for him because he wasn't taught to do things for himself. I was like a second mother now, I didn't mind. School wasn't arranged for me at all. When I came here nothing was organised. I was home for nine months without going to school, without any kind of education things at all.

My first impression was that everything was so narrow, all the corridors, and I felt so squashed and that feeling never leave me.

My mother used to expect me to do everything in the house and they used to beat me a lot. And then one day I was seventeen, I just picked up a plastic bag, carrier bag, put some clothes in it and left.

Ken Morgan

I was born in 1950 in Clarendon, Jamaica. My story is a kind of reverse of the 'soon come' situation. My mother had five children and Jamaica was a tough place back then. My father was in Britain, a couple of my aunts and so on were in England, and when I was nine years old one of them sent for me. A lot of people put the money together for the fare; it's family. I didn't stay with my father because they had this thing with children, I had to stay with a woman, so I had to stay with my aunt. She didn't have any children; she wanted me to complete their family kind of thing and take some pressure off my mother, supposedly to offer opportunities to another generation.

Jamaicans are usually located like Dalston, Hackney, Clapton, Stoke Newington. We rented premises in all those places, moved around about. My father was living in Clapton. I would only visit him from time to time at weekends; I would go and check him out.

I didn't go back. I was British. I had a British passport. It's Jamaica; we export people. We export sugar, we export rum, we export bauxite, but we export people. You find Jamaicans in every corner. It's a small country, population less than three million. We export people. If there are no jobs here [in Jamaica] it creates a lot of problems. It creates violence. Nobody says it that way but that's exactly the reality, and family here help family.

Armet Francis

I never met my father. My mother [Dorette] left when I was three so I grew up with my grandparents and the children of my mother's siblings. They [the adults] all left more or less at the same time after the Second World War. They migrated to England. So, the grandchildren, if there were any, were left behind and so were the women. My mother was slightly different in that she came to England.

I had a cousin whose mother lived in the area but was staying with my grandparents, so there were two of us [children] in that specific house but there were cousins all around.

I had to help my granny because all her kids had left ... I was a farm hand. I learned a lot about how to plant things and how to nurture them etc. It was a tough environment for a kid in the sense that we were farmers. Farmers are a tough old bunch, things like: you're barefoot, you're up at five in the morning. It was a farm but for me it was school.

I think I missed my mother – from the age of three, I missed her. Because all my cousins were somewhere else there was that small unit where you could be quite lonely. You wake up in the middle of the night and think about darkness; it's a very frightening thing for a child [and experiencing a hurricane] ... you have to grow up fast.

My grandparents were very strict. My grandfather ran a dry goods and rum shop and he was quite prominent in that community. I was five or six when my grandfather taught me how to roll tobacco leaves ...

There's a picture of myself, my grandfather and grandmother; someone [a travelling salesman] was passing through and they had a camera and they took a picture so that they could send it to my mother in England.

Everybody left. So all the things that my grandparents planned had gone. So what are you left with? It's a bit sad, I think. You're [grandparents] doing this [working hard] for your kids ... This was the whole community – the people who migrated.

I think, because my mother had gone somewhere else and my uncles had gone somewhere else, it gave me the feeling that I also wanted to be somewhere else ... If I got a good beating from my granny I would say, 'I want to go to see Mum,' and so I'd get a bigger beating after I said something like that or, 'You ain't my Mum anyway!' I used to run up trees. It was just enough as she couldn't go up there and I knew how to get up there really fast. But she'd break a bit of a twig and put it down at the bottom and said, 'When you're ready to come down bring it.'

It took seven years before [my mum] could send for me. I didn't recognise my mother [when I arrived with a guardian]. I had this idea in my head because I'd only seen a picture of her. The first thing I realised was that I didn't know anybody and then my guardian left. Obviously she knew my mother. So I didn't have long to work it out, but then I realised she was a complete stranger; and the second thing I realised was that everyone was a complete stranger. I didn't know anybody. And probably the hardest thing for a child to do is to work out who do you trust and how do you make sure that nobody knows that's what you're thinking.

The last time [my mother] saw me I was three. I don't think we ever really bonded; I had bonded with my granny, I had to. So I always compared her to my grandmother because we didn't have that shared identity.

My brother [who was five years younger] was born here so all his sensibilities are here, whereas I was born in Jamaica so I would always start to question, but he would just accept and everything that had happened to him. Me I would go, 'Why are you doing that?' I'd get into fights all the time.

You don't write to a five-year-old so I didn't know I had a brother. And, apparently, my grandmother didn't want me to come. She didn't want me to leave her. But my mother didn't tell me [about my brother] and it's probably why it took so long to get me here because, in a funny way, once I left, there was nobody, as granny considered me to be her last child, so she didn't want me to leave.

Here to Stay: At Home and At Play

Ethlyn had a number of wonderful phrases that she'd brought over with her from Jamaica. One of my favourites was: 'Whilst the grass is growing the horse is starving.' Applied to the immigrant ideals of 'working some money' (to save and prosper), it meant that, whilst it was sensible to save up for a better future, it was also necessary to pay attention to how you lived in the present. West Indians took this notion to heart in investing in their homes, especially in their front rooms.

Our front room was the room on which care and money were lavished. All the other rooms were tired-looking, the lino was cracked, the wallpaper scuffed, the furniture – bought for its cheapness – was perfunctory. But the front room was special. It was never a living room, more of a show room to display acquisitions to friends, a temple to my father's vanity and need – in this three-bedroomed house with seven kids – to have a room of his own. The front room was often out-of-bounds for the children (at least while the fathers were in the house). Every West Indian seemed obliged to surrender to the allure of 'doing up' the front room. As a child, Don Letts found it particularly strange: 'My parents weren't even sociable, I don't think they used the room more than four times a year.'

All of my parents' West Indian friends shared an uncanny aesthetic sensibility. Their front rooms were decorated in ways that were almost identical, as if some wholesaler had managed to offload a job-lot of glass fish and doilies.

In a sense, the front room was the West Indian equivalent to the Victorian parlour. As Michael McMillan showed in his installation and book, 'The West Indian Front Room', the pride of these aspiring migrants, in having come to England and bettered themselves, was often reflected in the decor of the front room. Floral wallpaper was ubiquitous, as was the drinks trolley with its plastic pineapple ice bucket. No front room was complete without a Blue Spot radiogram and expensive three-piece suite (usually bought via HP) which, years after delivery, still retained the protective plastic covers.

There was no point having a drinks trolley, of course, without guests to entertain. The front room as a place to socialise was a hangover from the West Indies.

There were no pubs in the West Indies; people drank at home. If you wanted to drink out-of-doors you might go and perch on a stool at the rum shop. So when West Indians came to Britain, pubs were not just alien, but the culture associated with them was odd. You couldn't go to a pub and ask for a bottle of rum and proceed to share it, as you would do in a rum shop, with your friends. In any event, pubs were not welcoming. So West Indians, who were effectively barred from pubs and other social clubs, tended to socialise among themselves.

A feature in the *West Indian Gazette* in November 1960 defended West Indians against complaints that they were noisy, arguing in mitigation: 'We have almost no facilities for recreation; no halls of our own, no club premises where games may be played. The fight for integration is often too gradual, leaving us no choice when not at work to either sleep or play the gram. Our voices are soft and we must learn to mute our melody while going forward.'

Blues parties (where Bluebeat records featuring ska music such as Prince Buster's 'Oh Carolina' and Derrick Morgan's 'Don't You Know' were often favoured) would be held, first in front rooms cleared of furniture and later in cellars and hired spaces. These impromptu social gatherings were initially free – with people bringing their own booze. By the mid-1950s, as the numbers of venues and those attending them had swelled, a charge might be levied on the door. Ultimately, investments in front rooms, blues parties and West Indian-run social clubs were all signs that the migrants were settling in the Motherland. West Indians were here to stay.

★

Mavis Stewart

It [the front room] was so special to a West Indian, because we were used to that small likkle room, and when you'll get a different room that you could put things in and entertain people, it was a big achievement for us. When your friends come along you want them to say, 'Oh look at those lovely plates. Look at those cups and saucers; oh, she's earning some loads of money.' Some people, if you go on holiday and you buy that black scroll, you would fold it and put it away, but not a West Indian. They put it on the wall to show people that 'I have been to Hastings, I have been to Bognor Regis, I have been to Margate, I have been to Paris' – especially one from Paris – they put it in the front. 'Oh this is my daughter.' 'Oh this is my granddaughter.' 'This is my mother.' 'This is when I get married' ... But they're all on the walls, sticking all around the wall.

The front room is a very, very special place. It's a place for socialising, eating and drinking. We also played music and we dance. It can also be a dangerous room where you do all the plotting and the gossip.

Linda Small

But that time it wasn't a lot of people. A lot of people were still living in their one room, so it was a bit posh. It was gorgeous, because when you rent a room you're lucky if you get two chair. Once I get my three-piece settee, you couldn't stop me. My living room start looking lovely and the more I come and see stuff I would buy it.

Friends came round and I could entertain them and open up the Stones ginger wine and some illegal Yankee whiskey. And we played Bluebeat music on the 'Blue Spot' radiogram and from anyone coming from 'home' is only two things we wanted from them: rum and records.

My favourite thing in the front room is like my favourite picture, is my religious pictures. Crochet on the table, crochet on the coffee table ... Every little thing.

All the girls at work, every time they see me at dinnertime and they would say, 'Could you make me a set for the dressing table, for our coffee table?' I was so busy making for other people that I had never had much for myself.

The traditional front room, like we older generation, we're going to die off. I mean, when I go, these are going in the skip. My two daughter front room is just basic – just settee, television a coffee table and they call my place clutter; [theirs] it looks so empty.

Michael McMillan

I grew up learning that 'cleanliness is next to godliness' and that, no matter how poor we were, if the front room looked good then we were respectable. While as children we weren't normally allowed into the front room unless there were guests, Sundays were an exception because it would have been ritually cleaned in readiness for some unknown visitor. Air freshener and furniture polish would mask the smell of the paraffin heater coming from the passage and big people would be chatting in the front room over the mellow voice of Jim Reeves crackling from the radiogram.

Mum would invite me in to meet a relative who I had never met before, who would tell me how big I had got. I would get mum two rarely used gold-rimmed glasses amongst many from the glass cabinet. Then I would wheel over the drinks trolley, from which she took her favourite drink, a bottle of Stone's ginger wine and ice from the plastic pineapple ice bucket. I'd sit down obediently on the settee, plastic-covered to protect the upholstery, the plastic sticking to me skin.

Bored, I would stare at a picture of a blue-eyed Jesus in 'The Last Supper' on patterned floral wallpaper or notice a fly fooled by plastic flowers and colourful crochet on a fake marble coffee table. The sun shines through the pressed lace curtains and I'm about to fall asleep when I overhear, 'I don't know why she marry him' and I am ordered out of the front room to check on the rice and peas cooking in the kitchen.[1]

Don Letts

Every Jamaican had a front room, locked off; my parents weren't even sociable, I don't think they used the room more than four times a year, and there's four boys in one room! There's this room, with nice carpet, the whole sofa, Queen on the wall, the ultimate sixties kitsch, and we were never allowed to use it. It's a pride thing; you have your front room, cabinets with glass doors with the glasses and saucers and plates that no one ever used, and the doily and the blown glass animals, and they were the status symbols of 'I've made it'. And it's funny they want to show off to their mates, 'I've made it', but they never had any mates over. They had their bar and their radiogram. They were small things but they meant a lot to my parents' generation.

Sue Brown

You had the Blue Spot radiogram; every black house had a Blue Spot playing forty-fives, playing the country and western crooner Jim Reeves, 'Welcome to my world', forty-fives, thirty-threes and seventy-eights. Jim Reeves was a good singer, one of the best.[2]

But I didn't know he was white, Jim Reeves, I remember the first time I was at home and I saw the album cover and I saw this white man and it just didn't compute, because I always heard the music all the time. I suppose it was very Christian-based.

Michael McMillan

The type of music played on the radiogram depended on what the front room was being used for ... on a Sunday, it was common to hear Jim Reeves and other religious-inspired music or a sermon broadcast on the radio.

I think the appeal of 'Gentleman Jim' lies not so much in the style of his 'silky smooth' ballads, but rather their content. In 'Distant Drums', for instance, he sings about transcending the trials and tribulations of everyday life in recurring themes of loneliness, love, infidelity and loss. And this echoes the intense desire and longing to go beyond the misery of oppression expressed through the hymns, spirituals and gospel music of the black church.

Carol Tulloch

I grew up in Doncaster and my father was a miner who, like many of the people we knew, had used the pardner hand to save for a deposit for a house or rented out rooms to each other. As a consequence a close-knit social network emerged. The care and attention for the home and how they chose furniture for the front room ran counter to the negative social representations of West Indians during the 1950s and 1960s. My father shares a philosophy with the white working class, which was that you should buy the best you could afford for the home because it meant longevity.

In our front room was a 1920s styled plastic cream telephone with a receiver on top – the kind Mae West would have used in her boudoir, my mum had on display on the radiogram. It didn't actually work because my dad had bought it for me as a toy and afterwards it had hung around the house and eventually found its way into the front room.

Sybil Campbell

A friend of a friend got me my room and it was easy to make friends. There were loads of house parties. You had ska, twist and

Bluebeats. Cars would pull up to you and they would ask if you were looking for a party and you'd say yes and they'd take you out and bring you back, with no strings attached. You were drinking your cherry B, VP wine – you'd get up with a headache but you'd still go to work!

John Fraser

In the West Indies pubs are only for social outcasts. The home is always the centre for social contact and that is where the West Indian does his drinking. Parties from 9 p.m. to 5 a.m., which upset the neighbours so much in Brixton, are normal behaviour for him. So are the juke boxes and calypsos.

Roy Hackett

We had a bloke called Owen Henry who had a radiogram and every Saturday night or Friday night we would buy up wine and beer and we meet at houses – 'cause those were the days that pubs shut, really shut at ten o'clock – and we had a jolly good time, but actually, you know, we always been stopped by the police. And at one stage Henry got arrested for that which is very unfortunate.

David Wheeler

There was one particular house in Bramley Road that a lot of coloured people lived. I say coloured, they were West Indians but I don't know from what island, and people were having parties every night, and lots of women going in and out and people were getting generally fed up. If music is played loud and it comes through the walls of my home, that's an infringement of my liberty.

George Mangar

All black people's houses have what we call a Blue Spot in it ... a radiogram. It was made in Germany; we all had one. Friday nights anybody who had a party, the neighbours – really in our country, they wouldn't have needed to be invited to come, but just come, you don't invite them. Here, you have to invite them, so half of them, nine o'clock, they call the police. Police come, knock knock, 'Can you turn it down?' 'No, why?' 'You're making a noise; the neighbours complained.' 'No; come and listen.' The police come inside, you give them a rum and coke; that's the God's honest truth; they come and have more fun than the next-door neighbour!

James Berry

When my friends and I went out socially to big public dances we sometimes found it hard to get a dance. If one girl refused you, all the others refused you too, and you got avoided and looked at sideways. So, a group of friends and I came together and decided to hold our own dances with the kind of music we liked.

Tony Bullimore

I think in the sixties – the fifties and sixties – it [Bristol] was a dull city. When the pub closed it was fish and chips and off home we go. Bristolians couldn't quite understand these new people that were coming to Bristol and the Bamboo Club, which became a famous social centre for West Indian people, plus it was multiracial. Lots of people would come there and the doors were open for anyone to become a member and I would say a small percentage of the membership were Bristolians that loved the music and the way of life.

Donald Hinds

These parties were indeed noisy, robust with a tantalising touch of eroticism as bodies touched in a slow grinding mento. In the beginning drinks were free. The parties were smaller then and everybody was known to the host, and the following weekend he would be at one of his guests' party. By the end of the fifties, it no longer made economic sense to adequately provide drinks for nearly one hundred people. Most of the 'guests' would prefer a more personal choice by buying their own drinks. The temptation was great! Drinks were sold and the parties became illegal. Police raids were intensified as more and more neighbours complained about the noise next door. It seemed that if you were enjoying yourself after midnight, you were beating your wife, up to no good, indulging in illicit pleasure and generally beyond the law. The neighbour was always worried about the soul of the people next door.

Ethlyn Adams
Yes they have blues party all over, in Hitchin, Stopsley, Letchworth, sometimes up Ipswich way. I never go to no blues party. It's bull party really. All men just stand up drink rum, and plenty blue foot and Irish gal doing dem dirty dancing. Me? I never go to dem places – not a one!

Clinton Cameron
The first place I lived they were good people and I loved living with them, but they were always having parties and being very cheerful – these were Jamaicans – and that was at the time when the sound system was just being introduced in England. Back in Jamaica, in Kingston, from about Friday every week there would be trucks driving round the streets with these huge boxes of speakers – music blasting out. That was the culture then; how it was. But I couldn't stand it. Then when I arrived here, one of my housemates in Leeds (another Jamaican) decided to build some of these big boxes in the cellar. I was really very, very conscious and a bit embarrassed really that people would make all that amount of noise and not pay enough attention to the neighbours. I couldn't stand the noise so I left .... .

Alford Gardner
You had house parties for a few years. Well, one club opened, the Lamport on Chapeltown Road in Leeds where everybody went

and then another one opened, Striga Club on Roundhay Road. And I mean the Lamport especially was the in-place. Everybody went to the Lamport, everybody. Every week there was a party somewhere ... A lot of West Indians, different West Indians. Every week there was parties. Parties everywhere – house parties. You could leave from one party and go to another party, especially when Bluebeat come to England. I went to a party and somebody brought a team – Guildford Blue Beat they called it – I was the man any time you had a party; don't forget to bring the Bluebeat records. For a man who wouldn't learn history ... but nowadays I am history – to me it doesn't look like seventy years. It doesn't look like it at all. No.

Viv Adams

We knew blues parties and went to a few, but we never held any in our house, because a blues party was an illegal spontaneous event, and you'd arrange for some guys to come with a sound system and all the furniture would be cleared out and the partici-pants would turn up and somewhere in the kitchen you'd set up a little drinks counter. I always remember that the thing they used to like at that time was whisky and fruit juice and have it like a shot and these men would have these shots; and there'd be patties and curry goat and, as the evening went on and the dancing became hotter and hotter and the drink was flowing, now would come the time for the goat. It would be purchased. You'd have a little cardboard plate with a dollop of white rice and this green curry, it was a unique curry and that was very pleasurable actually. Jamaicans were not very outdoor people as far as pubs and clubs were concerned. There was no culture for it. The only thing in Jamaica was the rum bar and that was such a masculine thing, they were raw places.

The relationship between black men and white women at that time seems to me a dangerous thing, because the girls always came across as being rough, drunken harlots really. A view grew amongst us that it was only a certain kind of English girl who would do that sort of thing. There was the other kind of English girl we'd call 'Miss Anne'. She was a dowdy but safe girl who was the right side of being decent. There was nothing in-between. I think in the culture it was believed that a white girl shouldn't fraternise with West Indians so those girls who were prepared to flout those rules were the girls who were risk-takers and saw black men as doing a different kind of dance, and it attracted a certain kind of girl.

Owen Townsend

Moss Side and Hulme was a totally different place back in the sixties and seventies. Princes Road was a two-lane road and it was the centre with Alexander Road, they were the centre of this community; after 5 p.m. Manchester City Centre was a ghost town. All the action, all the fun, enjoyment, entertainment was Moss Side.

There was the Reno and the Nile, one play reggae, one play soul. You had restaurants, you had blues parties. From Brookses Bar to Princes Road, you had three or four clubs, on top of that you've got the blues dances, you've got the shebeens. A blues dance was like an occasional party, so Friday night, Saturday night. The shebeen was seven days a week, more or less twenty-four/seven. They weren't licensed, they were called illegal, but only in the sense that the drinks were sold and the tax man wasn't getting a cut; but they were the hub of the community, especially for young people like myself who were not long come from Jamaica – where now you have the internet and mobile phone, all correspondence [then] was by letter, which takes weeks to reach or telegrams and usually all they tell you is bad news. So between the parents here and Jamaica, the communication was infrequent – you can't jump on the phone and talk to your mum or your dad from Jamaica or vice versa, you lost that communication. Even though they left us young, if we had that link then it wouldn't have made us strangers really. We'd have some shared experience even if it was just over the phone, and that caused certain problems.

Back to the club scene and the party scene, that was just unbelievable. You have your house, you got your cellar or your room, you have your sound and people just come in and dance, eat food, drink beer. People follow sound.

Almost everybody had a sound and every weekend every sound is playing somewhere. After you go to the dance hall or concert hall or the Polish Club down here, various larger venues, you can go to a blues. So the sound would play at a dance and then at a blues and you could go from Friday night straight through to Sunday morning.

I've seen four blues on one street and every one is packed. I've seen coaches from Birmingham and London park outside blues as if they're going to a big dance.

People worked hard and everybody looked forward to the weekend, let off a bit of steam. It's a business as well. A house with a cellar or an attic, you can make money from it; you can run a blues and people doing hairdressing or dressmaking in the attic. So that supplement your wages so you can build a house back home or look after your family back home. You couldn't go if you were only sixteen or seventeen, you might bump into your aunt or someone; it was close-knit, everybody knew everybody.

The police used to raid them on a regular basis because technically they were illegal, but the prime reason for raiding them was to get free drinks, they'd take the drink, but people would just carry on.

Peter John Nelson

I started going to blues in my late teens. My dad was a minister, I had to be home for ten o'clock, so I used to get home for nine, and when he was asleep we'd sneak out and get back at three in the morning. We went to any blues parties that was going, and

then we started having one or two West Indian clubs like the Carib
– that was in Cheetham – and one called Ebony and there was a
beat club. I liked the Carib, because the decor inside reminded you
of the Caribbean – bamboo, palm trees all that,

The blues, that was your lifeline. And one thing with reggae,
they're singing about things that are happening at the present, so
the music were about the politics and the social condition at the
time; so by listening to the records to have an idea what's happening
in Jamaica. They played roots and culture music.

The sound systems played in the blues and the cellar parties. You'd
have an afro, and wear bell-bottom trousers, flares, and your trousers would be on your hips, and you'd have a dashiki, and African
floral shirt, that would be a roots thing. You'd have your afro and
walk down the street, 'Yeah man, I'm African.'

There was an incident when we know the police is going to raid
us and we got everyone to wee in the bottles – the whisky bottles
– and the police came and they took it all away. Oh man, that was
murder, we couldn't go on the street for weeks, the police were
mad. They were MAD!

Tommy Brogan

I do remember they would only allow usually under five black people
in a pub in town [Manchester]. After that you weren't getting any
more, no one else was getting in and you couldn't – like four guys
couldn't go as a group: they would actually have to hide around
the corner, one would go in and wait five minutes and then the
other, they would come separately.

But the Reno was like, for all the black and mixed race people,
it was like home; because a lot of the lads, when they came there
and they had never been there, it freaked them out. They had never
seen that many mixed race people together and the dads would be in
there, you just couldn't believe it. Many buckle, thinking like, 'Wow, I
never knew this existed'; they just always was on their own. So when

you went down there you must have felt like that yourself. It was like, 'Hey, there is more than one of me' – you know what I mean?

Dorothy Jasper

I was born in Manchester in 1936. My dad was originally from Liberia. He was a seaman until after the war, then he became a miner, and me mum was an insurance collector for Pearl.

[Moss Side was] bloody lovely. Because there were so many black people. There weren't that many in Cheetham Hill. African families dotted round but when you went to Moss Side you saw West Indians – because I didn't know what West Indian was – West Indians and all that. I loved it. You worked hard all week and you knew at the end you were going to Moss Side.

First club I ever went to was The Mayfair on Oxford Road. It was a West Indian club. But across the road was Frascatti's bar, a big, big bar where all black people went. Where the swimming baths is, near The Mayfair. At first we couldn't go in, because I was only seventeen and the police was always round there picking up young girls, so we used to stand outside and dance to the music.

A lot of Africans went to The Mayfair and they knew me dad, so there was no way I was getting in there, or Eva or Margaret, 'cause we were all shine girls together. They wouldn't let us in then, until we was eighteen. Shine girls or shine boys is a mixed race person; back then they didn't say that or half-caste. As soon as I was eighteen I started going in the clubs [like the Reno]. It was another world.

We were into calypso then. It was more or less all calypso and Nat King Cole and the black singers from America.

It was me, Eva, Margaret, Pearl, Doris Walker and a Maltese girl, I can never remember her name. And we all used to get dressed, we used to go up to Aunty Annie's, which was Eva's mother.

We'd all go there, get dressed and have a bottle of blue – it was a wine. A massive big bottle like that and we used to buy it between us and have a drink of that before we went out. And we all used to get sozzled and then take a blue heart out of Aunty Annie's pills! It would keep you up all night. Clubs would only open until two o'clock back then, you know. And so what we would do is go to the shabeen.

Before there was shebeens we'd come out and anybody who was having a party we'd gatecrash. 'Cause they didn't like you being there, especially if you're a shine girl. They didn't like it, 'cause most of the girls, white girls, were going with Americans, 'cause the American GIs were here then. They just didn't like you there, most white women. So we used to go and gatecrash.

And we also went to the Nile. But I can count on me hands how many times I went to the Nile. It was a place where women went ... It was like older women. Some would take their shopping with them and go in and they were there for the night, put their groceries at the side and get bladdered. One opened a tin of – I don't know whether it was dog food or cat food – and ate it 'cause she was hungry. It was very rough. Very rough.

The maxi was in then. You know the maxi skirts, the long skirt with the split up the side. Ballerina shoes, which they're wearing now. You know flat ballerina with the little bow on? Then, because you were bopping – it was kind of fading out, going into the calypso music, but you still did a bit of bopping.

You always wore a black skirt, everybody had a black tight skirt with a split up, and these like, like a Mexican top, Jane Russell blouse, just off the shoulder, here. We were out for fun and we got on very well with the men [but] you didn't go to bed with anybody. Well, we didn't. I hated being called baby and honey, you know [by American GIs], and I always liked Jamaicans.

I didn't meet [my husband] until I was nineteen so there again, in-between that little space of time, all this is what happened in that little space of time. When I met [him], I started staying in then. But he used to go out to all the blues parties every Friday and Saturday. All the men went out, you know. And women, if you were living with a guy, you stayed in. And that was it. If you went to live with a guy, you stayed in. That was the end of your going to clubs and that is the truth, that. Because most black women would think you're a slut if you were living with a man and you went out like that. If you went to live with a man, you were making up a home. You didn't go out without him. Never. But he would go out where he wanted.

Apart from the clubs we had like, blues, but you had it in the house. Blues in the front room. And they would sell drinks. Aunty Ida had a blues in the front room, she had the blues there and made a fortune.

Sonia Saunders

Augh, those dreaded house parties ... thing about the blues party and even the front room is that it was for the big people, adults. The children weren't invited. The front room was sacrosanct, a designated area marked off for our father's entertainment. It was adjoined to the living room by a connecting door and I remember that, to ensure we, the children, couldn't access it, he removed the handles from the lock so the door couldn't be opened into the front room.

Occasionally, we were dragged along to the blues parties. They only ever seemed to be in a front room, packed with people, laughing their heads off, animated talking, as if people were arguing, gold teeth on full display; and the smells, cigarette smoke, alcohol and curry goat and rice on the stove.

Mostly, I was very bored; we had to sit there for what seemed like an eternity – largely ignored by the big people, who were doing their thing. I do have an old, dog-eared black and white photo with four of my siblings at this particular blues party. I'm wearing a home-made red and white polka dot dress.

I'm squashed in a single chair with my older sister and my younger brother, slightly bewildered, sitting on her lap. On the chair beside us are my two older brothers, about eight and ten years old at the time, in stiff tweed suits – their Sunday best.

It's funny looking back, though, 'cause it does make you think that it marks something, especially as there was always talk of us going back to Jamaica, what with all the attention to the decoration of the front room and the hysteria about not missing out on blues parties, that maybe an unspoken decision had been made to stick and stay in this country.

Colonisin' Inglan in Reverse

Apart from West Indian tastes in music (reflected at blues parties) and the rituals around the treatment of hair (for men the Saturday-morning visit to the barbershop; for women the Friday-evening straightening of hair with hot copper combs in the kitchen), the expression of West Indians' Caribbean-ness seemed to revolve around food, church and cricket. Their investment in all three seemed emblematic of West Indian life.

Almost everyone I interviewed was disappointed by the blandness of what was on offer when they came to the UK, especially the food. Bert Williams had to resort to adding mustard to everything 'just to give it a little bite'. But within a decade West Indian spices had made their way to Brixton market, to stalls that had never seen their like before. The new foods included ackee and salt fish, yam, callaloo, jerk chicken, curry goat. It was only a matter of time before the British palate would yield to the charms of West Indian flavours.

Perhaps the most obvious and immediate influence of West Indian migrants culturally was found in other areas of retrenchment. Lord-loving West Indians boosted the dwindling numbers of church-goers. They did so by forming their own churches after they faced rejection when trying to join mainstream ones. West Indians who were Hindus or Muslims found more welcoming places of worship.

Finally, West Indians transformed the way that cricket was played and watched.

'Let's be honest, cricket can be a pretty dull affair,' Viv Adams reminds me. 'You go to Lord's and you see a schoolboy with his father keeping the score, quiet, shh. The West Indians would be commenting on every ball bowled, turning it into more of an event and social occasion than sporting performance. The crowd wasn't just there to watch the thing. It was a chance to express yourself.'

Even Ethlyn, who was no great fan of cricket, could appreciate that West Indians, with their whistles and drums, and makeshift maracas (pebbles inside of empty beer cans) added another layer of experience to the game.

Food, religion, cricket – all were occasions of communion. They also marked a change in the cultural landscape, as West Indians began to occupy places and spaces from which they'd previously felt excluded.

At the beginning of mass Caribbean migration to Britain, the folk singer Louise Bennett riffed on the fever and stampede among young people to leave their islands, predicting that, with time, West Indians would come to colonise England in reverse. Bennett was being ironic. But all cultures need renewal and rejuvenation if they're to survive. And if at first West Indians felt marginalised, they and the British public soon came to realise that their culture could not be ring-fenced.

They soon found means of expressing their Caribbean-ness within British culture but in ways that were distinct too, as was evident when England and the West Indies found themselves on opposing sides at cricket grounds.

*

Bert Williams

Oh man, it was just eat, because you don't taste; when I first came here to England we used to buy the English mustard just to let the food have a bit of taste. We used to get pepper sauce from home.

We couldn't even get rice; we used to get that Carolina rice, which is a split rice which the English use for rice pudding.

Shirley Williams

And Indian pickles, mum used to bottle it up in plastic bottles and send it from Guiana, because dad used to get free plastic bottles from his job as a pharmacist, and she'd secure it with reels of tape so it didn't leak, and pack them in the boxes for me.

Bert Williams

One good thing. When we first came here, the butcher wouldn't charge you for trotters and pig's tail at that time, and pig's head. The ears and things. That was a nice part, because we used to use a pig's tail in the soup, so you'd boil the peas with the pigtail in and then you'd put your rice in. That's beautiful.

But if we wanted proper rice we had to either go to Brixton to get it or send word, so people from London would come down visiting and they'd bring it. My brother and sister would come down and bring yam and cassava and coco; that sort of thing, you couldn't get that in Brighton at all. They would bring plantain, sorrel, a lot of Jamaican product. But they might only come every two months – like you see in the prisoner of war films. But what we did, we bought the ordinary food, the beef and the chicken, and we just do what we'd do in the Caribbean with it, if you do fried chickens or curries or anything like that.

Agnes DeAbreu

I missed the kind of food you could get back home. It wasn't just the food, though, is how we cook it. It was funny how some things were more primitive than back home. Even though back in St Vincent we didn't have a stove, we had a wood fire. Our kitchen was separate, not in the house. We used to cook what we grew on the land. Unfortunately there was not many places to get Caribbean food but there was a shop owned by an English lady and she used to try and get yam. I don't know where from but she could get it.

Ethlyn Adams

It was just Mrs Henry selling West Indian food in Luton, in the market. Bageye [my husband] used to cuss some bad words, say she charge too much. No one else was selling so you had to go to her. You'd go for a pound of yam, long so, and the end bit would be rotten. But don't bother ask Mrs Henry to chop off the rotten part. She would tell you, 'Is so me buy it; it so it must sell.'

Don Letts

My parents, hardcore Jamaicans: chicken, rice and peas, ackee, salt fish, plantain, dumpling, sweet potato, yam, callaloo, the works.

Every Saturday we went to the market, you didn't have a choice. Rain, cold and fucking freezing wearing short trousers, not wanting to go. You'd have to go with your mum and dad to Brixton market and it was very much an Afro-Caribbean thing back then – not this trendy thing it is now – totally Jamaican food. The main bit was Granville Arcade, which is now the food village or whatever, but that was just packed with every representative from every Caribbean island.

Bert Williams

Going to Brixton was like going back home really, I was very comfortable there, just being amongst black people; especially when you live in Brighton and you feel you're the only one here, there was others, but you felt you were the only one. So going to Brixton was like going back home. There's black people there, and you didn't just go for the food, you go to feel good about yourself. You do go to eat though and the first thing you do, before you do your shopping, is go and have some food, because they had West Indian restaurants; and the only place you could get music as well, West Indian music, was in Brixton.

Not only that, you were picking up new words as well, new things, that was the idea of buying the records, listening to the music. That time it was the Trojan label really selling; you've got to remember that in the sixties, reggae music, it gave you messages, new words were coming out and the conditions in Jamaica. It gives you a reminder of what Jamaica was like, I loved it.

Don Letts

The market, I'm thinking with hindsight, was a really buzzing hive of cultural activity but, coming from a ten-year-old's perspective on a Saturday morning, it was a pain in the arse and you couldn't wait to get home to watch TV.

At the market they'd be getting their ground provisions; maybe not ackee, that was expensive, it was a luxury. It was a little slice of back home. It was like you'd picked up a bit of Kingston, Jamaica and plonked it in the middle of London and then took away the sunshine and dropped the temperature SEVERAL degrees.

It wasn't just the food; you had the barbershops, which were key central bases where the men would come and talk shit – politics and whatever else. I went to a guy who was a barber in Jamaica and he opened up in his basement. You'd have your record shops that would spring up and cater to the community so it was this kind of oasis of sub-culture.

Bert Williams

It was a home from home, you walk around Brixton and you walk from shop to shop. There was English guys selling stuff as well, it wasn't all Jamaicans, but you'd target where the black guys are selling stuff. You talk to them, 'Wha'appen?' 'Wha'gwan?' You know. You could come out with the lingo and stuff like that. When I first came to England nobody understood me ... nobody, when I talk everybody says, 'Pardon?' And I hated the word pardon. Every time they say, 'Pardon? I beg your pardon?' Because they didn't under-stand you. So going to Brixton was like, you could come out with all your verbals.

Pastor Phillip Burris & Pastor Strachan
The Birmingham Gazette, 13 September 1958
Many of our people are unsettled here. I try to encourage them, but they are embarrassed and uncertain about British life, and that often keeps them away from the churches, although they went at home in Jamaica.

When I was small in Jamaica our ministers came from England and we heard about living by the Bible and thought that in England we should find that even more in practice than at home. But some of our people have been discouraged at not finding this. You have passed Christianity on to us, but it is stronger in the West Indies than it is here.

Linda Small
Back home when you go to a church, you're welcome, no matter which church you walk into; you're welcome ... When I come here there was a church on Rectory Road, and it's still there now, and I walk in and when I walk in everybody turn and look. It was just a church, so I went and sit down, and I look round and I noticed there was no black people in here, so maybe that's why they're looking. Anyway, I listened to the minister and when the service finish and I get up to walk out and he called me and he asked me not to come back ... and I went home and I'm still trying to work out, 'How did I get home?' Because it's the first time in my life ... I was shocked to know that you're going into a church and they ask you not to come back!

Keith Waterhouse
Daily Mirror, 10 August 1953
The mission room [on Coldharbour Lane, Brixton] is maybe the size of the front room parlour, and it's a Boys' Brigade meeting hall as well as a church. There were something like forty coloured men and women there and the pews were full. The way they held their service is unorthodox by our standards. It goes on for three or four hours, and it doesn't follow any set form. Anyone who has

anything to say gets up and says it. Then maybe someone will start singing and the others join in. The service goes on until no one else wants to get up and speak.

A young man in white trousers and a flashy tie was singing as I stopped in the doorway. It wasn't anything you'd find in *Hymns Ancient and Modern*.

A man got up and beat rhythmically on a tambourine. A few started stamping their feet. The rest were clapping their hands. Brother Service, the pianist, quickened the tempo. A man and a girl danced, jive fashion, down the aisle, the rest cried: 'Praise de Lawd! Glory, Glory! Hallelujah!'

A middle-aged Negro woman got up. She wore an orange dress and an enormous straw bonnet.

Another man got up and waving his hands about as he spoke. 'Brothers 'n' sisters, ah've got news for you. Ah don't trust mah furniture. Ah don't trust mah wife. Ah don't trust no bankin' account. Ah'll give you a piece of information. Ah don't trust nobody but de man Jesus.'

I don't think I have ever been in a more sincere church in my life. I looked at the woman who started it, a little American Negress in a green suit and spectacles. Her name is Marcella White, a Pentecostal missionary. She started her church in people's homes and moved into the mission hall when the congregation got too big.

Most of the people are Jamaicans. Some of them were out of work. The way they looked at the mission hall you'd have thought they were all millionaires, they were so happy. Two men shook my hand and spoke as I left. 'Come again, brudder,' said the first one. 'This here's a coloured church – black, white, any colour.' The other said: 'Any time you're passing, man. Ain't no colour bar here.'

Don Letts

My parents, Valerie and St Leger, came over in 1954. They were churchgoers all right, you mad? My parents weren't party animals by any means; they didn't drink, that I saw, they didn't smoke. But my father had his own sound system, it was called St Leger's Superstonic Sound. But it wasn't like sound systems today, in basements with one red light and people burning ganga. He would do his sound after church services, in the church hall on a Sunday afternoon.

The church was St John's. After service they'd gather in the hall which was at the back of the church and it was a kind of way to ease their pain after having to put up with a lot of shit over the week; and it was obviously a way for them to stay in touch with each other, and also get news from back home. It was much more of a community thing, much more of a social affair than people letting their hair down and partying till four in the morning; my parents weren't that way inclined. They would have played early r&b, Fats Domino – Jamaicans love Fats Domino – early crooners, Brooke Benton, Perry Como, Nat King Cole and some of the emerging reggae sounds, but back then it wasn't even reggae – it was ska and Bluebeat. So you're talking about Prince Buster, Toots and the Maytals. They might even drop a bit of country and western, because one thing about my parents' generation, I don't know what it is, but the old Jamaicans love a bit of country and western, Jim Reeves.

Learie Constantine

The white man had not been used to a black man in his midst competing on terms of equality with him on the cricket field, making runs and being cheered. I got anonymous letters from time to time saying, 'You can't play cricket for toffee and if I had anything to do with it I wouldn't pay you in washers. Why don't you go back to your country? You are not wanted here!' Time after time these letters came and my heart was almost broken, but my wife, I want to pay her this tribute, said, 'Let us turn round and fight, Learie!' So, I played for Nelson for nine years and won the

Championship on seven occasions and were runners-up on the other two. I became pretty popular, although I say it myself.

Gloria Constantine

My parents had a very hard time being accepted in the town. I think they were very unhappy. People used to pass them on the other side of the road when they saw them coming and a lot of people ignored them, more or less.

Dad always used to say when he went to Nelson, on one or two occasions, he shook hands with people who would be doing this with the hand to see if it rubbed off ... It was my mother who decided we're not moving. We are staying here! He would have gone back home after the first year, but she said, 'No!' and that's when they took me up.

Learie Constantine

BBC Third Programme, 1943

We must admit, being the first coloured professional cricketer who has come to the Lancashire League, that I had a job to do to satisfy people that I was as human as they were and, in truth and, in fact, I carried a burden. At first you know, the 'strangeness' ... what we discovered later on to be 'strangeness' we thought at one time it was prejudice and we took that as true.

Trinidad Guardian,

Lord's cricket ground, 30 June 1950

Across this sacred sward of cricket, when the last English wickets had fallen to the West Indies, swept wild rejoicing crowds. Leading them was the gleaming black-faced calypso singer, 'Lord Kitchener'.

Right around the ground he went on an African war dance, all in slow time.

Kitch, with a khaki sash over a bright blue short carried an outsized guitar which he strummed wildly.

'Do you see that patch of ground moving over there?' said a cricket wit. 'That is W. C. Grace turning in his grave.'

Llewelyn Barrow

Well, boy, that day, I think since I leave Trinidad, that day in Lord's when the West Indies win the cricket match, was the best I ever feel, up to that time, as a black man in England. West Indies beating England at Lord's? We start throw fire in them, we beat them bad-bad ... it was more than proud. We was proud of the cricket team, of course. but we was proud of weself too ... we start to make one set of noise ... Eventually we leave the grounds and we go down Park Street singing and beating anything we could find, dustbin, old wood, anything.

Lord Kitchener

After we win the match [at Lord's in 1950] I took my guitar and I call a few West Indians, and I went around the cricket field, singing. And I had an answering chorus behind me, and we went around the field singing and dancing. That was a song I made up. So, while we're dancing, up come a policeman and arrested me. And while he was taking me out of the field, the English people boo him, they said, 'Leave him alone. Let him enjoy himself.' And he let me loose, because he was embarrassed. So I took the crowd with me, singing and dancing, from Lord's, into Piccadilly in the heart of London ... So we went a couple of rounds of Eros. And from there we went to the Paramount, a place where they always had a lot of dancing.[1]

Clyde Walcott

In those days, coloured people or black people – whatever you want to call them – were more or less given a hard time. And they said how, and this was after the first test, proud they felt to go in to work or school the next day or the Monday or whatever it was, having beaten England.

Sam King

After that, the British people, realising the minority people from the colonies here had beaten them at cricket, we were not as stupid as a lot of them assumed or wanted us to be stupid. And, even in the factories, gradually, it starts permeating, that if you teach these people machinery, they will be good machinists. And in the forties a few of us were engineers or whatever it is, and then they realise, if you give them the opportunity, they will be good non-commissioned officers, and if they had education, they'll be officers. Yes it was a milestone for the people from the colonies.

Brian Osborne

After the match, I remember speaking to some of the West Indian guys in Baldock who played for Dad's team and they were really having it. They were really happy about the win and giving it to us verbally, but in a nice way! Not long afterwards that calypso came on the radio on the BBC and became very popular, and that was the first time I'd ever heard calypso music.

Colin Babb

The point about cricket and watching it was the reconnection with home. Many of the cricketers were immigrants themselves, playing for the Lancashire League, for example. They had similar experiences to the people who were watching them. Conrad Hunte came in the fifties to work in a car factory in Lancashire – he played for the West Indies. Cricket was front and centre of Caribbean life. It was the best way of celebrating being Caribbean, watching with all of the other West Indians, whether it was in Old Trafford, the Oval, Edgbaston – all places with substantial West Indian populations. People would start queuing from two o'clock in the morning to ensure they got a ticket.

It was, you know, a case of, we're catching hell here but cricket can be a respite – and a chance to show our flair, style. It was exciting and English people hadn't seen it before. West Indians didn't see themselves as West Indians until they came to England – as it was a way of unifying, of getting them together – and what underpinned that was cricket. Honestly, it was a respite, too, from inter-island, inter-racial rivalries.

It was a way of releasing all the pent-up frustrations of life in England. A cricket ground was one of the few public places where West Indian people could get together and express ourselves – in ways we couldn't in any other venue or public space. Men who came in the fifties and sixties didn't see friends so often, as they were working unsociable hours. At cricket you might see friends you hadn't seen for years, literally.

And the way of celebrating? The 1963 series, especially at the Oval – many people hadn't been in the country all that long and to see the West Indies beat England three to one. We invented the pitch invasion. Basil Butcher, a cricketer from Guyana, remembers the English press calling it 'The Charge of the Dark Brigade!'[2]

Donald Hinds

[In] Barbados, every Barbadian boy was born with the gift of playing cricket. I saw this when still working on the buses in the 1950s. Every garage for London Transport had its own cricket team and I played for the Brixton team. All of us seven or so black bus conductors were from Jamaica, and it was presumed 'Yes, you're from the West Indies you can play cricket!' So I got in. And then by 1956, London Transport had set up a recruitment office in Barbados, so there were a lot of Barbadian guys coming over – and you couldn't possibly choose me over someone like Clarke who, if I had his talent, I wouldn't have been on the buses, I'd have been trudging from county to county to see if I could get into one of the teams. He was that good. He was a conductor. He could have been playing for the West Indies team. That good.

Harwood Williams

In the fifties and into the sixties, when the guys came here from the Caribbean, the [cricket] club was used as a kind of base. Word would get round and someone from the person's family here in the UK would get in touch with the club. A person from that family would then meet and greet the person coming here at the club and find a place for them. The club was a home away from home and a place where you could share knowledge of where the jobs were and how to get accommodation in the area.

Gary Younge

The black community's social life revolved around our cricket team, the Stevenage West Indians Sports and Social Club, or SWISSC. Both my father and elder brother used to play for SWISSC and I used to score for them. About twice a year SWISSC would have a big party where each person would bring a dish (because there were no Caribbean caterers in the area), and a DJ who understood black music, generally from another town or someone's friend from London, would play calypso and reggae until the early morning.[3]

Ian Wooldridge, 1963

It seemed that half the West Indian population of London was crammed into the two tiers of seats at the Nursery End. They chattered, they laughed, they rose like passionate hot-gospellers to exhort one another to still noisier support. Their gaiety was contagious: it spread down to the wings of the wonderful old grounds and met up again among the waistcoats and gold and scarleties beneath the Long Room windows.[4]

Basil Butcher

I remember when I got my hundred at Lord's on a Saturday afternoon [in 1966] and it seemed as if the whole of Lord's was overfilled with people running on the pitch. Some of them were West Indian friends of ours from back home and you couldn't stop them, especially how after they were going on after every ball as I approached my hundred. Man, you would have had to kill them to stop them! It was boom, and the game just stopped for a couple of minutes. They were full of joy and happy for me, man, slapping me on the back and so on. And the Guyanese who had run out to see me – some of them wanted to talk to me about how they recognised me from Guyana, and how they knew my father and that kind of thing.

Conrad Hunte, 1966

When Butcher hit that winning stroke ... I raced back towards the pavilion trying to avoid my countrymen. I was brought down by a perfect rugby tackle. I lost my bat in the process. I lay there on the ground, terrified at being trampled upon as I looked up into the jubilant and excited faces of my compatriots. I need not have feared for my life or for my bat. Some West Indians got hold of my feet as I kicked and struggled to be free, others got hold of my arms and shoulders, some supported my waist and back, and carried me shoulder-high through a clear path in the crowd to the pavilion steps.

Viv Adams

Watching the West Indies play cricket against England was a great experience, one of the greatest. Why? It was a great experience – us getting one over, giving it to the Englishman. I was enamoured of the West Indian cricketers because of that. Because the whole history of England in the West Indies is one of emasculation, it's about the emasculation of the black man. They took away my manhood and here was the West Indies cricket team restoring it. Yes they can colonise us, rule us for hundreds of years, but we can damn well beat them at their own game.

The Englishman has the same intense feeling when he does well, he wears his Englishness as a badge of honour, it is something sacrosanct. In the past the black man was too quickly bought. So watching the West Indies, I can speak for myself, made me feel better about being here. The Tebbit test? What about it? What is he on about? To want England to beat the West Indies is to want to beat myself up.

I remember we had lots of flamboyant cricketers but Rohan Kanhai was especially flamboyant. He'd come in and be out with the first ball or he'd score 200 in the first half hour. He was fun to watch, the West Indies were always great fun to watch. Look at the way the black man walks. He can't just walk down the street, walking down the street is an existential experience, he has to show you who he is! It was the same experience watching the rhythm of the cricketers, you were reminded of the rhythm of being back in the West Indies. That's why people started bringing their drums and their horns, every damn t'ing!

Gone to Foreign

There's a mantra you'll hear as the elders gather at almost every West Indian funeral in Britain: 'Bwoy, this country too cold to bury. Don't mek me bury here.'

Nothing much has changed since I was a child – the setting may have been different (christenings and weddings then, rather than funerals) – but the same sentiment was loudly expressed. Men and women, their old-time talk fuelled by rum 'n' coke, still assumed that one day 'Yes Lord, if God spare my life', they would turn back towards the West Indies. They yearned to be buried in the same place as parents they hadn't seen since they left for Britain half a lifetime ago.

Some did return to homes in the Caribbean, but the majority did not. Throughout my childhood my parents seemed to live irritably in a state of temporariness, neither able to leave England nor return to Jamaica. 'Don't get too comfortable,' Bageye would warn us kids. 'We're only passing through.' It meant that we lived like the Trinidadian poet Roger Robinson in 'Month One': 'He kept his suitcase full of clothes in the cupboard to stop it flying back by itself. He never actually unpacked.'[1]

The plan was always a five year one. Caribbean migrants would come to Britain and 'work some money' and then return to their homes back on the islands. But the five years stretched to ten, ten became fifteen, and one day we woke up to the sight of our parents changing the hall wallpaper. And then we knew we were here to stay. Although our parents never gave up the dream to return, they never went back to live there.

In the exciting times of migration back in the 1950s and 1960s when someone left Jamaica to come to England, it used to be said with some envy and a little awe they had 'Gone to Foreign'. Now it is more often said in reverse – about Black Britons who have been wrongly classified as illegal immigrants, stripped of their British passports and sent 'back home' to Jamaica and other islands – a foreign land to many of them.

The forced and premature return has interrupted an unspoken narrative; you left the West Indies poor but are expected to return wealthy. But when you return, is it home you're really going back to? When I took Ethlyn back to her birthplace for a brief visit over a decade ago, she was extraordinarily upset. She found that Outlook Avenue, the genteel residential area of Kingston where she grew up, bore little resemblance to the gentility of the past. Today, the kindest word you'd use to describe it is 'slum'. And perhaps it's kinder to hold on to that old romantic image. It's safer too.

In Jamaica I met some of the pioneers to Britain, who in later life sold up and returned the West Indies. These returnees have increasingly become the targets of criminals. Tragically, scores of them have been murdered and as Carolyn Cooper says, it doesn't make sense to put themselves in harm's way; they're better off staying in Britain.

But the heart trumps reason and folk are still returning, albeit to gated communities patrolled by guard dogs. The majority of returnees have settled without incident, but they do face problems with high levels of violence, as do all inhabitants. The expense of living and healthcare, as well as missing family and friends, has led some returnees to come back to the UK.

Ethlyn finds herself in a dilemma. When I asked her to reflect on her time in Britain, she says, 'There's been no real happiness. Real happiness? No, and home is home, after all.' But with siblings, children and grandchildren in Britain, seventy years on from the great adventure, where is home for the Windrush generation?

★

Anonymous Jamaican
Journey to an Illusion, 1966

If I dream tonight, you can bet your life it will be about Jamaica. I think so often about going back that the idea of returning has become as inevitable as death ... I was eighteen when I left Jamaica and I remember boasting to some of my friends that I would be back before I reached twenty-five. My plan was to get a job and study electrical engineering by correspondence course and evening school. I was unemployed for six months. When I eventually got a job as a porter, all ambition was knocked out of me. Instead of correspondence course I did my football coupon [the pools]. All I wanted was to get a better job ... I don't mind much about that promise of returning in six or seven years because all the chaps to whom I made that promise are all over here.[2]

Agnes DeAbreu

I felt British with a British passport, but in St Vincent I'm Vincentian. You did feel part of it, it's the Mother country and the Queen and everything and the English language, but I feel I'm Portuguese even though I'm Caribbean and Vincentian. My husband [Gunn] thinks he's more Scottish – he's really mixed. On his mother's side is Indian and black and on the father's side he's Scottish and Carib, but he feel a bit Scottish, but whose side is he going to take? He knows the history a bit but never really gone into it.

When we first came to England we'd send postal orders home to our parents at Christmas. When my dad knew I'd got the kids in just one room he said, 'You should come back and bring the kids and stay,' but I said no. Some people did do that, they let the wife and children go back while they make the money, but I say, 'No, whatever happens we have to stay together. Whether it's hard or soft you go together.'

But previously, when I was expecting Trevor, Gunn wanted to go to Trinidad, because he had a sister there and we got a trunk and started to buy things together and she got a place and he sent postal order to her, but he got back the money as the sister had disappeared. She moved and moved and never kept in touch but I'm glad we never went there. He's always had it in mind that we'd go back, but he just blanked it out of his mind when we didn't make it to Trinidad.

Bert Williams

When I first came, before I joined the RAF, I keep seeing visions of Jamaica and, if I have a dream, even now, the scenery is all banana trees. A lot of my dreams the scenery is always of that Ticky Ticky, bush, that's where I play. Another thing I'd say, I never wanted my bones to rest here, but not now I'm getting old.

But I'm born and bred Jamaican till the day I die, and I hate losing my Jamaican accent; and I know I have but I hate it. That's the only thing I wouldn't like to lose. I feel like that's my only identification. All the time I worked for the health authority my accent was heavy, no one's ever mistaken me for something else.

I came in 1960 and went back for the first time in 1972. They thought I was rich but I was as poor as everyone else. But you were only allowed to take £25 out. My mum had died and my dad had a new young girlfriend. It wasn't emotional, I'm not an emotional person. I went back because my dad was ill.

I flew to Kingston. When you go to the bar people beg you for money, who you know. I say, 'I never know you turn beggar man.' They'll take the shoes off your foot, no shame. They're all mouth, not violent; it turns violent if you don't mouth them back, you've got to hold your own. Since my dad died, that's when I feel, 'Oh sugar, I'm the head of my own family now, Oh sugar my bones going to rest here now. I'll get cremated.'

Wayne Thompson

The only problem I had in Britain was the system of management. I had all the right qualifications, but I was passed over for promotion so many times. The attitude was that you were never going to be as good as a white man. But I bided my time. I knew I was going to come over here [to Jamaica].

'No problem,' that's Jamaica's slogan, and we were caught by that. We said, 'Let's take life down a few steps and relax a little.'

Reginald Davis

I only met my father for about four hours [before I left for England], he was on duty and so on, but he was so glad to see me; and that four hours, he left me feeling that I'm not alone, I have a father, and not only that, but I have sisters, so I no longer feel lonely, but I was longing. I came back to look for him. About 1970, I come back on a airline to Montego Bay. I come and see my sister. I search for him [my father] but I couldn't find him because he had died.

I didn't feel anything because, for four hours, meeting somebody, I still feel lonely, but not lonely, because at that time, at twenty-five or thirty, I was settled in my way of life.

I'm happy to retire here in Jamaica. I came and I met my wife. I was lonely I wanted a companion. We met and I don't regret anything, we alright now, but at my age now, she'll look after me. She's full of fun.

When I come home I see many things that I can identify myself with. I see people that – we don't have racist problems – I see people that respect me, and not only that, I know it suit me, because I come home and feel accepted.

My sisters, them that have known me for years, when I come here now I have sisters that I didn't know; they hug me up and kiss me and so on. My father was a fair complexion and my mother was a Maroon, so she's very dark. They accepted me with open arms, but I was scared they would reject me because I wasn't a lawful child.

My family come and look for me now, for more than one reason; I am in a position that they can say, 'Uncle Reg, lend me a money,' right, and I give them it, do everything that family should have done.

Eric Robinson

I served my sentence. At the time of leaving England, I'd had enough, I wanted to get on to the next stage. I feel happier now. I can help other people less fortunate than myself.

In England initially, when I wanted to buy something, I used to send a white person to the shop to get it for me. He'd get it at a reasonable price. Here I send a Jamaican who has always lived here. Otherwise they take one look at me and think, 'You've travelled, you've had plenty, we want what you've got,' and they'll charge me excess.

Reginald Davis

Sometimes, the experience come by who you relate yourself to in the community. Not at all times. Those who want to come and rob you are the few, but they respect you; they'll rob you without hurting you. But if you come and live like you're better than them, you don't speak to them, they don't only rob you, because they want something from you, they hate you before.

A couple of man climbed the ackee tree, about eight o'clock – we don't go to bed yet, so we leave the door open – so they come through and take out the thing where the money was, and they come in the bedroom. I lie down and my missus lie down, chatting, and one of them hold my wife with a knife, but she bit his hand. It a kitchen knife; they didn't come here to kill us, they want money. And then, one stand beside me; I kick him over and pull his hand and broke the knife in his hand and when it dropped he runs out. I didn't call the police. If they want to hurt us they could have. Even today that man see me and call me Uncle Reg ...

Brinette Rose

It was only in Jamaica that people started calling me English. At first I felt insulted, but now I feel there's a lot of things I learned in Britain to be proud of.

I felt that we were working very hard in Britain and not getting very much in return. Put it this way: as black people in Britain, we couldn't go and live in the countryside. It doesn't seem to work. But out here we fit in.

I don't trust any Jamaicans. I'm wary because the dollar is devalued against the pound: they look at you and think, fifty to one. The rumour goes round that the English have a lot of money. Some people despise you for that. We don't have a gun yet, but I want to get one.

Michael McMillan

How the returnee readjusts may also depend on the culture and society they grew up in and this ambivalence with what it represents for them now.

My father used to tell me a story called 'Johnny just come' about a man who returns home to the village of his birth from a long period abroad in the colonial centre of Britain. Local people eager to see how their prodigal son has changed through his dress, mannerisms and language gather round. The returnee sees a rake lying on the ground and has no memory of what it is or how it is used. He accidentally steps on it and it hits him in the head and suddenly he remembers its name and function with 'deh blasted rake lash me in deh head.'

Derek O'Connor

I was captivated. I always knew something was lacking, but I couldn't identify it. I never felt totally at home in England. But once I came back to Jamaica I felt, yes, now the pieces are fitting together. Smelling the sea and the earth, the flood of memories came back.

At first, I only needed to stand somewhere, not even say a word, and people would come up and say, 'How long you been back?' As much as I wanted to come out here ... I realised that I and the Jamaicans are not akin to each other.

Diana Wilson

Although my parents came from here, they never talked about it. Jamaica was as foreign to me as anywhere else in the world. I had no concept of the place and I didn't know anybody here. I didn't even come for a preliminary visit.

I was working for a big city firm in London. I didn't experience any discrimination working in the City. I just saw a lot of people who were going to burn out before their thirtieth birthdays, and that was one thing that I was determined not to do. I came here out of a sense of adventure.

Ken Morgan

About 1993, we had a family funeral, so we came to Jamaica, and then all hell broke loose on the way back. At the check-in at the Norman Manley Airport, you know, they took me aside and instructed me that I need to speak to the British authorities at the High Commission. They wrongly took my passport and I was stuck. I couldn't go back.

I was so ashamed. The way you were raised in Britain, as West Indian, there is something that is unsaid, but you understand. You don't come back to Jamaica unless you've made it. You don't come back to Jamaica unless you have the means to establish yourself here. I was so ashamed.

Since I've been here [Jamaica] I've learned how to navigate this country. If you're going to survive somewhere, you've got to burn the bridge behind you. The bridge was burned for me. In your mind, you cannot hold on to England, if you're going to survive here. Jamaica is not that kind of a place. The people who have maintained links are the people who this place will defeat.

I found myself cursing everything English. I cursed England. I cursed it. It was my way of getting it out of my system. Probably you call that denial, I don't know what the scientists would call it.

If you reject me, I reject you too. I reject you back. I reject you more than you reject me.

I was asked, 'When you get back your British passport?' – assuming I get it back – 'When you get back your British passport what you going to do?' Like it's a birthday present. It's my passport!

I haven't re-applied for a British passport. The people who have contacted me, I have instructed them that I will not take the visa that they're offering. The returning resident visa that they're offering, because that's a visa that gives me indefinite leave to remain. I'm a British citizen. You don't give me indefinite leave to remain. If you don't want to give me the passport, keep it.

Waveney Bushell

I still feel I'm Guyanese, I feel that I've adopted this country [Great Britain] in terms of feeling comfortable having lived here so long, that I can talk their language and so on, but I don't feel I'm British; I just speak like the British, which I did when I was at home. I'm Guyanese, my heart is not British and that's the important thing now.

It was a good decision to come here. I've been able to study. I've got a Masters and I feel I can hold my own intellectually, but it stops there unfortunately. It's sad in a way that I live in a country that I don't feel I belong. It's because I don't feel [I am accepted]. I feel it would be like when I was a little girl at school, and you're standing to be chosen to play rounders, in a circle, and she's always the captain, the girl who can play rounders well, and I was a little skinny girl who could never hit the ball far, and she would come, and every time she came I would always be left out. I feel like that, that the analogy that I have to give, living here; it's pretty sad.

I felt extremely angry about Windrush scandal. And I'm very angry with Mrs Theresa May who was the head of the Home Office then, because she reflects the thinking about who they want to get rid of. How can that be done to people who've been living here all along? Some people went away and when they came back, some were imprisoned, you know. They weren't even allowed to ring their family. It's so degrading and it just shows what people think of us. I am still angry about that church service to which they were invited, and people boast that they went. And I say, 'What! After what they did!'[3]

Carolyn Cooper

I feel sorry for the Windrush generation and people caught up in the scandal. After living for so long in England and then being treated like that, I would just try to leave, I don't know. But, you see, people have made their lives there, their children are there, their grandchildren are there; where they going to go, to come home to Jamaica and people kill them? Because this is a culture of violence, in many ways, and returning residents are prime targets. Yes man!

And so, you have these huge houses, and local criminals just prey on them. To me it's just a tragedy that someone who work so hard in the UK, doing menial jobs many times, buy a little house. Fortunately it appreciates significantly, you sell it, come home and within two-twos some grudgeful Jamaican kills you. It doesn't make sense. You have to stay in the UK.

Viv Adams

I've never doubted the fact that I am British, I was born British and I was conscious of being British. My father was a policeman with the regalia of Britishness around him. The uniform, the badges, the Queen's motif on his lapel. They were symbols that he was working for this organisation that defined me, in terms of my nationality. I never entertained the idea of being English because, to put it bluntly, the English are those people that we used to laugh at when we drove around, the little funny man.

I think England is a better country for Caribbean people being here. They don't necessarily recognise it, but I go back to the days when there were no significant amounts of dark-skinned people from the other countries being here and the indigenous people were ossified, dull, washed-out people, they had no sense of vibrancy about them. I'm talking culturally, they didn't have fashion sense, it took West Indians to come here to show them how to dress, flamboyant and style. They didn't know what style was.

One example; we'd have a different shirt for every day of the week, and some of them would be coloured, but an Englishman would never wear a coloured shirt, he'd only one shirt and a number of detachable collars, that's all he would change, and that was the norm.

The English working class were a downtrodden people, they were courageous but they were a people that had been downtrodden by their ruling class, so they didn't believe and embrace that this country was there for them. They gravitated towards the bottom and so when the West Indians started to do other things, it was like an eye-opener to the English man.

England puts a canopy over people, a canopy that forces them into being kind of persons that are not natural to them really and they adjust to that, but it's not a natural way for them to be, because the English style of seeing the world is a unique frame of reference.

Naipaul talks about going to the theatre in London, and he says, you go to the theatre and you enter the theatre alone, and you sit and enjoy the performance alone, and when you come out into the external world alone as well; and what he's saying is that, in the West Indies, the theatrical performance is an event of its own, which is not against you.

I remember going to the cinema in Jamaica, it was like a carnival event, and it was just an ordinary black and white movie. The guy next to you would be talking to you, and he'd go and buy some peanuts and he'd share his peanuts with you; and the guy in front of him would pass his cigarettes around. You'd never see these people afterwards but it was like they embraced a culture that was accommodating; you had warmth as well. But I never believed that that was a natural reference point [in England]; the natural reference point in England required misery.

Having said all that, because the experience of wanting to leave the island had been so deeply ingrained in me from year dot, it was anathema to me to want to return to that state that I'd known before; it wasn't a question of it being a sign of failure, it would be a sign of destruction.

I have ambivalent feelings about it sometimes; sometimes I think it was a mistake to have come, but you can't reassess things historically like that, because at the time it was a wise thing to do; because one wanted that and one did not have a sophisticated understanding of the alternatives and where they could possibly lead. And so I mustn't look a gift horse in the mouth, because coming to England has enabled everything that has happened to me to happen, and I'm not sure, because of the structure of our family life, if any of those things would have happened in Jamaica. You don't get university degrees in Jamaica unless you are seriously middle class, seriously middle class. England was very good for me in terms of that.

Victor Williams
The Colony, BBC TV, 1964

Well, England to me really when I went home, it was more or less like a land of paradise, happiness, everything that is gay, and you could live ever so comfortable without any form of misery or anything like that, you know, and I had that kind of impression more or less, when I was going to school. But after advancing up in age and beginning to read books and things like that, finding out for myself that it isn't altogether the way how I thought it was. It appears now to me as if everybody has got to struggle through life so as to make the grade, if you intend to make the grade at all. I would like to see if I can go home some day even better off than how I did come in the country; and the only way of doing that, and achieving the goal in that respect is to see if I can get myself a job, and try to keep the job, the best possible way. Ignore any form of ignorance that might be an embarrassment to me, and things like that, because, it has already been said, if a man wants good, the nose has got to run.

Charles C.
The Colony, BBC TV, 1964

Sometimes we think we shouldn't blame the people because it's we who've come to their country and troubled them. On the other hand we think, if they, in the first place, had not come to our country, and had spread a false propaganda, we would never have come to theirs. But then we say, if we had not come we'd be none the wiser, we would still have the good image of England, thinking that they are what they are not, and the English would be ignorant of us.

Rena Khublall

I went back to Guyana a few times and I didn't like the way things were going there, I didn't think my children would have been able to cope. Working wise, school wise, it would have been difficult for them, because of lack of opportunities, I wouldn't have been working, what would I have been doing? All my life I worked over here. From the time I came right up until four years ago. Had I been in Guyana, what would I have been doing? Having a couple of chickens and a little kitchen garden and cook all day.

Arthur France

I went back the first time in 1975 having arrived in 1957. In the earlier days it was harder. When my dad died in 1965 we couldn't afford to go back, we just sat here and cried.

I wanted to go back to see my mum in 1975. And when you went back, the whole village was waiting for me. And when I went into the village, my mum said to me, 'You have to give them some money. Help this lady, things not good for her.' Then there was this business man who lived on the other side of the island and I had this blue silk shirt that I'd never worn and my mum said, 'He was good to your dad, you have to give him that shirt', so I had to give him the shirt. And then there was someone, I had to give him my suit.

My father used to buy things like flour in bulk and my mum used to give it away, she'd say, 'I'm just making a little parcel for this person,' and if he had some meat, she'd give it away. She would say, 'We'll have to make a little parcel and give it to someone,' and then she'd have to say to my dad, 'The flour done, you know,' but she was always like that [laughing]!

Funny, but it's always in your mind that you're going back, but you have your children and your grandchildren. Lots of people – some always dream of going back; funnily enough, some who were born here, their parents wouldn't go back but the children, they've gone to live out there.

When I was a child, I was born free. If I'd stayed down there I would have been more independent. My brother, you couldn't even get him to come to England for a holiday, and there's no way you could match what he's achieved. Those people who stayed behind, they achieved quite a bit.

One guy I was at school with, he has a big furniture business, and I was looking at it; you know, it would be nice to set up a project with black children, and take them out of this country for a period of time, to live in one of the Caribbean island. England is still a very racist country in many ways, it's institutionalised; you go to the Caribbean and you see the prime minister is black and all of the authorities. Our cousin Shirley was saying, when her son was seven years old, she didn't want her son to grow up in England.

Mahalia France

I think, for dad, home was always the Caribbean, it was never the house we live in now. Home was back home. So you got the impression that they were here in the physical sense, but spiritually and emotionally that's where they want to be. In one way they want to go back to a life of being a child: running around naked in the yard or going across the yard to the kitchen, not going into a red or grey brick building where everything's under one roof without the freedom of just going outside, sitting on the veranda or sitting underneath a tree and just shelling nuts or anything like that.

So always hearing the word 'home' kind of makes you think, 'OK there's another home as well.' In my case, obviously going back to the island, you do have fond memories. It's funny. The other day, I bought a pack of lychees from the supermarket and I thought to myself, 'Imagine if we had a tree'; and I thought, 'Just a minute, my grandmother had a tree in her yard.' It was always Nanny's yard, never Nana's and, as you get older, you think, how fortunate.

You hear these stories, like mum – they'd go chasing lizards and pop them on the outside stove and watch them wriggle and you think, ugh! But there's a different element of adventure, doing your own risk assessments and … you know, bathing on the veranda with the fire flies. Even though times have changed and things have developed back home, from what I remember it was quite basic, but it was much more basic when my parents were there as children. And in one way there's an essence – not all of it can be captured – and it kind of gets diluted further and further down the generations.

Albert 'Johnny' Anderson

Well going back is OK, but what are you going back to? When I was at home we would have to be in by 8 p.m., and would get a telling off if we were late. I had to be in bed by 8:30 p.m., so I grew up to be in bed by then, even at the age of twenty-one. Even when I went back in 1968 my father said, 'It's nine o'clock, it's time for bed.' I said, 'I came here to visit you, you better be a good father. I came here to visit you and all my friends, and I want to go and have a drink with my friends, and if you're going to lock the door, that's up to you, but I'm going to have a drink.' So I came home at four o'clock and the door was open. I talked to him the following morning, I said, 'Let's talk man to man.' I said, 'I am the breadwinner now.' I said, 'You are working but you're not bringing in enough, I am the breadwinner so we're going to talk man to man and the childhood days thing has got to stop.'

He stormed up the yard to Doctor's Cave where he took the boat out. So I went out because, at that time, a child should never talk back to their parents, but you see, I was twenty-nine years old.

Years later, I did go back, intending to stay. But it never work out. It was tough, rough and tough. And I come back to England.

Louise Smith

I tell you something, the truth and nothing but the truth; I can't go back to Jamaica now to live. I would if I was strong because my niece was here and they gone home live on Mandeville, beautiful place me a-tell you, Mandeville. Oh it so. I would go out there. If I had me husband alive and buy a house in Mandeville on the roadside – not up the hills again with the goat, I can't climb hill, only goat climb the hill up there – you see, I would.

Another thing, I settle. Now here [in the UK] me have me children and everybody grow up and I'm happy. I have a few good friend and we all meet I am happy here. If, say, my mother was alive and me father and all me aunties I would go but they're all gone. Nobody is out there now, just one or two niece and nephew.

Constance Samuel

My husband came first to England and I followed in 1961. My husband always used to say, 'I won't like to stay in England until I'm sixty and when he saw how some of the English people he worked with at Fords Motor Company died before they had time to enjoy their retirement, that really frighten him. He left at fifty-five. We sold our house and used that money to come back home [to St Vincent] in 1987.

We hired a container and then we had to pay to get it out of Customs, but you don't have to pay that surcharge any more if you're coming home for good. I brought back mostly everything from my front room in England. It was difficult then and even now people will make sure you have to pay for everything, because they think as you come from England that you have money. And that 'red eye' attitude has stopped a lot of people coming back home to live because they would say: 'Me ain't goin' back home cah deh people dem too grabalicious.' But I don't take any notice and pay my own way for everything.

My health is better since coming back and I have no regrets returning, because this is home, and it doesn't matter where you go, you will always want to come back home.

Alford Gardner

I've never planned to go back to live. I've always gone back for holiday, that's all. Before she died this partner of mine, my wife, when I was made redundant at Barnbow and had a few pounds and said to her that time – I mean the family was young – 'We will go to Jamaica,' because we could just afford. But she says, 'No no, I'm not travelling, I don't fancy going to Jamaica at all, too far.' Anyway, she wasn't interested, so we didn't bother.

Well, years passed, my life is me myself and I. Me? My family. Myself? Music. I? Sport. I don't bother with politics, I don't bother with religion, let them keep it.

If I had to do it all over, I wouldn't change a thing. I wouldn't change a single thing.

Epilogue
We Are Here Because You Were There

The motley crew of West Indians who assembled at the chapel in Luton in 2015 for Bageye's funeral – zoot-suited older guys; women with outsized hats that appeared as big as themselves; and track-suited Rastas – were quieter than I'd expected. Perhaps they were unsettled by the unfamiliarity of it all. There were audible whispers and murmurs of doubt that Bageye's will was being respected:

'A wha' dis?'

'Lord, I t'ink it gwan be a cremation?'

'But man, a West Indian must be bury.'

'Nah must!'

'Every damn t'ing turn upside down in dis damn country.'

Were these elderly West Indian friends (some of whom were soon to follow Bageye) to be denied the last chance to gather around a grave; for the men to be robbed of the spades to fill the hole; and for the women to wail with pitiful hymns as the coffin was lowered into the ground?

Even though my siblings and I were arguably betraying a tradition, it felt momentous to me, that we were not only laying to rest the last of the West Indians, but also confining to the grave the very idea of being a West Indian.

A stranger, about my age, came up to me after the ceremony. He was trembling, his voice creaking and cracking with emotion. 'This man, Bageye ... ' he said, 'has done great things.'

I did not know what he meant or what to say to the stranger. Eventually, I told him that the last time I'd seen Bageye, he'd won an accumulator at the bookies. He, Bageye, was delighted; he told me he'd always been lucky. I finished telling the anecdote to the stranger: it was meant to be humorous. The stranger didn't laugh.

But Bageye and his generation *had* been lucky. Of course they'd made their luck through fortitude and endurance. Few of the people I interviewed for this book saw their lives as anything but a triumph. They scoffed at paying attention to minor humiliations and derided me for introducing words like 'micro-aggressions' into the catalogue of transgressions they'd had to endure since their arrival in the forties, fifties and sixties.

But sometimes, when the interviews became too cosy and celebratory, with the elders saying that they didn't really have anything to complain about, I'd throw in the bomb: Enoch Powell's inflammatory 'Rivers of Blood' speech. On 20 April 1968 the Shadow Minister envisaged terrifying years to come: the black man would have the whip hand over the white man; racial wars were coming; the Thames would overflow with much blood like the Tiber in days of ancient Rome. Powell warned of a dystopian future where little old white ladies cowered from black men; where Britain would be overrun with ever-growing numbers of 'charming, wide-grinning pickaninnies.'

'What about Enoch Powell?' I'd ask the elderly West Indian interviewees.

'What about him?' they'd answer.

'Everyone was alarmed at [Powell] saying things like that,' conceded Bibs. '[But] we took it with a pinch of salt.'

A pinch of salt?

Don Letts was twelve at the time of the speech. He recalled that, before 'Rivers of Blood', 'in the playground it was, "Oi, Lettsie." The day after the speech it was, "Oi, you black bastard, nigger this, golliwog, Brillo bonce"; it literally polarised Britain overnight. And these kids weren't political, it was just something in the air that was rubbing off from some of their parents.'

A few years younger than Don Letts, I also remember playground taunts that, now that the truth-telling 'old Enoch' had spoken, my Jamaican family and I should pack our bags as we were no longer welcome.

But we weren't going anywhere. When the Windrush generation started to change the wallpaper, to humour the authorities, to take setbacks on the chin, to take Enoch Powell with a pinch of salt, they gave their children a big advantage. They showed how they might triumph from and through adversity.

Enoch Powell's 'Rivers of Blood' speech was a betrayal of the Windrush generation. But the groundwork had already been prepared. The Commonwealth Immigrants Act of 1962 effectively closed the door on further migration of unskilled labourers from the West Indies, and confirmed that the much ventilated 'immigrant problem' was now colour-coded; it was the 'colour problem'.

Joyce Trotman looked back to 1962 with the realisation that the hostile environment was not a twenty-first-century invention; it was there from close to the beginning. 'Very quickly,' says Joyce, 'we were converted from "Children of the Empire" to "Citizens of the Commonwealth" to "Foreigners and Immigrants".'

The politicians may have been responsible for introducing such policies, but the population did not show an inclination to dissent. 'I think they think we owe them something. I don't know, this kind of funny feeling,' says David Wheeler about the West Indians and their descendants in this country. 'They seem to think well, you owe us from our old days. Now maybe, maybe we do. But not the working class of this country.'

Some mordant wits have likened the West Indian story in Britain to that of the famous five stages of grief: denial, anger, bargaining, depression and acceptance. It's handy shorthand for a contentious and contested history. If in part it does truthfully characterise the West Indian experience, might it also encompass characteristics of the indigenous population's experience of West Indians?

In the wake of the Windrush scandal, Carolyn Cooper summed up that which almost all of the West Indians I have spoken to believe: 'The British government, the police, all of those institutions of authority, they just need to accept that black people have a right to be here. As Ambalavaner Sivanandan's famous quip goes, "We are here because you were there".' The British Empire ensured that its citizens in Britain and its former colonies in the West Indies were (and are) inextricably linked.

West Indians have had their allies, from day one, whether it was through small interventions like Hilary Alderson defying her friends and dancing with a black man, or Mae Maven rolling up her sleeves and putting her millinery skills to good use at Carnival. 'I didn't really have a problem with the arrival of people from abroad,' says Mae. 'I thought it was the beginning of what I thought much later; when I can't afford to go around the world, I'll be very pleased for the world to come to me.'

The Caribbean world did come to Britain and forced a realignment of the culture. The achievements of the Windrush generation are many. But the afterglow of their presence is found in their children and grandchildren who have 'stopped talking tripe' and have moved from the margins to the centre. Along the way they redefined the very notion of what it is to be British.

As Bageye would say, 'Argument done!'

List of Contributors

Eddie Adams was an activist who lived in Notting Hill in the 1950s.

Ethlyn Adams was born in Kingston, Jamaica in 1932. She arrived in the UK in 1959 and mostly lived in Luton, and now lives in Brighton. She worked as a machinist at Vauxhall Motors.

Viv Adams was born in Kingston, Jamaica in 1948. He flew to Gatwick in 1962 and lived in Luton and London. He is the author of *The Enigma of Desire*. He is also a poet and has worked as a teacher, civil servant and broadcaster. He now lives in southern Spain.

Hilary Alderson was born in Leeds in 1940. She worked as a hairdresser. She lives in Barnby Dun.

Albert was interviewed for *Journey to an Illusion*.

Albert 'Johnny' Anderson, was born in Montego Bay, Jamaica in 1940. He lives in London. He has worked as a musician and a DJ.

Colin Babb, a writer and journalist, was born in London to parents who migrated to England from Guyana and Barbados in the early 1960s. He is the author of *They Gave the Crowd Plenty Fun: West Indian cricket and its relationship with the British-resident Caribbean diaspora* and *1973 and Me: The England v West Indies Test series and a memorable childhood year*.

Babs married a West Indian in the 1950s and was interviewed by *Picture Post* in 1954.

Deen Bacchus was born in British Guiana and lived in the Notting Hill area during the 1958 riots.

Guy Bailey was born in Jamaica and came to the UK as a young man. In 1963, he went for a job interview to work for the Bristol

Omnibus Company and was refused because he was black. That decision galvanised members of the black community to initiate the Bristol Bus Boycott.

Hubert 'Baron' Baker was born in Jamaica and came to the UK in 1944 to serve in the RAF. He was one of the few West Indians to greet the new arrivals of the HMT *Empire Windrush* when they disembarked in 1948. He became a community worker and political activist. He died in 1996.

Llewelyn Barrow was born in Trinidad. He was a spectator at several England v West Indies test matches.

James Berry was a poet. Born in Portland, Jamaica in 1924, he arrived in the UK in 1948. Berry was known for using a mixture of West Indian dialect and Standard English in his own work. His poetry collections include *Fractured Circles* (1979), *Anancy Spiderman* (1988) and *Windrush Songs* (2007). He died in 2017.

Bibs was born in Jamaica and moved to Notting Hill in the 1950s.

Ishmahil Blagrove is a writer and film-maker. He is the author of *Carnival: A Photographic and Testimonial History of the Notting Hill Carnival* (London: Rice N Peas, 2014).

Bodelyn was born in Jamaica and came to the UK with the ambition of working as a nurse.

Ben Bousquet was born in St Lucia and came to the UK in 1957. He was a Labour Party councillor for North Kensington. He was the subject of the first documentary about race on BBC Television in 1958. He died in 2006.

E. R. Braithwaite was a writer from Georgetown, British Guiana, and author of *To Sir, With Love*. He was born in 1912 and died in 2016.

Rudy Braithwaite was an activist in the Notting Hill area in the 1950s.

Tommy Brogan was born in Moss Side, Manchester in 1956. He was a merchant seaman.

Sue Brown was born in Birmingham, UK, to Jamaican parents who came to the UK in 1955 and 1958. She is a poet and broadcaster.

Cyril Buckley was a traffic manager for the Bristol Omnibus Company. He was interviewed for *Round Up*, BBC Home Service, 1963.

Tony Bullimore was a yachtsman who opened the Afro-Caribbean Bamboo Club in 1966. He died in 2018.

Vanley Burke was born in St Thomas, Jamaica, in 1948. He arrived in the UK in 1965. He lives in Birmingham and is a photographer.

Pastor Phillip Burris was a Jamaican-born pastor of the Church of God of Prophecy, one of the earliest West Indian churches established in the UK in the 1950s.

Orville Burrowes lived in the Notting Hill area in 1958 and witnessed the violence during the riots.

Waveney Bushell was born in Buxton, Demerara, British Guiana in 1928 and she arrived in the UK in 1956. She lives in Croydon and was a teacher.

Basil Butcher was born in British Guiana. He played cricket for the West Indies in the 1960s and 1970s.

Charles C. was interviewed for the BBC documentary *The Colony* in 1964.

Clinton Cameron was born in Mendez, Jamaica in 1939. He arrived in the UK in 1959 and lived in Leeds. He has worked as a tailor, a bus driver, an area officer of tertiary education and is a political activist.

Dawn Cameron was born in Leeds. She works in research and project management in the arts and cultural sector.

Earl Cameron is an actor who was born in Bermuda in 1917. He arrived in London in 1939. His many films include *The Heart Within* (1957).

Jennifer Campbell was born in Kingston, Jamaica. She moved to Barking, Essex and works as a nurse.

Sybil Campbell was born in Jamaica. She came to the UK in 1961 and worked as a canteen assistant.

Wilbert Augustus Campbell aka Count Suckle, the Sound System Bomb, was born in Jamaica and stowed away on a cargo ship to Britain in 1954. He was one of the first black DJs and nightclub owners in Britain and was massively influential in bringing Jamaican music to Britain and in particular, the London party scene. He died in 2014.

Colin Carter was born in Barbados. He is a writer and funeral director.

Ian Charles was born in St Kitts and Nevis. He is a cofounder of the Leeds West Indian Carnival.

Donald Chesworth was a member of the policy committee, London County Council, 1952–1965.

George Clark was a community worker in Notting Hill in the 1950s.

Pauline Clark's Jamaican family was split between those who remained and those who left for the UK.

Dennis Clifford was a police constable active during the Notting Hill riots.

Wallace Collins migrated to the UK from Jamaica in 1954. He is the author of *Jamaican Migrant*.

Hughbon Condor was born in St Kitts & Nevis. He moved to Leeds in the UK and is a designer for the Leeds West Indian Carnival.

Yvonne Connolly was born in Jamaica and came to the UK in 1963. She was appointed the first female black head teacher in 1969.

Gloria Constantine is the daughter of Learie Constantine.

Learie Constantine, the Trinidad-born cricketer (quick bowler and superb batsman) was the first black player to be a professional in the Lancashire League, joining Nelson Cricket Club in 1928. He distinguished himself playing for the West Indies and became the UK's first black peer. He gave a biographical talk on the BBC Third Programme in 1943. He died in 1971.

Carolyn Cooper was born and lives in Jamaica. She is an academic and writer. Her books include *Sound Clash: Jamaican Dancehall Culture at Large.*

Vincent Coventry was a police inspector during the Notting Hill riots.

Charles Coyne was stabbed and hospitalised during the Notting Hill riots. He was interviewed for *Sleeping with the Enemy*, BBC Radio 4, 2007.

Theresa Creek (not her real name) was interviewed for the Mass Observation project in 1939.

Stanley Crooke was a British Rail signalman and was interviewed for the BBC documentary *The Colony*.

John M. Darragh was a social surveyor of West Indian employees in Birmingham in the 1950s.

Reginald Davis was born in Falmouth, Trelawny, Jamaica, in 1933 and arrived in the UK in 1960, and worked as an engineer. He has now returned to live in Jamaica.

Velma Davis was born in Trinidad and arrived in the UK in 1957 to live in the Notting Hill area.

Agnes DeAbreu was born in St Vincent and the Grenadines in 1940. She arrived in the UK in 1958 and lives in London. She worked in department stores.

Karihzma Delpratt was born in the UK and her parents were from St Thomas, Jamaica. She is a dance teacher.

Devon left Jamaica in 1955. He was interviewed for *Journey to an Illusion*.

Sydney Alexander Dunn was a Pastor and later a Bishop in Handsworth. He was interviewed fo the BBC documentary *The Colony*.

Vivian Durham was a Jamaican journalist.

Allen Ebanks arrived in the UK in 1957. He settled in Birmingham before moving to Leeds. He worked in the engineering and transport sectors and then became a postman. He was interviewed for *A Journey Through Our History*.

Johnny Edgecombe was born in 1932 in St John's, Antigua & Barbuda. He arrived in the UK as a young man and became a British jazz promoter. His involvement with Christine Keeler inadvertently alerted the authorities to the Profumo Affair.

D. G. Ednie was the regional controller of the National Service Hostels in 1948.

Dennis Feist was a police constable active during the Notting Hill riots.

Arthur France was born in Mount Lily, St Kitts & Nevis in 1936. He arrived in the UK in 1957 and was the co-founder of Leeds West Indian Carnival.

Mahalia France was born in Leeds and is a teacher.

Armet Francis was born in St Elizabeth, Jamaica and moved to London in 1955. He is a photographer and was interviewed by Shirley Read, 2013, 'An Oral History of British Photography', © British Library Board, C459/214.

John Fraser was a Lambeth councillor.

Norman Fraser was a police constable active during the Notting Hill riots.

Alford Gardner was born in Kingston, Jamaica in 1926. He first arrived in the UK in 1943 to join the RAF and then in 1948 he returned on the HMT *Empire Windrush*. He worked as an engineer.

Carlton 'Stanley' Gaskin was born in British Guiana. He came to the UK to join the RAF during World War Two, and returned on the HMT *Empire Windrush* in 1948.

Elizabeth May Gilman was born in Leeds and worked in a munitions factory during World War Two.

Barbara Gloudon was born and lives in Jamaica, where she is a theatre impresario.

Olive Gordon was born in British Guiana. She came to London in 1952 and was a dressmaker.

Ainsley Grant was born in Jamaica and was living in the Robin Hood Chase area of Nottingham during the riots of 1958. He was interviewed for *Journey to an Illusion*.

Shirley Green wrote a biography of Peter Rachman in 1979, *Rachman: The Slum Landlord whose Name Became a Byword for Evil*.

C. W. W. (Charles Wilton Wood) Greenidge was born in Barbados in 1889 and had a life-long association with the island and the West Indies. He was a Member of Commission on Development of British Guiana and British Honduras in 1947 and later was a Member of the Legislative Council of Barbados. He lived most of his life in Barbados.

Roy Hackett was born in Jamaica. He came to the UK in 1952 and was a co-founder of the Commonwealth Coordinated Committee in Bristol in 1962.

Stuart Hall arrived in Oxford in 1951 as a Rhodes Scholar from Jamaica. The small number of West Indian graduates and undergraduates in Oxford included V. S. Naipaul from Trinidad, who was at Christ Church. A leading cultural theorist, he lived most of his life in London thereafter and worked as a professor at the Open University among others. He died in 2014.

Horace Halliburton was a Jamaican civil servant who came to the UK in 1948.

Lucile Harris was born in Jamaica and came to the UK in 1948 on board the HMT *Empire Windrush*.

Alfred Harvey was a DJ and a Soho celebrity in the 1960s.

B. F. Harwood (not her real name) was interviewed by the Mass Observation project in 1939.

Mr Hazel was born in Trinidad and lived in Rachman-rented accommodation in the Notting Hill area.

Russ Henderson was a jazz musician and steel band player who was instrumental in the founding of the Notting Hill Carnival.

Edwin Hilton Hall was born in Jamaica. He came to the UK in 1948 on the HT *Empire Windrush*.

Donald Hinds was born in Jamaica. He is a writer, journalist and historian. He is the author of *Journey to an Illusion*. He was also interviewed by Robert Wilkinson, 2012–2014, 'Oral History of Oral History in the UK', © British Library Board, C1149/25.

Phyllis Hines was born in St James, Jamaica. She arrived in Leeds in 1960 and worked as a nurse.

Sheila Howarth was born in Leeds; her parents were from St Kitts & Nevis. She is a teacher and was a Leeds West Indian Carnival Queen.

Darcus Howe was born in Trinidad. He arrived in the UK in 1961, intending to study law. He was a broadcaster, journalist and activist; his work included being editor of *Race Today*, as well as presenting Channel 4's *The Bandung Files* from the mid-1980s. With John La Rose, he led the New Cross Massacre Action Committee campaign for an inquest after a fire at a house party in south London killed fourteen black teenagers. He died in 2017.

Conrad Hunte was born in Barbados and moved to the UK in 1956. He worked at a bus plant in Lancashire before playing cricket in the Lancashire League and eventually playing for the West Indies. He died in 1999.

Eric Irons was born in Jamaica. He joined the RAF in 1944 and he was Britain's first black magistrate. He died in 2007.

Nelly Irons was born in Nottingham and was married to Eric Irons.

Franklin Jackson was born in Prospect, Clarendon, Jamaica in 1950. He came to the UK in 1965. He is an entrepreneur, DJ and former pub landlord in Manchester.

Mary Jacobs was a teacher from Birmingham. She married Jake Jacobs in 1948.

Mr James was interviewed by *Picture Post* in 1954.

Wilmer James was born in St Kitts & Nevis; he arrived in the UK in 1961. He is a Leeds West Indian Carnival engineer.

Dorothy Jasper was born in 1936 in Manchester, UK. She married a West Indian man when she was nineteen years old.

Jessie married a West Indian man and was interviewed by *Picture Post* in 1954.

Mr Johnson was born in British Guiana.

Patricia Jones (not her real name) was interviewed for the Mass Observation project in 1939.

Colin Jordan founded the far right British Peoples Party in 1939 and launched the White Defence League in 1956.

Archippus Joseph was born in Montserrat in 1932. He arrived in the UK in 1954. He was called up for National Service in 1957.

Ken was born in Trinidad. He was interviewed for *Journey to an Illusion*.

Sylvie Kershaw was born in the Notting Hill area and was on honeymoon in Ilfracombe when the Notting Hill riots broke out. She was interviewed for *Sleeping with the Enemy*, BBC Radio 4, 2007.

David Khublall was born in British Guiana. He arrived in the UK in 1961. He lives in Wembley and has been a tailor, a handyman, a carer and a social worker.

Rena Khublall was born in British Guiana in 1940. She moved to the UK to join her husband, David, and has worked on production lines and has been a pension clerk.

Sam King was born in Jamaica. He served in the RAF during World War Two and returned to the UK on the HMT *Empire Windrush* in 1948. He was the mayor of the London Borough of Southwark.

Lord Kitchener was born Aldwyn Roberts. He was a Trinidadian calypsonian who arrived on the HMT *Empire Windrush*. He famously composed the calypso 'London is the Place for Me'.

George Lamming was born in Barbados. He is a poet and novelist and he is the author of *The Pleasures of Exile* and *The Emigrants*. He came to Britain in 1952 on a ship also bringing the author Sam Selvon. Lamming dedicated his novel, *In The Castle of My Skin*, to his mother – who fathered him.

Louise Lange was interviewed for *Sleeping With the Enemy*, BBC Radio 4, 2007.

Mike Laslett O'Brien is the son of Rhaune Laslett, who was one of the founders of the Notting Hill Carnival.

Nella Last was interviewed in 1939 for the Mass Observation project.

Wilford Lawson was born in Montego Bay, Jamaica. He first arrived in the UK in 1954 as a stowaway. He was sent back to Jamaica and returned to the UK two years later in 1956.

Dorothy Leigh was from Long Eaton, Derbyshire. She met her Jamaican husband on the dance floor at the Rialto Ballroom in the 1950s. She was interviewed for *Sleeping with the Enemy*, BBC Radio 4, 2007.

George Leigh was born in Jamaica. He came to the UK to serve in the RAF during World War Two. He settled in Long Eaton, Derbyshire, where he married Dorothy. He was interviewed for *Sleeping with the Enemy*, BBC Radio 4, 2007.

Don Letts is a British DJ, musician and film-maker. His parents moved to the UK from Jamaica.

Bet Lowe was born in London. She worked as a teacher. She married Jamaican Chick Lowe, who came to the UK on the ship the *Ormonde* in 1947.

Stephen Marks arrived in the UK from Jamaica in 1960 and settled in Manchester.

Mae Marven was an active member of the Kensington Residents Forum. She volunteered as a costume-maker for the Notting Hill Carnival.

Michael McMillan was born in the UK to parents who were from St Vincent and the Grenadines. He is an artist/curator, playwright and educator. His installation 'The West Indian Front Room' opened in London in 2005 and has been reproduced in many cities around the world.

Ruben McTair was born in Trinidad and lives in Huddersfield. He has been a regular at the Leeds West Indian Carnival for many years.

George Mangar was born in British Guiana in 1937. He arrived in the UK in 1959 on a scholarship to study medicine.

Roy Mitchell arrived in the UK in 1944 as a RAF ground crew in World War Two. He lived in Leeds. He was interviewed for *A Journey Through Our History*.

Charles Moorcroft was born in Jamaica and came to the UK in the 1940s to join the Royal Air Force.

Ken Morgan was born in 1950 in Clarendon, Jamaica and came to London when he was nine years old. He is an entrepreneur.

S. D. Morton worked for the Ministry of Labour in 1948.

Chris Mullard was the chair of the Notting Hill Carnival.

V. S. Naipaul was born in Trinidad and came to the UK on a government scholarship in 1950. He is the author of *A House for Mr Biswas* and many other novels and works of non-fiction, winning the 1971 Booker Prize. In 1989 he was awarded the Trinity Cross, Trinidad and Tobago's highest national honour. He received a knighthood in Britain in 1990 and the 2001 Nobel Prize in Literature. His early days in Britain were later memorialised in a fictional biography, *The Enigma of Arrival*. Naipaul died in 2018.

Peter John Nelson was born in Jamaica. He came to Manchester in the UK in 1960 aged ten years. He joined the army and also worked as a welder.

Ron Nethercott was the south west regional secretary of the Transport and General Workers Union at the time of the Bristol Bus Boycott in 1963. He was interviewed for *Round Up*, BBC Home Service, 1963.

Derek O'Connor was born in Jamaica. He left Jamaica to join his parents when he was seven years old and relocated back to Jamaica more than twenty years later. He was interviewed by Emma Brooker for 'All Gone to Look for Jamaica', the *Independent*, 1995.

Brian Osborne was a thirteen-year-old schoolboy from Baldock who was present at Lord's for the Test match between England and the West Indies in 1950.

Anne Partridge (not her real name) was interviewed for the Mass Observation project in 1939.

Kate Paul was born in Jerusalem in 1940. She moved to Birmingham to become a teacher and kept a journal chronicling her life. This included stints sharing accommodation among West Indian migrants.

Brian Phillips, aka Bushwacker was born in St Kitts & Nevis. He is an active member of Leeds West Indian Carnival Committee.

Mandy Phillips was born in Dominica and was a volunteer in getting the first Carnivals in Notting Hill up and running.

Trevor Philpott was a journalist who worked for *Picture Post* in the 1950s before moving to the *Sunday Times*.

Edward Pilkington is a journalist and the author of *Beyond the Mother Country: West Indians and the Notting Hill white riots.*

Maizie Pinnock was born in Jamaica and settled in Leeds in 1962. She worked as a nurse. She was interviewed for *A Journey Through Our History.*

Susan Pitter was born in Leeds to Jamaican parents. She was Lady Mayoress of Leeds 2000–2001 and is one of the driving forces behind the Leeds West Indian Carnival.

Marjorie Price (not her real name) was born in Antigua. She arrived in the UK in 1959 and worked as a nurse.

John Prince was born in Antigua. He arrived in the UK with his wife in 1957. He worked first in a steel plant before building a career in education.

Trevor Rhone was born in Jamaica. He was a playwright and screenwriter for the film, *The Harder They Come.* He died in 2009.

Eric Robinson left Jamaica for the UK in 1954. He returned to live in Jamaica forty years later. He was interviewed by Emma Brooker for 'All Gone to Look for Jamaica', the *Independent*, 1995.

Rashida Robinson was born in Trinidad. She moved to Leeds, UK and worked as a nurse. She was one of the Leeds West Indian Carnival Queens.

Brinette Rose was born in Coventry to Jamaican parents. She relocated to Jamaica in 1993 with her husband, David.

Constance Samuel was born in St Vincent and the Grenadines. She came to the UK in 1961 and returned to St Vincent and the Grenadines in 1987.

Norman Samuels was born in Jamaica. He joined the Bristol Bus Boycott Campaign in 1963 and was the first black person to drive a bus in Bristol in 1964.

Sonia Saunders was born in the UK in 1962 to Jamaican parents. She is a writer and a historian.

Everine Shand was born in Jamaica. She came to England as a child to join her mother. She is a neighbourhood support officer for the Royal Borough of Kensington and Chelsea.

Lord Silky was born in St Kitts & Nevis and has been a regular contributor to the Leeds West Indian Carnival since its inception.

Linette May Simms MBE was born in St Catherine, Jamaica in 1930. She worked for London Transport as a bus driver.

Dorothy Skinner was born in Manchester in 1940. Her son was born to a West Indian father in 1957.

Corinne Skinner-Carter was born in Trinidad. She came to the UK in 1955 to train as a teacher. She retrained as an actor for film and television.

Linda Small was interviewed for 'The West Indian Front Room' in 2005.

Bernice Smith was interviewed for the BBC programme *The Colony* in 1964.

Louise Smith was born in St Thomas, Fonthill District, Jamaica. She came to the UK and lived in Birmingham. She married a fellow Jamaican and worked as an auxiliary nurse.

Paul Stephenson was born in 1937. He served in the RAF from 1953–1960. He was a social worker and became a political activist, leading the Bristol Bus Boycott in 1963.

Mavis Stewart was interviewed for 'The West Indian Front Room' in 2005.

Pastor Strachan was a Jamaican-born pastor of the Church of God of Prophecy, one of the earliest West Indian churches established in the UK in the 1950s.

Chris Stredder was a nurse who witnessed the violence of the Notting Hill riots in 1958. She was interviewed for *Sleeping with the Enemy*, BBC Radio 4, 2007.

Carol Sydney was born in Westmoreland, Jamaica in 1943 and was brought up by her grandparents when her mother went to the UK in 1952. She joined her mother in Essex a few years later. She was interviewed along with Don Sydney for Evewright Arts Foundation 'Caribbean Takeaway Takeover: Identities and Stories.'

Don Sydney was born in Trinidad. He arrived in the UK in 1961 where he worked as a mental health nurse in South Ockendon.

Wayne Thompson was born in Jamaica. He came to the UK as a child and lived in Brixton. He always dreamed of returning to Jamaica and did so with his wife and children more than twenty years ago. He was interviewed by Emma Brooker for 'All Gone to Look for Jamaica', the *Independent*, 1995.

Owen Townsend was born in Westmoreland, Jamaica in 1950 and came to the UK in 1965 to join his parents in Manchester. He worked as a builder.

Joyce Estelle Trotman was born in Stanleytown Village, Demerara, British Guiana in 1927. She came to the UK in 1955 to study to be a teacher. She worked as a teacher in many schools, starting off in Bermondsey, London.

Carol Tulloch was born to Jamaican parents in Doncaster, UK. She is an artist and a curator. She is a professor at the University of the Arts, London, and was interviewed for 'The West Indian Front Room' in 2005.

Sydney Vass was a Police Inspector who was posted to Notting Hill police station in 1958.

S. Victor was born in Jamaica. She arrived in the UK in the early 1960s. In 1964 she returned to Jamaica to collect her children before coming back to the UK, where she settled in Manchester.

Clyde Walcott was born in Barbados. He was a West Indian cricketer whose unbeaten 168 helped his team beat England in its first Test victory at Lord's in 1950. He died in 2006.

Keith Waterhouse was a British novelist and newspaper columnist especially for the *Daily Mail* and the *Daily Mirror* until his death in 2009.

Rene Webb was born in Trelawny, Jamaica in 1919. He joined the RAF during World War Two. He settled in the UK in 1947. He was a postal worker and a campaigner who often addressed issues of housing and unemployment as a speaker at Speakers' Corner in Hyde Park, and was a supporter of the radical United Coloured People's Association.

Angela Wenham was born in Barbados and has been an active member of the Leeds West Indian Carnival for several decades.

Mrs Werner was the manager of The Calypso Club which opened in 1957 as The Calypso Dance and Social Club. It served as the centre for local West Indians to gather for a 'council of war' on the second day of the Notting Hill riots.

R. Westgate (not her real name) was interviewed for the Mass Observation project in 1939.

David Wheeler lived in the Notting Hill area during the riots and befriended West Indians.

Edie White (not her real name) was interviewed for the Mass Observation project in 1939.

Bert Williams, MBE was born in Ticky Ticky, Manchester, Jamaica in 1944. He first came to the UK in 1960 to visit his sisters and later joined the RAF. He helps run the Brighton and Hove Black History Group.

Francis Williams was born in Jamaica and she settled in Leeds in 1961. She was active in the trade union and was a shop steward in Social Services, where she worked for twenty-four years.

Harwood Williams was born in Saint Kitts & Nevis in 1970, and played cricket for the West Indies.

Shirley Williams was born in British Guiana and came to the UK when she was eighteen to train and work for several decades as a nurse.

Victor Williams was born in Jamaica. He was interviewed for the BBC documentary *The Colony* in 1964.

Diana Wilson was born in Staffordshire, UK, to Jamaican parents. She is a corporate lawyer who returned to her parents' homeland in Jamaica at the age of twenty-seven in 1993 to work for the Citizens National Bank. She was interviewed by Emma Brooker for 'All Gone to Look for Jamaica', the *Independent*, 1995.

Ansel Wong was born in Trinidad in 1945 and is the former chair of the Notting Hill Carnival. He has worked for a number of public and charitable organisations including the Windrush Foundation.

June Wood was born in Jamaica and was brought up by her grand-parents before joining her parents in the UK.

Ian Wooldridge was a sports journalist who worked mostly for the *Daily Mail*.

Elizabeth Young (not her real name) fostered West Indian children in the 1960s.

Robert Young was born in Jamaica and has lived in Manchester, UK, for most of his life.

Gary Younge is a British journalist, author and broadcaster. His books include *No Place Like Home, A Black Briton's Journey Through the Deep South*. His parents moved to the UK from Barbados.

Acknowledgements

Homecoming was inspired by the memories and reflections of my parents, Ethlyn and Clinton (Bageye). It could not have been completed without the many pioneers who were interviewed for this book. The identities of some interviewees have been disguised and some names changed. I am thankful to all of them for their time and contribution.

The book has been enriched by the generosity of a number of individuals and institutions who opened up their archives. They include the National Archives; The Mass Observation Archive; BBC Radio and Television Archives; The Oral History collections at the British Library; Manchester's oral history project 'Ghosts: Disappearing Histories'; Archives of the Birmingham Black Oral History Project; and Archives of The Essex Record Office.

I am grateful to the following for permission to reproduce material: *Enigma of Arrival* by V.S. Naipaul is reproduced with permission of Pan Macmillan through PLSclear; *Familiar Stranger: A Life between Two Islands* by Stuart Hall is reproduced with permission of Duke University Press; *Journey to an Illusion: The West Indian in Britain* by Donald Hinds published by Heinemann, reproduced by permission of The Random House Group Ltd. © 1966; *No Place Like Home: A Black Briton's Journey through the American South* by Gary Younge is reproduced with permission of Pan Macmillan through PLSclear; *The Pleasures of Exile* by George Lamming is reproduced with permission of Pluto Books Ltd through PLSclear; *To Sir, With Love* by E.R. Braithwaite published by Vintage Classics is reproduced with permission of David Higham Associates Ltd.; *Windrush: The Irresistible Rise of Multi-Racial Britain* by Trevor Phillips and Mike Phillips is reprinted by permission of HarperCollins Publishers Ltd © Mike and Trevor Phillips, 1998.

Thanks especially to Don Letts for sharing the personal histories from his film *In Those Days*. I'm grateful to the Evewright Arts Foundation for the inclusion of interviewees from the exhibition 'Caribbean Takeaway Takeover: Identities and Stories'. Michael McMillan's landmark exhibition from 2005, 'The West Indian Front Room', has been a major inspiration.

The committee of the Leeds West Indian Carnival and the Jamaica Society (Leeds) were early and enthusiastic supporters of this oral history.

As with all my work, *Homecoming* has been a family affair. My partner, Jo Alderson, spent tens of hours transcribing these interviews and helped select and edit the material. My sister, Sonia, provided much of the key research, along with my nephew, Robert, and siblings, Lurane and Clint.

The support of my friend and agent, Sophie Lambert, has been invaluable. I'm grateful to my editor, Bea Hemming, and the rest of the team at Jonathan Cape, for their work on the book.

Homecoming also benefitted from my Arts Council England project 'Writing the Everyday Stories of Diverse Britain', managed by Speaking Volumes, which enabled me to hold writing workshops with Caribbean people in Manchester, Leeds and Birmingham; and to forge strong working relationships with my co-tutors, Sue Brown, Deanne Heron and Edson Burton.

It was a challenge to ensure that as many contributors as possible from across the Caribbean region were represented in *Homecoming*. In that regard, I am indebted to Sharmilla Beezmohun who, as well as being a sharp-eyed copyeditor, has been a great fount of knowledge.

The Caribbean voice sings throughout *Homecoming*. I have been humbled by the dignity, humour, stoicism and humanity of the pioneers who have encouraged me to try to compile a commendable book and to endeavour to lead a commendable life.

Walk good.

Notes

Introduction

1 V. S. Naipaul, *A Way in the World* (London: William Heinemann, 1994), p. 119. Naipaul came to Britain in 1950 to study at Oxford University on a Trinidad government scholarship.

2 George Lamming, *In the Castle of My Skin* (London: Penguin Classics, 2017), p. 3.

3 Stuart Hall and Les Black, 'At Home and Not At Home: Stuart Hall in Conversation with Les Black', Cultural Studies, 23:4, 2009, p. 675.

4 Sam Selvon's *The Lonely Londoners* is the seminal novel of the arrival of the Windrush generation to Britain. His amiable cast of characters, shepherded by the pioneer, Moses, navigate the forbidding landscape of penury, piecemeal work and loneliness, with comic pragmatism. Though Andrea Levy is best known for her post-World War Two novel, *Small Island*, her first novel, *Every Light in the House Burnin'* is a semi-autobiographical story of a Jamaican family living in London in the 1960s. Levy's father sailed to England from Jamaica in 1948 on the *Empire Windrush* and was joined by his wife six months later.

5 Chinua Achebe, 'The Art of Fiction', No. 139, *The Paris Review*, Winter 1994.

6 Derek Walcott, *The Gulf and Other Poems* (London: Jonathan Cape, 1969), pp. 127–9.

7 Ishion Hutchinson, 'A Voice at the Edge of the Sea: An interview with Derek Walcott', *Virginia Quarterly Review*, Winter 2015.

England Was No Muma to Me

1 George Lamming, *The Pleasures of Exile* (London: Pluto Press, 1960), p. 214.

2 Lord Beaverbrook was a British-Canadian newspaper proprietor and politician. A Cabinet Minister during both World Wars, he also held the title of First Baron of Fleet Street. Lady Jeanne Campbell, a socialite and journalist, was the granddaughter of Lord Beaverbrook, who dissuaded her from making a career in acting. Instead, she moved to America, becoming a correspondent for the *Evening Standard*. In the 1950s and 1960s Jamaica was promoted as the resort of choice, an idyllic island, for the very wealthy, like

Beaverbrook and his granddaughter. As well as the Beaverbrooks, American politician Lyndon Johnson regularly visited on his yacht. Noel Coward bought a villa on the island, not far from Golden Eye, Ian Fleming's home on the north coast where he wintered and wrote the Bond novels, and the hell-raising Hollywood actor Errol Flynn partied hard in Jamaica and bought an island just off the coast of Port Antonio.

3   Obeah, a Jamaican folk religion, is feared by some as a form of voodoo, focused on the power of ancestors, involving drumming, spirit possession, ritual sacrifice and herbalism. Obeah was outlawed by the British in the late nineteenth century but is still widely believed in and practised in Jamaica.

4   Louise Bennett-Coverley aka 'Miss Lou', was a renowned poet, singer and folklorist. Her first collection of patois poems, *Verses in Jamaican Dialect* (which she called 'nation language'), was published in 1942. For several decades, the *Jamaica Gleaner* featured her poems in its Sunday editions.

5   Anancy (or Anansi) stories originated from Africa and were brought by the enslaved to the Caribbean. In these folk tales, Anancy is a trickster whose cunning overcomes adverse circumstances and adversaries. The fables were kept alive by slaves on the Caribbean plantations, who embraced strategies from the fables to circumvent the harsh slave regime.

6   Published in *A Story I Am In: Selected Poems*. (Northumberland: Bloodaxe Books, 2011), pp. 72–3.

Last One Out Turn Off All the Lights

1   Hannah Lowe, *Ormonde* (London: Hercules Editions, 2014), p.12

2   Wallace Collins, *Jamaican Migrant* (London: Routledge & Kegan Paul, 1965), p. 51.

3   Donald Hinds reflects on his own life as an adult coming to Britain in *Journey to an Illusion*. In the book he also interviews a number of people who are either anonymised or, like Devon, just given their first name.

4   'One People, One Nation, One Destiny' is Guyana's hopeful motto for a country made up of 39.8 per cent East Indians and 29.3 per cent Afro-Guyanese. The 1957 elections held under a new constitution exposed growing ethnic divisions within the Guyanese electorate: the People's National Congress (PNC) founded by Forbes Burnham (African) and the People's Progressive Party (PPP) founded by Dr Cheddi Jagan (Indian). Britain intervened in the election, sent in troops, suspended the constitution of Guyana and expelled the PPP from office. Since independence in 1966, Guyanese society has been characterised by ethnic and racial divisions as the result of misinformation

and political manipulation. The legacy of the racialised politics of struggle between Burnham, the 'man on horseback' championed by some Afro-Guyanese, and Jagan, lionised by many Indo-Guyanese, remains.

5   V. S. Naipaul, *The Enigma of Arrival* (London: Penguin Books, 1987), p. 99.

6   The SS *Almanzora* was requisitioned as a troopship during World War Two. At the war's end, she was tasked with ferrying troops to and from their homelands and repatriating European nationals. In addition, on 21 December 1947, the ship docked at Southampton with a number of former military men from the West Indies who had fought for Britain in the war.

7   The twenty-year-old Trinidadian fledgling singer Mona Baptiste travelled on the *Empire Windrush*. There were more that seventy other Trinidadians on board, including the calypsonians Lord Kitchener (Aldwyn Roberts) and Lord Beginner (Egbert Moore). All quickly found work as musicians. Within two months of arriving in the UK, Mona Baptiste and Lord Beginner appeared on the BBC's *Light Programme* with Stanley Black and his Dance Orchestra.

8   The only source for this is anecdotal. It is quoted in Hennessy, *Never Again*, but attributed to Sam King, who is quoted in *Forty Years on: Memories of Britain's Post-War Caribbean Immigrants* (London: South London Press, 1988), p. 4. And in *Citizenship and Immigration in Postwar Britain* by Randall Hansen, p. 57.

9   George Lamming, *The Pleasures of Exile* (London: Pluto Press, 1960), p. 212.

Before You Go to Britain

1   George Lamming, *The Emigrants* (Ann Arbor: University Michigan Press, 1994), p. 108.

2   E. R. Braithwaite, *To Sir, With Love* (London: Vintage, 2005), p. 37.

3   'Before You Go to Britain' was the name of a pamphlet compiled by the Migrant Services Division Pamphlet. 'Before You Go to Britain' (nd: file dates 1954–1956 CO 1028/34, The National Archives).

4   'How to Live in Britain', a pamphlet by the British Council, offered advice to immigrants. It was an appendage to 'Before You Go to Britain' (nd: file dates 1954–1956 CO 1028/34, The National Archives).

Take Courage

1   Attlee responded to the letter on 5 July 1948 criticising the MPs and defended those who had arrived on the *Windrush*, saying: 'The majority of them are honest workers, who can make a genuine contribution to our labour difficulties at the present time.' 'Letter from Prime Minister Attlee to an MP about immigration to the UK', 5 July 1948 (HO 213/715).

2   Donald Hinds, *Journey to an Illusion* (London: William Heinemann, 1966), pp. 48–49.

3   George Lamming, *The Emigrants* (Michigan: Ann Arbor Paperbacks, 1994), p. 108.

4   Donald Hinds, *Journey to an Illusion* (London: William Heinemann, 1966), p. 49.

5   Wallace Collins, *Jamaican Migrant* (London: Routledge & Kegan Paul, 1965), p. 56.

6   V. S. Naipaul, *The Enigma of Arrival* (London: Penguin Books, 1987), p. 118.

7   Stuart Hall interviewed by Maya Jaggi. *Personally Speaking: A Long Conversation with Stuart Hall* (London: Media Education Foundation, 2009), p. 7. Other Oxbridge Trinidadians whom Hall found 'considerably more congenial' included J. O'Neil Lewis, Doddridge Alleyne, Willie Demas and Eldon Warner. See Hall's posthumously published memoir, *Familiar Strangers* (London: Allen Lane, 2017) pp. 161–2.

Tin Baths and Paraffin Heaters

1   Harold Wilson gave his speech to the House of Commons on 22 July 1963. He opened by suggesting: 'I beg to move that this House deplores the intolerable extortion, evictions and property profiteering which have resulted from the Rent Act 1957, and demands that Her Majesty's Government take immediate and drastic action to restore security for threatened tenants.'

2   While there was no law against race discrimination, Constantine argued that his right to accommodation had been violated. Mr Justice Birkett agreed. An innkeeper had a duty to provide reasonable accommodation and the judge rejected the defence that the hotel offered alternative lodgings; it had still failed in its duty. Constantine was awarded five guineas in damages. It was not until 1965 that the Labour Party committed to a general statute against racial discrimination with the passage of the Race Relations Act.

3   Local government investigations of the practices of Rachman and the other slum landlords is found in Donald Chesworth's correspondence, reports and papers relating to Notting Hill housing and social conditions (1957–1963). See also Edward Pilkington, *Beyond the Mother Country: West Indians and the Notting Hill White Riots*, pp. 57–8, and Shirley Green, *Rachman: The Slum Landlord whose Name Became a Byword for Evil*, pp. 90–91.

4   Michael de Freitas, the self-styled 'Michael X', assumed the mantle of black leader in London in the 1960s but had also worked as an enforcer for London slum landlords, including Rachman.

5   Donald Hinds, *Journey to an Illusion* (London: William Heinemann, 1966), p. 49.

If You Can't Get a Job

1 E. R. Braithwaite, *To Sir, With Love* (London: Vintage, 2005), pp. 39, 42, 43.

2 The National Assistance Act abolished the Poor Law system that had been established during the reign of Elizabeth 1. It founded the National Assistance Board to provide public assistance by allowing for means-tested payments, which were taken from National Insurance contributions. The Act created a safety net for people who, through circumstances such as old age or disability, could not pay into National Insurance. A Working Party set up by the government in December 1953 concluded that, 'Because the fields in which "coloured" immigrants are suitable for, employment are somewhat limited by their physique and the reluctance of some employers, for various reasons, to take them on, the proportion of unemployment tends to be higher than in the case of white workers and coloured people are principally, for that reason, rather more liable than white people to become a charge on National Assistance.'

3 Donald Hinds, *Journey to an Illusion* (London: William Heinemann, 1966), p. 113.

4 Maizie Pinnock's account appears in Melony Walker's oral history project, *A Journey Through Our History: The Story of the Jamaican People in Leeds & the Work of the Jamaica Society* (Leeds, 2003).

5 London County Council (LCC) was the local government body for the County of London (1889–1965), and was known for its liberal leanings. In the early 1950s, very few West Indian children travelled to Britain. 'By 1958, however,' as Jordanna Bailkin notes in *Afterlife of Empire*, 'the child and female entrants from the West Indies exceeded the number of men. The Commonwealth Immigrants Act allowed the entry of dependants of migrants already in Britain. *The Times* initially described the influx of West Indian children as beneficial, as it contributed to the creation of "normal" [Caribbean family units].' But migration put strains on the West Indian family. In 1956, Miss Doris Nicholls, a West Indian, appeared on British television pleading for someone to foster her baby; over 100 people responded. Jamaican and Trinidadian parents also placed 'Homes Wanted' advertisements in *Nursery World*. In 1959, the LCC devised a scheme to help West Indian parents repatriate their children from Britain.

6 In his book, *Britain at Work: Voices from the Workplace 1945–1995*, Wilf Sullivan, TUC Race Equality Officer, argued that, despite black workers joining trade unions in large numbers, they were not welcomed by the UK trade union movement or the TUC. Migrant workers, despite claims otherwise, did not

constitute a threat to the jobs. Following World War Two there were acute labour shortages. However, in the 1950s and 1960s, the unions maintained the position that black workers failed to integrate with white workers. But, as evident from official correspondence, most of the problem was the result of prejudice. In a 1963 letter to the Transport Minister Ernest Marples, Dr Richard Beeching, Chairman of British Railways, admitted: 'Some of the staff are reluctant to accept coloured workers. The railway trade unions – as a whole – are opposed to colour discrimination. Nevertheless, there are clear indications that the existing staff at certain stations and depots would stop work if coloured people were taken on.'

7 The colour bar was a phrase denoting racial discrimination against black people. Reporting on Aneurin Bevan MP's official opening of the new headquarters of the League of Coloured Peoples, *The Times* (27 February 1954) reflected Bevin's reproach to Britain. 'He said there was a belief among some people in Britain that there was no colour bar. He wished he could believe it, but he knew from his experience in London that coloured people had great private difficulties. "We are not quite as advanced on this colour question as we like to think we are," he said. "There are colour prejudices and colour bars and difficulties under which coloured people suffer which are a reproach to Britain".'

8 Wallace Collins, *Jamaican Migrant* (London: Routledge & Kegan Paul, 1965), p. 56.

9 Cyril Buckley was interviewed for the BBC's *Round Up*, 30 April, 1963.

10 Donald Hinds, *Journey to an Illusion* (London: William Heinemann, 1966), p. 74.

Rum, Coke and Molotov Cocktails

1 In the two square miles of Notting Hill, there were estimated to be between 5,000–7,000 Caribbean people, many of them single men, living in over-priced rented accommodation of the type made infamous by the slum landlord Peter Rachman. These young men were often stereotyped in news outlets as the cause of drug dealing, vice gangs, prostitution and other forms of criminality in the area. By the late 1950s the post-war labour shortage was over, and many West Indians were paid for the kind of menial labour long abandoned by the white working class, but that didn't stop the propagandists alleging the black people were responsible for the rise of unemployment among the white working class. This only fuelled white fascists' prejudice.

2 George Lamming, *The Pleasures of Exile* (London: Pluto Press, 1960), p. 81.

3   Anti-West Indian sentiment was stoked and engineered by numerous right-wing organisations such as the League of Empire Loyalists, the National Labour Party, the White Defence League and, most notoriously, the British Union of Fascists. Oswald Mosley who founded his movement in 1932, was originally galvanised by his hatred of communism; during World War Two he was a supporter of Hitler. Living in Paris in the 1950s, he hurried back to contest a seat for the London borough of Kensington (which included Notting Hill) in the 1959 general election. He staged local campaign speeches and meetings. His rallying call became black repatriation, to drive black people into the sea.

4   Wallace Collins, *Jamaican Migrant* (London: Routledge & Kegan Paul, 1965), p. 121.

Glue Gun Revolutionaries

1   The Notting Hill riots witnessed the public emergence of the two active right-wing groups in the area, The White Defence League (WDL) and the National Labour Party (NLP).

2   Corinne Skinner-Carter spoke about her memories of Claudia Jones in 1996 at a special symposium organised on the life and times of Jones. The presentations from the symposium were subsequently written up by Marika Sherwood, with Donald Hinds and Colin Prescod, as *Claudia Jones: A Life in Exile*.

3   *Notting Hill Carnival: History – Carnival and the Performance of Heritage* (Open Learn from the Open University, 2011).

4   The calypso was composed before the 'Rivers of Blood' speech and refers to previous comments/statements/speeches where Powell voiced his antipathy toward West Indians and migration.

Would You Let Your Daughter Marry a Negro?

1   Wallace Collins, *Jamaican Migrant* (London: Routledge & Kegan Paul, 1965), p. 67.

2   Kate Paul's diary is found in *Journal: Volume One 1958–63* (University of Sussex Library's Mass Observation Repository, 2000). The quote also appears in David Kynaston's *Modernity Britain: A Shake of the Dice, 1959–62*. Kate Paul's *Journal* as a whole reflects the liberal principles of her student days when she was actively anti-apartheid, anti-nuclear weapons and anti-politicians.

3   E. R. Braithwaite, *To Sir, With Love* (London: Vintage, 2005), p. 174.

Soon Come

1   Claudette Crawford-Brown, quoted in Brook Larmer, 'The "Barrel Children"', *Newsweek*, 18 February 1996.

Here to Stay: At Home and At Play

1   In addition to my interview with Michael McMillan, I have quoted from the interviews conducted by him for the book that accompanied his installation, 'The West Indian Front Room' at the Geffrye Museum, London in 2006. Michael McMillan, *The Front Room* (London: Black Dog Publishing, 2009).

2   Jim Reeves was enormously popular in the Caribbean and amongst West Indians in Britain. 'Welcome to My World' was a favourite record of his that I heard in almost every West Indian household in Britain, especially on a Sunday. Country & western music generally seems to have found a place in the hearts of West Indians, the music having initially arrived when GIs stationed in the West Indies during and after World War Two brought their music to their bases.

Colonisin' Inglan in Reverse

1   Lord Kitchener's famous anecdote was recorded in Mike Phillips and Trevor Phillips, *Windrush: The Irresistible Rise of Multi-Racial Britain* (London: HarperCollins, 2009), p. 103.

2   Colin Babb, *They Gave the Crowd Plenty Fun: West Indian Cricket and its Relationship with the British-Resident Caribbean Diaspora* (London: Hansib Publications, 2015), p. 33.

3   Gary Younge, *No Place Like Home: A Black Briton's Journey Through the American South* (London: Picador, 1999), p. 7.

4   Ian Wooldridge, *Cricket, Lovely Cricket: The West Indies tour, 1963* (London: Hale, 1963), p. 30.

Gone to Foreign

1   Roger Robinson, *The Butterfly Hotel* (Leeds: Peepal Tree Press, 2013), p. 25.

2   Donald Hinds, *Journey to an Illusion* (London: William Heinemann, 1966), p. 190.

3   A service of Thanksgiving to mark the seventieth anniversary of the arrival of the *Empire Windrush*, 'Spirit of Windrush: Contributions to Multicultural Britain', was held at Westminster Abbey on 22 June 2018.

Select Bibliography

Achebe, Chinua, 'The Art of Fiction', No. 139, *The Paris Review*, Winter 1994.

Babb, Colin, *They Gave the Crowd Plenty Fun: West Indian Cricket and its Relationship with the British-Resident Caribbean Diaspora*. London: Hansib Publications, 2015.

BBC Caribbean Service, 'Going to Britain?'. London BBC Caribbean Service, 1959.

Bailkin, Jordanna, *Afterlife of Empire*. Berkeley: University of California Press, 2012.

Bennett, Louise, *Selected Poems: Louise Bennett*. Kingston: Sangster's Book Stores Limited, 1982.

Berry, James, *A Story I Am In: Selected Poems*. Northumberland: Bloodaxe Books, 2012.

Blagrove, Ishmahil, Jr., *Carnival: A Photographic and Testimonial History of the Notting Hill Carnival*. London: Rice N Peas, 2014.

Braithwaite, E.R., *To Sir, With Love*. London: Vintage Classics, 2005.

Brooker, Emma, 'All Gone to Look for Jamaica', *Independent*, 17 September 1995.

Carberry, H.D. and Dudley Thomson, *A West Indian in England*. London: Central Office of Information, 1950.

Collins, Wallace, *Jamaican Migrant*. London: Routledge & Kegan Paul, 1965.

De Mello, Martin, ed., *Moss Side Stories*. Manchester: Commonword, 2012.

Farrar, Max and Guy Farrar, *Celebrate! 50 Years of Leeds West Indian Carnival*. Huddersfield: Jeremy Mills Publishing, 2017.

French, Patrick, *The World Is What It Is: The Authorized Biography of V. S. Naipaul*. London: Picador, 2008.

Fryer, Peter, *Staying Power: The History of Black People in Britain*. London: Pluto, 1984.

Green, Shirley, *Rachman: The Slum Landlord whose Name Became a Byword for Evil*. London: Hamlyn, 1981.

Hall, Stuart, *Familiar Stranger: A Life Between Two Islands*. London: Allen Lane, 2017.

Hall, Stuart and Les Back, 'At Home and Not At Home: Stuart Hall in Conversation with Les Black'. Cultural Studies 23: 4 (2009), pp. 658–87.

Hall, Stuart and Maya Jaggi, *Personally Speaking: A Long Conversation with Stuart Hall*. London: Media Education Foundation, 2009.

Hinds, Donald, *Journey to an Illusion*. London: William Heinemann, 1966.

Hutchinson, Ishion, 'A Voice at the Edge of the Sea: An interview with Derek Walcott'. *Virginia Quarterly Review*, Winter 2015.

Johnson, Buzz, '*I Think of My Mother*': Notes on the Life and Times of Claudia Jones. London: Kalia Press, 1984.

Lamming, George, *In the Castle of My Skin*. London: Penguin Classics, 2017.

Lamming, George, *The Emigrants*. Ann Arbor: University Michigan Press, 1994.

Lamming, George, *The Pleasures of Exile*. London: Pluto Press, 1960.

Levy, Andrea, *Every Light in the House Burnin'*. London: Tinder Press, 1995.

Lowe, Hannah, *Ormonde*. London: Hercules Editions, 2014.

McMillan, Michael, *The Front Room*. London: Black Dog Publishing, 2009.

Naipaul, V. S., *A Way in the World*. London: William Heinemann, 1994.

Naipaul, V. S., *The Enigma of Arrival*. London: Penguin Books, 1987.

Patterson, Sheila, *Dark Strangers: A Study of West Indians in London*. Harmondsworth: Penguin, 1963.

Phillips, Caryl, 'Interview: George Lamming Talks to Caryl Phillips'. *Wasafiri* 26, Autumn 1997, p. 13.

Phillips, Mike and Trevor Phillips, *Windrush: The Irresistible Rise of Multi-Racial Britain*. London: HarperCollins, 2009.

Philpott, Trevor, 'Would You Let Your Daughter Marry a Negro?' *Picture Post*, 30 October 1954.

Pilkington, Edward, *Beyond the Mother Country: West Indians and the Notting Hill White Riots*. London: I.B. Tauris, 1988.

Robinson, Roger, *The Butterfly Hotel*. Leeds: Peepal Tree Press, 2013.

Selvon, Sam, *The Lonely Londoners*. London: Penguin Classics, 2006.

Sherwood, Marika, with Donald Hinds, Colin Prescod and the 1996 Claudia Jones Symposium, *Claudia Jones: A Life in Exile*. London: Lawrence and Wishart, 1999.

Sullivan, Wilf, 'Britain at Work: Voices from the Workplace 1945–1995'. TUC Library Collections, London Metropolitan University, 2012.

Walcott, Derek, *The Gulf and Other Poems*. London: Jonathan Cape, 1969.

Walker, Melody, *A Journey Through Our History: The Story of the Jamaican People in Leeds & the Work of the Jamaica Society*. Leeds: The Jamaica Society (Leeds), 2003.

Wooldridge, Ian, *Cricket, Lovely Cricket: The West Indies Tour, 1963*. London: Hale, 1963.

Younge, Gary, *No Place Like Home: A Black Briton's Journey Through the American South*. London: Picador, 1999.

Index